Contents

CW01499919

Napoleonic Britain

Napoleonic Britain

A Guide to Fortresses, Statues and Memorials of the French Wars 1792–1815

David Buttery

Pen & Sword
MILITARY

First published in Great Britain in 2023 by
Pen & Sword Military
An imprint of Pen & Sword Books Limited
Yorkshire – Philadelphia

ISBN 978 1 39908 437 6

A CIP catalogue record for this book is
available from the British Library

Typeset by Mac Style
Printed in the UK by CPI Group (UK) Ltd, Croydon, CR0 4YY.

Pen & Sword Books Limited incorporates the imprints of After
the Battle, Atlas, Archaeology, Aviation, Discovery, Family
History, Fiction, History, Maritime, Military, Military Classics,
Politics, Select, Transport, True Crime, Air World, Frontline
Publishing, Leo Cooper, Remember When, Seaforth Publishing,
The Praetorian Press, Wharncliffe Local History, Wharncliffe
Transport, Wharncliffe True Crime and White Owl.

For a complete list of Pen & Sword titles please contact

PEN & SWORD BOOKS LIMITED
47 Church Street, Barnsley, South Yorkshire, S70 2AS, England
E-mail: enquiries@pen-and-sword.co.uk
Website: www.pen-and-sword.co.uk
or
PEN AND SWORD BOOKS
1950 Lawrence Rd, Havertown, PA 19083, USA
E-mail: Uspen-and-sword@casematepublishers.com
Website: www.penandswordbooks.com

To Sharon Whitmore, who was a great travelling companion on our 'Martello Marches' and the Nelson Trail, and Stuart Hadaway, whose historic knowledge is always appreciated.

List of Colour Plates

Maps
Map 1: Central London I.
Map 2: Central London II.
Map 3: St Paul's Cathedral.
Map 4: Central Edinburgh.
Map 5: Surviving Martello towers.
Map 6: Irish Towers.
Map 7: Invasions of Ireland.
Map 8: Museums and Heritage Centres.

Photographs
1. Napoleon I, Emperor of the French, whose ambitions threatened British interests – Ernest Crofts.
2. The bust of Nelson above the tombstones of his parents.
3. The former Wrestler's Inn in Great Yarmouth, where Nelson stayed with Lady Hamilton.
4. The Norfolk Pillar in Great Yarmouth commemorating Nelson's victories.
5. A First Rate, three-decked ship of the line possessed devastating firepower.
6. One of HMS *Victory*'s gun-decks.
7. The entire ship is a treasure trove of Royal Navy artefacts.
8. Walking in Nelson's footsteps is an unforgettable experience.
9. The stern of HMS *Victory*.
10. The tunnel entrance that Nelson walked through in Portsmouth before joining his final command.
11. Arthur Wellesley, Duke of Wellington, Britain's greatest commander – Sir Thomas Lawrence.
12. Apsley House (No. 1 London), the Duke of Wellington's London residence.
13. The Duke was given a giant statue of his greatest enemy to adorn his home.
14. The drawing room of Apsley House.

46. Edinburgh's Nelson Monument designed in the shape of an upturned telescope.
47. The Duke of York's statue on the esplanade before Edinburgh Castle.
48. The Marquess of Anglesey's statue looks out over the Menai Straits.
49. The River Procession in Nelson's honour was a unique event in London's history.
50. Greenwich Dock, where Nelson's body was brought ashore and later loaded onto his funeral barge.
51. Nelson's spectacular tomb had been intended for King Henry VIII's use.
52. Wellington probably would have approved of the impressive but straightforward design of his tomb.
53. The memorial to Admiral Collingwood – the 'Forgotten Hero of Trafalgar'.
54. Generals Pakenham and Gibbs killed at the Battle of New Orleans in 1815.
55. A dramatic memorial commemorating the death of Captain Robert Faulknor.
56. Captain John Cooke's memorial, one of two Trafalgar captains commemorated near Nelson's Tomb.
57. The memorial commemorating over 20,000 officers and men buried in the grounds of the Old Royal Hospital, Greenwich.
58. Ensign Ewart's tomb on the esplanade before Edinburgh Castle.
59. The equestrian tomb of Colonel Edward Cheney.
60. Jemima Nicholas volunteered to fight the French and is buried in St Mary's Churchyard.
61. A monument over the grave of the first French soldier killed in the invasion of Ireland in 1798.
62. Irish exile Wolfe Tone presents his invasion plans to General Bonaparte.
63. Fishguard Fort.
64. The Royal Oak public house where negotiations took place.
65. A mural depicting General Humbert and his army.
66. Nelson's uniform jacket at the National Maritime Museum, Greenwich.
67. The remarkable ship in a bottle at Greenwich.
68. The captured Eagle of the 45th French Line Regiment in Edinburgh Castle.
69. A recreation of a Napoleonic POW dormitory at Edinburgh Castle.
70. The Royal Welch Fusiliers Museum has some particularly realistic Napoleonic mannequins.

Introduction

There are few places on earth with a richer history than the small group of islands in the North Atlantic Ocean known as the British Isles. They have witnessed some of the great events in human history and boast an incredible number of historical sites connected to famous wars, personalities, social history and political events. Britain has played a far larger international role than one would expect from such a small nation, whose United Kingdom is currently comprised of England, Scotland, Northern Ireland and Wales.[1] Such an extensive heritage means travellers are spoilt for choice, with an abundance of churches, stately homes, battlefields, cathedrals, palaces, castles and fortresses to visit. This guidebook concentrates on the Revolutionary and Napoleonic Wars of 1792–1815, covering some of the famous personalities, military fortifications and commemorative monuments for conflicts that had far reaching effects upon Europe and the entire world.

The demand for social reform in Europe accelerated during the eighteenth century and the successful rebellion of the colonists against British rule during the American War of Independence of 1775–83 revealed that the world was changing rapidly. Even so, the French Revolution that began in 1789 shocked the world as one of the most powerful regimes in Europe was bloodily overthrown. Outraged by the executions of King Louis XVI and Queen Marie Antoinette, along with many nobles and priests as well, the great European powers gathered to crush the young French Republic emerging in their midst before its revolutionary ideology could spread.

Yet the inexperienced revolutionary armies proved surprisingly resilient and not only withstood incursions into French territory but eventually marched over their frontiers and took the offensive. After a series of revolutionary governments, France fell under the sway of General Bonaparte who seized power as First Consul in 1799 and eventually crowned himself Napoleon I, Emperor of the French, on 2 December 1804. Under his inspired leadership, the imperial armies won remarkable victories until Napoleon overreached the

---

1. Wales was officially recognized as a country by the International Organization for Standardisation (ISO) in 2011.

limits of his power as France proved unable to withstand the financial strain or maintain the political will to fight a series of wars that lasted over 20 years.

Britain remained France's implacable foe throughout this period with only a brief period of peace from October 1801 to May 1803 that was predictably short lived. For over two decades Britain devoted vast amounts of men, money and equipment to defy Napoleon and ultimately restore the French monarchy. During this time, the British people suffered financial hardship, threats of invasion and lost over 300,000 men in conflicts on land and sea from 1802 to 1815 alone. Estimates vary but over a million civilians lost their lives in Europe and at least five million soldiers and sailors died during the Napoleonic Wars. As these conflicts spread to India, Canada, the United States and South America, many historians now consider them as 'world wars' due to their social, economic and political repercussions around the globe.

As the world was profoundly changed by these wars, it is unsurprising that so many people wish to learn more about them, especially when they see so many monuments and statues have been created to commemorate organizations or individual participants. There is also great interest in fortresses built or adapted to defend British shores against invasion, along with curiosity about the vast numbers of prisoners of war held in Britain and what became of them. The recent bicentenary events held to commemorate the Battle of Waterloo on 18 June 1815/2015 and Napoleon's death on 5 May 1821/2021 sparked even greater enthusiasm, with new monuments dedicated to figures of the era even though these wars were fought 200 years ago. Statues, tombs and fortresses from the period are significant to those who study the era and learning more about them can lead to an increased understanding or simply satisfy a well-justified curiosity about the past. The intention of this guidebook is to assist enthusiasts who wish to discover what historic sites Britain has to offer and how to find them, along with providing relevant background information.

Vice Admiral Nelson and the Duke of Wellington are widely recognized as Britain's foremost military heroes, with the scale of their achievements overshadowing even those brave individuals who fought in more recent conflicts. Both of them rose to prominence during the Georgian period and, as many of the sites covered in this work are closely linked to them, it begins by providing brief details of their careers and relevance to British military history as their names crop up throughout this book. Especially significant sites are highlighted as Case Studies and examined in greater detail, such as the circular redoubt at Harwich and HMS *Victory*. Chapters 3 and 4 examine the fortresses built to defend British shores against invasion along with older strongpoints adapted to accommodate or withstand modern weaponry. Some are remarkably well preserved while others have fallen into ruin but all provide intriguing reminders of how seriously the British government and people felt about the invasion threat.

Huge numbers of men died during the wars so the British raised monuments to commemorate this tragic loss of life and the sacrifices made. The Victorians were especially proud of the role their nation played in resisting and defeating Napoleon and erected statues to celebrate the achievements of famous individuals, regiments and ships but modern monuments have also been raised as recently as 2021. Chapter 5 explores the vast range of statues and monuments to be seen in Britain but, in light of recent protests, also pauses to examine different interpretations of the past and the conclusions that can be drawn from these publicly displayed reminders of British heritage.

The manner in which our ancestors were laid to rest is a specialized field of study among historians and enthusiasts are known as taphophiles who study funeral rites, monuments, headstones and tombs. Hundreds of gravestones and tombs were dedicated to those who fought in the wars against France and Chapter 6 includes a specific study of relevant memorials in London's St Paul's Cathedral, along with a concise selection of examples chosen from around the country based on the author's first-hand experiences. Despite the length of the time that has elapsed, people continue to lay flowers and other offerings on the graves of distant relatives, renowned members of regiments and famous individuals they admire. There is much to be learned about the impact of the wars against France upon the British by the way in which they honour their dead.

Although many are aware of French ambitions to invade England during the wars, the fact that invasions actually took place in Ireland and Wales is little known and deserving of further study. Chapter 7 examines these small incursions, revealing how close they came to success and examining their relevance along with providing descriptions of what can still be seen at the relevant sites today. Chapter 8 provides details of some of the main museums and heritage centres that have exhibitions covering this period while the final chapter provides information about travelling around Great Britain, offering practical advice on the best forms of travel, where to stay, where to eat and general advice on how to get the best out of a historical tour in Britain. Although many readers are likely to be British enthusiasts, this chapter also attempts to make provision for those travelling here from countries outside the United Kingdom.

I have spent a lifetime travelling around the British Isles and am often surprised at just how much there is to see connected with the Revolutionary and Napoleonic Wars. There have been many occasions when I have come across statues, graves, buildings or monuments unexpectedly and therefore realize that a book of this size cannot hope to be truly definitive due to the number of sites that could be included. Even so, this guidebook makes a valiant attempt to cover as many locations as possible but concentrates upon the most famous and relevant examples with an emphasis on those I have personally seen during my travels.

These islands contain a wealth of sites often found in picturesque locations and viewing them should be a pleasure, so I wish you good fortune on your historical quest in this diverse and extraordinary country.

David Buttery

Chapter 1

Sailing with Nelson

Vice Admiral Lord Nelson stands out as a unique figure even among the outstanding pantheon of British military heroes who came to prominence during the wars against France. Rising from virtual obscurity to a senior rank in the Royal Navy, he fought in four wars, four major sea battles and host of smaller actions during a truly remarkable career.[1] His grasp of naval strategy and occasionally unconventional tactics brought him success but it was his inspiring style of leadership that made him so valuable to the British war effort. He was respected by officers and ordinary seamen alike and widely considered to be England's greatest hope against the French Navy so, when he fell at the Battle of Trafalgar in 1805, he was truly mourned as a national hero.

Over a thousand books have been written about Nelson, along with films and documentaries, and he became a household name in his own lifetime. The fact that he died at the height of his career during the most decisive naval battle of the age ensured his fame and numerous ships, roads, public houses, official institutions and residences have been named in his honour along with statues and monuments raised in his memory. Nelson's Column in the City of Westminster (London) is one of the most famous monuments in the world to be dedicated to an individual and, over 200 years after his death, he remains Britain's greatest naval hero. Although many of the main sites connected with Nelson are located in England's capital, his fame was such that there are many others scattered around the British Isles for enthusiasts to visit.

An Unlikely Hero

Without prior knowledge of Nelson, it is easy to form an incorrect impression of his character when looking at one of his famous portraits for the first time. Most paintings depict him in later life and his prematurely white/grey hair

---

1. These were the American War of Independence and Wars of the First, Second and Third Coalitions against France. He fought at Cape St Vincent, Copenhagen, Aboukir Bay (The Nile) and Trafalgar along with important sieges, large-scale raids and numerous minor actions at sea.

makes him appear older than his actual years (Nelson died aged 47). Nelson's usually immaculate uniforms and ostentatious display of medals imply that the subject was a conservative reactionary and stern disciplinarian – but nothing could be further from the truth. Far from being a martinet, Nelson not only helped fellow officers with their careers but also cared deeply for the ordinary seamen in his commands, doing what he could to relieve the hardship they suffered at sea and gaining their respect and even devotion. He lacked a wealthy patron and had to make his own way in the Royal Navy through determined self-promotion, sheer talent and devotion to duty. At a time when many of his contemporaries hailed from the upper classes and benefitted from influential connections, this made his rise to flag rank even more remarkable.

It is even more difficult to reconcile his scandalous and very public love life with the impression that his famous portraits convey. The Admiralty tolerated

Admiral Nelson's portraits can give a misleading impression of this enigmatic man – Lemuel Francis Abbott.

instances of political and social indiscretion because of his proven talent and national renown, but an officer of lesser value would have paid a heavy price for such behaviour. Yet the pleasant but determined face that stares back at the viewer from these images of Nelson gives little hint that their subject was an unconventional military maverick who was prepared to take extraordinary risks to further his career and win victories for his country.

Horatio Nelson was born on 29 September 1758 at Burnham Thorpe village in the county of Norfolk on the east coast of England. He was the son of Edmund Nelson, the village parson, and his wife Catherine (née Suckling). Catherine bore Edmund eleven children but only eight survived into adulthood, with Horatio (who preferred the name Horace as a child) being the sixth. Constant pregnancies and childbirths affected his mother's health and she died when he was 9. Through the influence of Captain Maurice Suckling (his uncle) he received the rank of Midshipman at the age of 12 and went to sea, which was typical as boys were employed by the Royal Navy at an early age to learn as much as they could about the service. Although his uncle offered occasional financial assistance and introductions, Horatio was obliged to make his own way in the service.

The boy learned quickly and served in the West Indies, the Arctic and East Indies, gaining a commission as lieutenant in 1777 in HMS *Lowestoft*. Two years later, at the remarkably young age of 19, Nelson was promoted to Post Captain and received command of the frigate HMS *Hinchinbroke* in the West Indies. Although his uncle's influence may have assisted with this rapid advancement, the Royal Navy did not bestow the command of costly men-of-war to young men unless they knew their business very well indeed.

Nelson took part in the disastrous expedition to Nicaragua in 1780 and suffered from frequent illnesses and fevers during his service in the Caribbean. Indeed, his health was poor throughout his life and he often complained of seasickness despite a long endurance of conditions at sea but he went on to serve in Admiral Lord Hood's squadron during the American War of Independence and gained some notoriety after this conflict by enforcing trade laws that limited the activities of American merchants in the Caribbean. In 1785 he met and courted Frances Nisbet on the island of Nevis (British West Indies) and they married in 1787.

By this time, he had earned a formidable reputation as a capable officer who was charismatic and utterly dedicated to his country's interests but when Mr Herbert (President of Nevis) first encountered him he gained an slightly different impression: 'Great God,' he reported later, 'if I did not find that great little man, of whom everyone is so afraid, playing in the next room under the dining-table with Mrs Nisbet's child.' This revealed a caring side of Nelson's character that he displayed time and again during his career by encouraging young officers to do well in the service and in his desire for a child of his own.

Shortly after his marriage, Nelson was placed on half pay, which meant virtual retirement as the Royal Navy needed fewer captains in peacetime. He spent the following years in Norfolk and was uncertain over whether he would receive another command or be forced to sell his commission and find new employment.

He spent the years 1787–93 ashore and during this time he and Fanny tried unsuccessfully to have children. Nelson busied himself with rural tasks such as helping to re-route the stream running through Burnham Thorpe and digging a ship-shaped pond in the Rectory garden but he also read newspapers, periodicals and navy seniority lists avidly, desperately hoping for appointment to another command. The outbreak of war with France resolved this dilemma as he soon received the command of a ship of the line (HMS *Agamemnon*) in 1793.

From this point Nelson began to gain official recognition as he played a major part in the capture of the island of Corsica from the French in 1794. During this campaign he was wounded while commanding an onshore battery during the Siege of Calvi as an enemy cannon ball struck the parapet before him, throwing up wood splinters and sand into his face. His right eye was severely damaged, which meant he was effectively blinded in that eye. The myth that Nelson wore an eye patch persists to this day but, although he never used a patch, he had some of his cocked hats modified by the addition of a small green eye shade to protect his sensitive right eye from direct sunlight, which proved particularly useful during campaigns in the Mediterranean.

Nelson had a talent for forming lasting friendships and, when the meritocratic Admiral Jervis became his commander-in-chief, he saw him as a promising officer and did his best to help him. In 1795–6 Nelson commanded a squadron ranging along the French and Ligurian coasts targeting enemy commercial shipping but the following year saw him raised to Commodore (temporary command of a squadron) when he fought under Jervis at the Battle of Cape St Vincent in 1797. During this fight against the Spanish, Jervis successfully split the enemy fleet in two and moved to engage the larger formation of enemy ships. However, Jervis had difficulty in turning the fleet at a sharp angle to attack them so it appeared that many would get away. Observing this, Nelson defied orders and steered HMS *Captain* (74 guns) along with two other ships out of formation to intercept them.

Boldly attacking the far larger *Santissima Trinidad* (130-guns), HMS *Captain* sustained serious damage and was partly dismasted. Undeterred, Nelson brought his ship alongside the *San Nicolas* and personally led a boarding party onto the enemy ship, resulting in a fierce hand-to-hand melee with the Spanish. Seeing that the *San Nicolas* was hard pressed, the *San Josef* came to her assistance but approached so closely that spars and rigging became entangled, effectively tying the ships together. Nelson took advantage of this situation as the *San Nicolas* fell and organized another boarding party, which he led from one enemy vessel to the other, crying 'Westminster Abbey or Glorious Victory!'[2] His men took both Spanish ships and Nelson later wrote 'on the quarterdeck of a Spanish first-rate, extravagant as the story may seem, did I receive the swords of the vanquished Spaniards, which as I received I gave to William Fearney, one of my bargemen, who placed them with the greatest sang-froid under his arm'. However, Nelson also received a blow to the stomach in this fight that gave him a hernia for the rest of his life.

This battle restored British fortunes and the Royal Navy consequently re-established a major presence in the Mediterranean Sea, which it had previously abandoned in the face of Franco-Spanish successes. Although Nelson had exceeded orders, his actions contributed to the scale of the victory so Admiral Jervis overlooked his disobedience but gave him little credit in his first dispatch. Nevertheless, as news of his brave exploits soon became widely known, Jervis acknowledged the role he had played and Nelson was promoted to Rear Admiral and received a knighthood. Capturing two enemy vessels at once was virtually unknown and this double-boarding action became known as 'Nelson's Patent Bridge for boarding First Rates' in the Royal Navy.

Following the battle, Nelson was ordered to cruise enemy coastlines and intercept shipping and eventually participated in the ill-fated raid on Santa Cruz to capture a Spanish treasure ship where he was shot and badly wounded, taking a musket ball in the arm. Midshipman Hoste recalled seeing his admiral come back on board 'his right arm dangling by his side while with his left he jumped up the ship's side and, with a spirit that astonished everyone, told the surgeon to get his instruments ready for that he knew he must lose his arm and the sooner it was off the better'. Following what must have been a painful amputation without anaesthetic, Nelson returned to England and was nursed back to health by his wife. Tales of Nelson's bravery spread rapidly but this terrible amputation damaged his already fragile health. Being right-handed, the loss of this arm was a dreadful handicap in as he struggled to master writing with his left hand to write the orders, dispatches and letters vital for his role. He paid for some bespoke items, such as a combined knife and fork for one-handed use, but his awful wound had made the already arduous life at sea even more difficult to bear.

2. Westminster Abbey is where many Kings, Queens and famous Britons are buried.

A lesser man might have retired from the service at this point but Nelson rejoined the fleet in the roads of Toulon, the greatest port of Southern France, in April 1798. The Royal Navy were blockading Toulon but a French fleet under Admiral Brueys managed to slip out of port and evade them nonetheless, carrying General Bonaparte's army and sailing east into the Mediterranean Sea. This fleet first landed at Malta and then at Alexandria where Bonaparte's army commenced an invasion of Egypt, which soon fell under French control.

Being aware that French military successes had overawed Europe and were affecting British morale, Nelson became determined to put heart into his men and reverse the course of the war if he could. Since boyhood he had been inspired by Shakespeare's most patriotic play *Henry V* and borrowed the phrase 'Band of Brothers' to refer to his captains to fire their enthusiasm. He was already renowned for his empathy with common seamen and had demonstrated this on several occasions, notably aboard HMS *Theseus* in 1797. Conditions aboard the ship were poor and ill-treatment by officers drove the sailors into a state of near mutiny but Nelson did his utmost to repair relations between officers and crew to the extent that they declared their willingness to fight and die under his command in an anonymous letter. His efforts to improve the lot of the men in his fleet met with considerable success but he was aware that only a great victory against France would turn the tide.

Accordingly, when they discovered Brueys's fleet at anchor in the mouth of the River Nile on 1 August 1798, he decided to attack immediately. Many of his captains were astonished as the conventional course was to anchor and attack at dawn as they had arrived in the late afternoon and only had a few hours of daylight left to fight the battle in. Nelson responded, 'I am of the opinion that the boldest measures are the safest'.

The French fleet was anchored in a line close to shore as Brueys anticipated a defensive battle rather than one of manoeuvre, hoping to inflict crushing firepower from his stationary ships against the attackers. After sighting the British approach, he also expected them to anchor overnight and attack next morning and was surprised when they sailed straight into action against him. The battle began that evening and raged on into the night with gun flashes and flares lighting up the sky. In spite of the risk of running aground, Nelson ordered some of his captains to sail close to the shore to get behind the enemy line so that their immobile vessels could be fired upon from both sides. This tactic proved successful and many French ships were subjected to a devastating crossfire. At the height of the battle, fires started by enemy gunfire on the flagship *l'Orient* raged out of control and she exploded in a fireball that lit up the night when they spread to the magazine. Fragments of wreckage rained down upon nearby vessels and the scene was so horrific that both sides briefly stopped firing with gunners watching aghast as this magnificent ship sank.

The French invasion fleet was effectively wiped out as a fighting force with four ships of the line and two frigates destroyed (most were run aground and burnt after capture) and nine ships of the line taken as prizes. Five thousand Frenchmen were killed or wounded with just under 3,000 taken prisoner. The British fleet was damaged and suffered around a thousand casualties, but did not lose a single ship. Nelson received a nasty wound to his forehead that bled profusely and suffered from concussion, though he continued to give orders until the end of the battle. Brueys died valiantly aboard *l'Orient* and only four French ships cut their cables and evaded capture.

Nelson's decision to fight on into the night was brave but bordered upon recklessness as night actions were difficult to control but the risk paid off, giving the Allied cause against France a badly-needed victory and destroying the myth of French invincibility. Men of all ranks in his fleet were delighted by their success and the prospect of significant prize money when captured ships were sold but the most important result of the Battle of the Nile was its effect on the strategic situation. With the French fleet defeated and scattered, Bonaparte was stranded in Egypt. Although he continued to campaign in the Middle East, his victories on land were short lived as his army was denied seaborne reinforcement or supplies and he abandoned his command in 1799. In contrast, Nelson received many honours for his victory, including the title Baron Nelson of the Nile, and became a household name in Britain.

Nelson paused to recuperate in Naples after the battle and became reacquainted with Lady Emma Hamilton who he had previously met in 1793. Although she was already married to Sir William Hamilton (a British diplomat) the pair fell in love and began an affair that soon became public knowledge as Nelson did nothing to conceal his infatuation with her. Sir William was 67 (over twice his wife's age) and did not appear to mind her spending so much time with 'the hero of the hour' but this scandalous affair drew severe criticism from senior navy officers. Even more damagingly, Nelson became embroiled in the politics of the Neapolitan court, which was in a sensitive situation being threatened by open rebellion and the danger of falling under French control.

Many believed the head wound Nelson suffered at Aboukir Bay might explain his erratic behaviour during the Neapolitan Campaign of 1798. He exceeded his authority by committing British forces to assist the Neapolitan monarchy suppress a Jacobin revolt and, when these pro-French rebels capitulated, Nelson refused to honour the surrender terms. He then disarmed and delivered the rebels into Neapolitan hands who put them on trial and executed the majority of the leadership. This bloody incident was a blemish on

Nelson's reputation but he was created Duke of Brontë by King Ferdinand IV of Naples in return for his help in putting down the revolt.

Nelson established a British presence in Sicily before embarking on a short tour of European courts and, although the hero of the Nile was made welcome, this ill-advised diplomatic venture failed to produce the results that he or the Hamiltons hoped for and made him appear slightly foolish. He returned to England in 1800, receiving an ecstatic welcome when he landed and stayed at Great Yarmouth and when he arrived in London some days afterward. In the wake of many national misfortunes, Britain needed a hero and Nelson was eminently suited to the role. However, his separation from his wife and decision to live openly with Lady Hamilton was widely criticized, especially as he made no attempt at secrecy. Doubts were expressed about Nelson's recent conduct in the Admiralty and many were relieved when he was promoted to Vice Admiral and returned to active service.

The League of Armed Neutrality of 1800 was a formal agreement between Russia, Prussia, Denmark and Sweden to stop the Royal Navy from boarding and searching their merchant ships and was designed to nullify the effect of British blockades on neutral shipping. The British were confiscating French goods from neutral vessels to damage enemy interests and, in response to this resistance from the northern nations, a large-scale raid was sent against Copenhagen in 1801. It was a punitive expedition led by Admiral Hyde Parker who was considered overly cautious but enjoyed the necessary seniority for such a command. Admiral Jervis suspected that decisive action against the Danes would only be won by aggression and daring so he appointed Nelson as his second-in-command.

Parker agreed to Nelson's counsel that they mount a two-pronged attack against the Danish fleet, which lay at anchorages around the capital city of Copenhagen. The plan involved fighting not only the enemy fleet but artillery batteries on shore and the ensuing battle was hard fought with around a thousand casualties on each side. At one stage, Parker believed that Nelson's squadron was losing the fight and sent a signal (using signalling flags) ordering him to withdraw. By this time Nelson was confident of victory and theatrically held up a telescope to his blind eye before his officers, declaring 'I really do not see the signal!'[3] continuing with the action that resulted as a tactical triumph for Nelson. An armistice was agreed with the Danes and Nelson soon gained overall command of the fleet and carried out cruising missions in the Baltic against French and neutral shipping.

---

3. Other sources use the wording 'Signal? I see no signal!'

On his return to England, Nelson received a peerage with the grandiose title of Viscount Nelson of the Nile and Burnham Thorpe. He took up residence with the Hamiltons dividing his time between London and his house in Merton while the Treaty of Amiens in 1801 brought a short period of peace between Britain and France. Although he had made generous provision for his wife, some felt she had been treated cruelly and openly breaking his marriage vows in a far more Christian society than today was scandalous in itself. His mistress had now borne him a daughter, whom they named Horatia and Nelson was delighted to start a family at last but did not legally acknowledge the child as his own until just before Trafalgar. When Sir William died in April 1803, Nelson tried to make some provision for Emma and Horatia in the event of his death, knowing that the resumption of hostilities with France was inevitable and that he would soon return to sea.

With the outbreak of war in early 1803, Nelson took command of the Mediterranean Fleet which resumed the blockade of Toulon. With Britain under threat of invasion, the Admiralty felt pressured to defend British shores but knew it was vital to bring the French fleet to battle and inflict enough damage upon it to prevent Napoleon bringing his army over the Channel. Ever the patriot, Nelson was aware of just how much his nation was relying upon the Royal Navy to fend off this threat and took great steps to instil his love of country in his men. He benefitted from having Admiral Collingwood (his best friend) as second-in-command and restored his practice of creating 'a Band of Brothers' among the captains in his command, taking care to listen to their concerns and involve them in his planning.

Eyewitness accounts of Nelson's physical appearance vary, with some portraits giving a misleading impression, but most agree he was fairly slight and narrow shouldered with his long hair giving him a somewhat wild and unheroic appearance. The Duke of Wellington recalled forming a poor first impression of him on the only occasion they met, writing:

He could not know who I was, but he entered at once into conversation with me, if I can call it conversation, for it was almost all on his side, and all about himself, and in really a style so vain and so silly as to surprise and almost disgust me. I suppose something that I happened to say may have made him guess that I was somebody, and he went out of the room … no doubt to ask … who I was, for when he came back he was altogether a different man … All that I had thought a charlatan style had vanished, and he talked of the state of this country [displaying] a knowledge of subjects both at home and abroad that surprised me …

Nelson was prone to vanity because he was sensitive about his humble origins and felt a pressing need for continuous self-publicity. Therefore, it is understandable that some people found his personality repellent on first acquaintance while others thought him highly charismatic, depending upon their outlook on life. Nelson's house at Merton was so filled with paintings and ornaments proclaiming his triumphs that it drew adverse comments, revealing that he was acutely sensitive about his image and tended to overemphasize his achievements. However, it is interesting to compare his concern over this with his heedless disregard of public opinion of the treatment of his wife and his domestic arrangements with his mistress.

The Emperor Napoleon believed a successful invasion of Britain as the only way to end the constant alliances of European powers against him and pressed Admiral Villeneuve to take decisive action with his combined Franco-Spanish fleet in order to bring this about. Villeneuve managed to make a large-scale breakout through the British blockade in early 1805 and headed for Martinique, hoping to evade Nelson's pursuit. With the Mediterranean Fleet out of the way, he then hoped to return and keep the Channel open long enough for an invasion force to cross. This plan failed though and, when he returned to Cadiz in Spain, the British fleet was still in pursuit. Knowing that Napoleon intended to replace him, Villeneuve left the Spanish port intending to bring Nelson's fleet to battle, which occurred off Cape Trafalgar about 11 miles off the Spanish coast.

As battle approached, Nelson made great efforts to inspire patriotic fervour in his men, relying upon inspiring devotion and duty to their national cause. This applied to all ranks but he also tried to improve living conditions and emphasize fair treatment to common seamen especially. His subordinates made it clear that they appreciated his efforts and, in a letter to Emma, he wrote 'I believe my arrival was most welcome, not only to the Commander of the Fleet but almost to every individual in it; and when I came to explain to them the "*Nelson touch*" it was like an electric shock.' He used this term only three weeks before Trafalgar and it is widely quoted today to illustrate Nelson's approach to naval morale, which ultimately proved highly successful.

The Battle of Trafalgar took place on 21 October 1805 and Nelson won immense respect from his ship's captains by openly taking them into his confidence regarding his battle plans. He emphasized that they were free to act upon their own initiative in combat as long as they acted aggressively, as he wanted to inflict a great defeat on the enemy. His predictions about Villeneuve's strategy proved uncannily accurate and his tactics focussed upon capturing or destroying enemy vessels to gain decisive results. This approach was summarized by a famous quotation from Nelson delivered shortly before the battle that 'No captain can do very wrong if he places his ship alongside that of the enemy'. He knew close-quarters gunnery and boarding actions were dangerously unpredictable but believed that Britain would only be spared from invasion by inflicting heavy losses on the enemy and felt great risks were justified.

Nelson formed his fleet into two attack columns and sailed straight at the enemy line of thirty-three vessels intending to pierce it in two places. After constantly reminding his men that their nation lay under threat of invasion, he raised the famous flag signal 'England expects that every man will do his duty' as they approached the combined enemy fleet. He knew they would initially come under heavy fire with no chance to respond effectively during their approach with this strategy. Once they closed with the enemy, his ships could deliver devastating broadsides into the Franco-Spanish vessels at close range. If the French line was successfully penetrated in multiple places by the British columns, they could isolate and overwhelm divided elements of the enemy fleet, which should lead to victory. Nelson led a column of eleven ships aboard HMS *Victory* while Admiral Collingwood headed a similar formation of fifteen ships in HMS *Royal Sovereign* and their attack was incredibly successful.

Nelson's flagship was fighting a close action with the ship *Redoutable* at the height of the battle when a French marine high up in one the fighting tops of the enemy ship's masts fired his musket at Nelson, mortally wounding him. He was carried below deck where he lay in incredible pain for hours but learned that he had won a great victory just before he died. His last words were 'Thank God I have done my duty.'

Over 12,000 casualties were sustained by both sides at Trafalgar with the French and Spanish suffering by far the greater proportion of these losses (the British suffered 1,314 killed or wounded) and many prisoners were taken. Eighteen French and Spanish ships were captured and one destroyed during the battle but only four of these damaged ships survived the heavy gales that occurred the following day and were sailed into Gibraltar as prizes. The combined Franco-Spanish fleet had received such a blow that French hopes of invading England were dashed for many years.

Trafalgar was the last great naval battle of the period and ensured that Britain remained the premier naval power for a century but, although it won the British a vital breathing space, it did not end the threat of invasion. Napoleon had already led the army he had prepared for the invasion inland on 26 August 1805 against Austrian and Russian armies but he never abandoned his plan to invade and defeat his most formidable enemy. Even after this naval catastrophe, Napoleon continued with extensive ship building programmes and attempted to acquire the national fleets of Denmark and Portugal to bolster the French Navy. The British continued building coastal fortifications for years and it was not until the Battle of Waterloo in 1815 that they finally considered the threat to be over.

While news of the great victory at Trafalgar was well-received in Britain, it was overshadowed by Nelson's death and a feeling of genuine national grief ensued as he was laid to rest in St Paul's Cathedral with full military honours (see Chapter 6).

Nelson's County

The people of Norfolk are immensely proud of their most famous son, remaining steadfastly loyal to his memory even when his politics and character flaws have been criticized over the years. Bernard Matthews, a Norfolk turkey farmer and food producer, achieved many things for his home county and saw Nelson as an excellent role model for the young. He proposed adding the words 'Nelson's County' to border road signs welcoming drivers to the region and, when local government protested at lack of funds, made a handsome contribution towards the cost. This phrase is widely used in Norfolk tourist information literature and local schools where Nelson's career is often studied.

Most towns along the east coast have pubs, medical centres and roads named in honour of Nelson or his victories, with street names such as Nelson Road, Nile Road and Trafalgar Road being commonplace. Great Yarmouth has dozens of roads named in honour of Nelson or Wellington and even boasts a 'Napoleon Place' in honour of the Emperor, which is almost unique in England although there is a Napoleon Road in Twickenham.

Many historians believe that Nelson had a Norfolk accent and several sources support this. For example, when he lay dying on the orlop deck of HMS *Victory*, one of his last statements to Captain Hardy was 'Do you anchor, Hardy,' which some Victorian historians misinterpreted as a question. It is far more likely that Nelson was actually ordering Hardy to anchor the fleet in the aftermath of the battle as 'do you' in the Norfolk idiom means 'you must'. Following his schooling, widespread travel and efforts to fit in with senior Royal Navy officers (who hailed from other counties) Nelson's accent may not have been broad but it is likely that he retained a trace of it throughout his life. Certainly when he gave a speech from a first floor window of the Wrestlers Inn his boast that 'I am myself a Norfolk man and glory in being so,' was well received by the crowd below.

Burnham Thorpe

The small village of Burnham Thorpe is a place every Nelson enthusiast should visit but is located in a quiet region of north Norfolk that is difficult to reach by public transport with travel by car being preferable. This was not the case in Nelson's day as goods landed on the nearby coast regularly passed through Burnham Thorpe, making it a far busier place than the peaceful rural village it has become today.

It takes just over three hours to drive from London to Burnham Thorpe travelling via the M11 and A1065. There are trains from London's Liverpool Street railway station to King's Lynn, which is the nearest large town, and taxis can reach the village in about 45 minutes from there. Alternatively the No 36 Coastline Bus from King's Lynn stops at Burnham Market, Burnham Overy Staithe and Wells-next-the-Sea. Nelson used to walk or ride to these locations from his village but be aware that the country lanes in this area are narrow, often lined with hedges (restricting views of oncoming traffic) and lack pavements so walkers should proceed with caution. Cycling or taking a taxi from the closest village of Burnham Market (1.3 miles/2km away) are safer options.

Burnham Thorpe is one of a group of villages named after the River Burn and is a charming place set deep within the English countryside. A small river runs through the village and used to be far wider but rarely exceeds 6–7ft/1.8–2.1m wide this far inland and the best local accommodation available is Whitehall Farm on Walsingham Road should visitors wish to stay overnight. The village is small so visitors can explore it swiftly even on foot but be aware there are few pavements, no village shop, narrow lanes (often a single car's width) and hardly any lamp posts so a torch or mobile phone light is required when walking back from the pub in the evening.

Walsingham Road runs through Burnham Thorpe and its turning into Church Lane at the northern end of the village leads to All Saints Church, which is the best place to start a tour. The church dates back to the thirteenth century and was renovated in the 1840s and for the centenary of Trafalgar in 1905. Internally it would have been far darker in Nelson's day, with tall boxed church pews, and its general appearance was probably far more dilapidated. It benefitted greatly from renovations largely made in Nelson's honour with its lime-washed walls and improved windows giving an impression of openness, light and spaciousness.

Nelson was baptised here and both his parents are buried at the northern end of the church chancel with large tombstones set side by side on the floor before the altar commemorating Edmund and Catherine. While Edmund's tombstone is plainly inscribed, Catherine's inscription is rendered in Latin and bears the Suckling family crest. A fine stone bust of their famous son was placed on the wall above during the Trafalgar centenary and now watches over them and there are two additional monuments to Edmund. Both are white stone plaques and one is set into the wall above his son's sculpture and the other is located in the right hand corner behind the altar and they record his service as Rector of this Parish 1755–1802. Nelson loved his village and spoke about being buried in this church but probably would have preferred his exalted resting place in St Paul's Cathedral.

The church contains many references to Nelson and his family, including his framed baptismal record, Trafalgar prayer, a photo of Nelson's medicine chest, reprints of *The Times* newspaper accounts and the family crest. Other relics include three large ships flags hung from the ceiling and the rood cross and lectern are constructed from wood taken from HMS *Victory*. There are usually books and other Nelson mementos for sale by the church door but there is rarely anyone in attendance here and All Saints Church relies upon people's decency by using an honesty box.

The fastest way visitors can reach the Lord Nelson public house from All Saints Church is by turning left into Church Lane from the entrance, proceeding along it until it rejoins Walsingham Road and the pub stands a few hundred yards further along it before the village playing fields. It was called The Plough in Nelson's day and he regularly came here, especially during his period ashore 1787–93, and he held a farewell dinner at The Plough after receiving command of HMS *Agamemnon*. It has a long history dating back to 1637 but is most famous for its association with Nelson and was renamed in his memory in 1807 (one of the first public houses to do so). The Lord Nelson has been a place of pilgrimage for enthusiasts ever since and is one of the few locations intimately connected with him that visitors can experience in much the same way as he did.

Even without the Nelson connection, it is a pleasure to take in the ambience and relax in this fine old English tavern that serves excellent food and drink. For many years only the main room and snug were open to the public with a serving hatch into a small back room acting as the pub's bar. Nelson held his 1793 farewell dinner upstairs, which is no longer open to the public, but both of the front rooms are still used for drinking and dining. A new entrance has been constructed at the side of the old pub so the former front door is rarely used but the hallway it opens into lies between the two rooms and this area probably predates Nelson's time judging by its uneven flooring and low adjoining doorways. The snug also contains an old mural of the Battle of the Nile that is atmospheric and well worth a look.

The Lord Nelson Pub in Burnham Thorpe.

The Lord Nelson closed for five years but reopened in 2021 after refurbishment and a large-scale extension that includes a new dining room, bar and kitchen at the back of the building along with a modernized garden area. The two original downstairs rooms are furnished in traditional style with high-backed wooden settle benches before the former bar and the entire pub is decorated with Nelson memorabilia including a large model of HMS *Victory* and numerous prints of Nelson, Lady Hamilton, the Old Rectory, the family coat of arms and various naval scenes. Plans are being considered to use the small building before the Lord Nelson as a museum to house exhibits taken from the former Nelson Museum in Great Yarmouth that closed in 2020. If this project goes ahead, it will house numerous exhibits directly connected with Nelson in the future.

A recent addition to the village is a chainsaw-rendered sculpture of Nelson, which was placed on the village playing fields overlooking the Lord Nelson in February 2022. This was carved by Henry Hepworth-Smith (forester and chainsaw artist) who used the trunk of a maple tree that formerly stood beside these playing fields. He based his design on statues and paintings of Nelson and spent two weeks creating this popular new addition to the village's 'Nelson Trail'. The Treasurer of the Playing Field Committee (Mrs Smith) remarked that 'It was going to be a large expense for us to remove the unsafe tree and stump. Instead it has been transformed into something amazing for a similar cost and it creates something very relevant to our village.'

Walking or driving from the Lord Nelson, take the first right and travel south along Creake Road, which runs roughly parallel with the River Burn. A row of cottages known as 'The Shooting Box' stand about half a mile down this road on the left with a small sign proclaiming their name. According to local legend, Nelson was actually born in one of these cottages as the rectory was being repainted at the time, but this has never been proved. They are all private residences but can be photographed from the lane if visitors are discreet.

Follow Creake Road for another half mile and visitors will see Nelson's Barn on the right-hand side. A plaque is set into the wall connected with this old structure and reads 'The Birthplace of Admiral Lord Nelson – The old rectory in which the Admiral was born stood twenty yards back from this wall. It was pulled down in 1803.' A smaller plaque below records how this memorial was presented by officers and men of HMS *Tyne*, flagship of the Commander-in-Chief of the Home Fleet, in August 1959.

The current 'Parsonage' was built approximately on the site of Nelson's birthplace and an interesting feature associated with him exists in its grounds. However, this is private property so visitors should knock on the Parsonage door and ask permission before entering the garden if they wish to see it. Nelson spent considerable time gardening and helping re-route the river running through the village during his five years ashore and he dug a large ship-shaped pond in this garden, which is still here. It is roughly 50ft x 15ft/15m x 4.5m but is currently clogged with rushes and appeared to be very shallow during the author's last summertime visit. It is to be hoped that the new owners of the Parsonage will eventually restore this pond to its former glory.

The small coastal village of Burnham Overy Staithe lies just over two miles from Burnham Thorpe and the most direct route to reach it is via Mill Lane, passing the first turning, and then turning left onto Wells Road that runs parallel with the coast. Nelson regularly walked or rode here to watch merchant shipping as a boy and is said to have learned to row and sail small boats within the tidal creeks hereabouts. Although there is little to see here that is directly connected with Nelson, it is a charming village where small vessels still ply the creeks and tourists embark on boat trips to see the coastal wildlife. If visitors have the time, it is well worth a short trip to this village to see where Nelson had his early maritime experiences and began to consider a life at sea.

Great Yarmouth

The town of Great Yarmouth was an important supply base for the North Sea fleet and being only 56.5 miles/90km from Nelson's village, he visited it many times. Following his promotion to Vice Admiral, he encouraged naval recruitment in Norfolk knowing that the southern coastal counties had been bled dry by press gangs and his county bred good seamen. The Royal Navy used Yarmouth Roads as an anchorage and made great use of the warehouses and armoury built along the banks of the River Yare that runs through the town. It takes around 2 hours 45 minutes to drive from London to Great Yarmouth and the best route is the M11–A1–A47. Regular train services run from Liverpool Street railway station, changing at Norwich and alighting at Yarmouth (2 hours 40 minutes). and coach services from Victoria Coach Station usually take just under four hours to reach the town.

The former Wrestler's Inn lies in central Yarmouth and is easy to locate just off Priory Plain as it stands virtually opposite Yarmouth Minster, which dominates the northern part of town. This building is on a corner at the edge of a car park and currently used by Aston Shaw Accountants, 7 Church Plain, Great Yarmouth, NR30 1PL. It is a fine two-storey building retaining many original features above ground-floor level. Serving officers from both the army and navy regularly frequented this inn and Nelson stayed here at least twice. In 1801 he met his new commander Admiral Sir Hyde Parker in the Wrestler's Inn before being rowed out to their ships in Yarmouth roads.

Two modern plastic plaques adorn the outside of the former inn with the first recording Nelson's stay here beginning 6 November 1800 and how he was made a Freeman of the Borough of Great Yarmouth during his visit. When the Mayor and other dignitaries came to make this presentation, Mr Watson (Town Clerk) saw Nelson place his left hand on the bible to take the oath and unthinkingly said 'Your right hand, my Lord,' to which Nelson replied 'That is at Tenerife!' The second plaque recalls 'James Sharman 1785-1867 – press ganged into Nelson's navy from this site of the Wrestler's Inn served with Nelson at the Battle of Trafalgar'. The Great Yarmouth Archaeological Society and the Nelson Society/Nelson Museum placed these memorials here.

On the second occasion he stayed here, Nelson and his entourage were mobbed by wildly excited locals all the way from the jetty to the Wrestler's Inn. They were so excited by his arrival that he felt obliged to deliver a speech to them from a first-floor window to calm the crowd, which was unlikely to disperse until he did so. He remained here several days in the company of Lady Hamilton and tarried so long that the Admiralty sent a messenger ordering him to hasten down to London and deliver his reports. The landlady was delighted to host such a Norfolk celebrity and asked his permission to rename her establishment 'The Nelson Arms' shortly before his departure. Nelson smiled and replied 'That would be absurd ... seeing I have but one.'

Great Yarmouth Minster (Church of St Nicholas) lies over the main road from the former Wrestler's Inn and Nelson came here to pray on 6 November

1800 and a small plastic plaque placed under a window on the south side marks the area in the south aisle where he did so to the right of the main entrance. The Minster is proud of its maritime connections and also exhibits models of ships among other nautical items on display here.

When he arrived on his 1800 and 1801 visits, Nelson disembarked from a ship's boat onto a large wooden jetty on the seafront before the town. This dated back to circa 1560 and was used by men-of-war anchored in Yarmouth Roads and fishing vessels and was considered a local landmark by the twentieth century. However, the elements took a heavy toll upon the structure and constant repair costs were difficult for the Borough Council to justify so it was demolished in 2012. The site where it once stood lies on the seafront half a mile south of Britannia Pier where a promontory juts out from the promenade with a historical information panel detailing the jetty's role in Yarmouth's heritage at its sea-facing end (placed here by the Nelson Society). A further half-mile down Marine Parade on South Beach Parade visitors will find some related relics including some of the jetty's oak pilings that now form part of a nautical montage in a flower bed before a row of hotels. They were placed here during a Great Yarmouth & Gorleston in Bloom event with a notice describing their history alongside.

Continue south along Marine Parade from the flower bed display before taking a right turn into King's Road. Walking or driving along this road will bring visitors to the front entrance of the former Royal Naval Hospital, which is listed as a Grade II building of historical importance. This huge building is now divided into residential properties but can be photographed as long as visitors do so discreetly. Visitors can gain entry on Heritage Open Days, see – www.heritageopendays.org.uk

Construction of the Royal Naval Hospital began in 1809 with Admiral William (Billy) Douglas (Port-Admiral of Great Yarmouth) laying its foundation stone. The hospital's construction cost over £120,000 during a project led by Mr Henry Peto (uncle of the famous Sir Samuel Peto) and consisted of four independent blocks around a courtyard on a site covering 15 acres and its facilities included wards, stores, bathrooms, mess rooms, kitchens, staff accommodation, a chapel, operating theatres and a mortuary. By the time it opened in 1811, French naval activity in the North Sea had lessened and 600 men wounded at Waterloo in 1815 were its first large intake of patients. It continued to treat wounded during the Victorian period but became a mental hospital for servicemen from 1863 and ended its days as a psychiatric hospital (St Nicholas Hospital) before closing in 1993.

A monument built to commemorate Nelson's victories is the most interesting historical site in Yarmouth by far and lies half a mile from the former hospital.

The monument's official title is the Norfolk Naval Pillar but is also known as the Nelson Monument or Norfolk Monument in the town. The quickest way to reach it from the hospital gates is to walk or drive westward to the crossroads before turning left into Admiralty Road. Continue along this for half a mile (the tower will soon become visible over the rooftops) until reaching the turning into Monument Road where it stands upon a raised area enclosed by iron railings.

Local debate about building a 'Norfolk Pillar' for Nelson began in October 1805 shortly after his demise. Raising public donations to fund its construction was straightforward because Norfolk people were keen to donate money for a monument celebrating the achievements of their county's greatest hero. Selecting a location proved more problematic, with the merits of sites at Norwich and Burnham Thorpe heatedly debated by the committee running the project. Eventually they decided that a coastal location was fitting for a great admiral and selected this site on the South Denes where it would act as a seamark as well as a memorial.

Although Sir Francis Chantrey submitted designs for a column with a statue of Nelson at its summit, the committee favoured plans by local architect William Wilkins, which initially envisioned a classical galley (ancient warship) as the focus of the monument. The predicted cost was £7,500 but Wilkins asked for and received a further £2,000 due to the difficulties of establishing deep foundations into the sandy ground. The foundation stone was laid on 15 August 1817 amidst much celebration and the column was completed on 1 June 1819, 24 years before the far more famous column was raised in London's Trafalgar Square.

The height of the fluted stone combined with the statue is 144ft/44m and there are 217 steps within it allowing visitors to climb to the observation platform above. The warship design was eventually rejected and a statue of Britannia stands at the summit that faces inland rather than out to sea. Some believe she was placed to face Nelson's birthplace of Burnham Thorpe but the reason was never officially recorded and remains the subject of speculation today.

Britannia is represented as a Greco-Roman figure, holding a trident in her left hand with her right arm outstretched and grasping an olive branch. She stands upon a globe that is inscribed with Nelson's motto from his coat of arms that reads '*Palmam Qui Meruit Ferat*' – 'Let him who has merited it take the palm.' The roof of the viewing platform below her is held up by six caryatids (classical female figures used to support a structure). The monument was restored in the 1980s and during the 2005 Bicentenary when the original statue and caryatids were replaced with copies after sustaining weather damage. The head of the original statue and a silver trowel used in the opening ceremony by the committee chairman are currently held by the Time and Tide Museum in Great Yarmouth nearby. See – www.museums.norfolk.gov.uk/time-tide

Two locally-famous deaths have occurred at this site. The first happened when Thomas Sutton (Superintendent of the Work) had a heart attack as the statue was raised before the opening ceremony and 'complained of a giddiness, was seized with a spasm, and instantly expired'. This led to the local legend that he had a heart attack because the statue was incorrectly placed facing landward but this is almost certainly untrue. The second fatality occurred in 1863 when Charles Marsh tried to climb from the viewing platform onto the Britannia's shoulders but missed his footing and plummeted to the ground before the horrified spectators gathered to see him attempt this feat for a wager. A legend has arisen that the sight of the statue's beauty when he stared into her face caused him to become so captivated that he fainted and fell but this is also apocryphal.

Captain Hardy recommended former Able Seaman James Sharman to be 'Keeper of the Pillar' who was an invalid at Greenwich Hospital at the time of its construction. Sharman was only 14 and working at the Wrestler's Inn when a press gang seized him and forced him to serve in the Royal Navy. He joined the crew of HMS *Victory* in 1803 and claimed to have helped carry the stricken Nelson below decks after he was shot at Trafalgar. A cottage was built for Sharman who conducted visitors around the monument and acted as the site's caretaker. He helped save several sailors from the brig *Hammond* (wrecked on the beach nearby in 1829) and Charles Dickens was so impressed after meeting him in 1849 that he based the character of Ham Peggotty in his novel *David Copperfield* upon him.

At the time of the pillar's construction, the area of South Denes was mostly scrubland, sand and shingle and there were few buildings. The famous painting of this scene by J.M.W. Turner gives a good impression of how isolated and beautiful the area was before the industrial estate that surrounds it today was constructed. Visitors will be impressed by the size and splendour of this structure and mystified by its obscurity as Nelson is an iconic naval hero not only in Britain but across the world. Interpretation panels placed around the monument convey details about its construction, symbolism and its part in Yarmouth's local history.

Observers will note that each of the monument's four sides bear names of sea battles on the pedestal below the column and names of ships that Nelson commanded during these battles on the column abacus above. The front (facing west and inland) of the structure provides its main focus and records the names Trafalgar – Victory. It also bears an inscription in Latin that translates as 'This great man Norfolk boasts her own, not only as born there of a respectable family, and as there having received his early education, but her own also in talents, manners and mind'. Dedications on its other sides record the names Copenhagen – Elephant (north), Aboukir – Vanguard (south) and Vincent – Captain (east).

The names of Thomas Sutton (Superintendent) and John Walker (Master Mason) are inscribed on the west side of the monument and those of Hon. Colonel John Wodehouse (Committee Chairman) and the other committee members are listed on the east side. The pillar is photogenic and easily approached but (at the time of writing) visitors are no longer permitted to ascend the internal stairs to the viewing gallery. In recent times volunteers maintained the site and allowed visitors to enter and climb to the summit but this was stopped during the Covid-19 Pandemic and their admirable local heritage project is yet to be resumed. Hopefully, this will change in the near future as the viewing gallery offers excellent views of Yarmouth and the coastline.

Norwich

Norwich is the only city in Norfolk and was considered England's second most important city from 1650 to 1750 with considerable industrial expansion continuing in Nelson's day. There is a direct train link to Norwich from London's Liverpool Street Railway Station (2-hour journey) with regular coaches running from London's Victoria Coach Station (3-hour journey) and drivers should take the M11–A11, which usually takes just under 3 hours.

Norwich Castle lies in the city centre and holds a number of Nelson related exhibits in the collection of the adjoining museum and art gallery (see Chapter 8). To reach 'The Halls' (NR3 1AU) visitors should walk along Castle Meadow on the north side of the castle, turn left into Opie Street and into Andrew's Hill, then walk on to Hall Plain. The buildings comprising the St Andrew's and Blackfriars' Halls date to medieval times and contain relics of old Norwich. Portraits of civic dignitaries are displayed here but the last known portrait of Nelson painted from life is of greatest interest. It was painted in 1802 by Sir William Beechy and commissioned by the City of Norwich showing the admiral in his prime, wearing full dress uniform and decorations. This huge original work was considered a faithful likeness by his contemporaries and currently hangs in Blackfriars Hall. For opening times and details see – www.thehallsnorwich.com/site/index.php

From The Halls, continue along Hall Plain into Princes Street and turn left into Tombland to find Norwich Cathedral. It is best to enter by the

Erpingham Gateway, which brings visitors into the cathedral close directly before the cathedral itself. The grassed central area is where statues of Nelson and the Duke of Wellington stand (see Chapter 5) and many of the buildings surrounding this area remain part of Norwich School (formerly the Royal Grammar School) that Nelson and his brothers briefly attended. Nelson was aged 8–9 during his time here and the building to the immediate left of the Erpingham Gate contains the former dormitory that he boarded in.

Deal

Deal is a delightful old seaside town on the south coast of England eight miles east of Dover. Driving to Deal from London via the M2–A2 should take 2.5 hours but coaches are available from Victoria Coach Station (London) and there are direct train links from London's St Pancras, Victoria and Charing Cross stations with most journeys taking just under 2 hours.

Nelson spent considerable time in Deal, especially when he used it as a base in 1801 after receiving command of Royal Navy forces tasked with preventing French invasion. Deal has no harbour so warships were obliged to anchor in Deal Roads, also known as the Downs Anchorage. The town has many nautical connections, which include a Victorian time ball tower that replaced the Semaphore facility located here during the Napoleonic Wars. The Hamiltons visited Nelson here several times and stayed at the former Three Kings Pub that is now the Royal Hotel. This is located at Beach Street, Deal, Kent, CT14 6JD and lies on the seafront only 38yds/34m (a minute's walk) from Deal Pier. This building's Georgian heritage is still obvious despite some modifications and the staff are proud of its connections with Nelson. For details about staying here see – www.theroyalhotel.com

St George's Church is located on 22 St Georges Road, Deal, CT14 6BA. It was built between 1706 and 1716 and Nelson worshipped here regularly as a committed Christian. It was badly damaged during the Second World War (Deal was bombed and even shelled many times) but has been restored largely in red brick with lead roofing and a white timber cupola. Yet it is the graveyard that will interest Napoleonic enthusiasts most as Captain Edward Parker is buried here. He was severely wounded in Nelson's raid on Boulogne on 15–16 August 1801 and recuperated in a house in nearby Middle Street but there are two houses where it is claimed he stayed, one of which boasting a plaque on its frontage. He died shortly after an operation to amputate his leg – see Chapter 6 for details of his tomb.

Nelson's London

London contains some of the most important locations relating to Nelson and most of these are more appropriately described in following chapters. For Nelson's Column see Chapter 5, his tomb in St Paul's Cathedral see Chapter 6 and The National Maritime Museum see Chapter 8.

Greenwich

Greenwich was a separate town in Nelson's time but is now a suburb of Greater London on the south bank of the River Thames. It is a 20-minute drive from the centre of London but it can be reached by bus, national rail network or the Docklands Light Railway (DLR) that is part of the London Underground system. For seriously dedicated Nelson fans, the author recommends travelling to and from Greenwich by boat, tracing the route of the river procession preceding Nelson's funeral (see Chapter 6) and a variety of boat trips are available from points along the riverbank, with those in the area of Westminster Bridge being among the most accessible.

Travelling to Greenwich by riverboat allows visitors a view of Cleopatra's Needle from the Thames, depending upon where they board. This stands on Victoria Embankment near the RAF Memorial and Golden Jubilee Bridge (Embankment is the nearest underground station). This is an ancient obelisk dating back to circa 1450 BC during the reign of Egyptian Pharaoh Thutmose III and bears hieroglyphics from that time along with inscriptions added during the reign of Rameses II commemorating his military achievements but has little or no connection with Queen Cleopatra. Built from red granite, the needle is 68.5ft/20.88m high, weighs 187 tons and makes an elegant and striking sight on the banks of the Thames.

This monument was gifted to Great Britain by the Ottoman Governor of Egypt and the Sudan Muhammad Ali Pasha al-Mas'ud ibn Agha in 1819 in gratitude for Nelson's triumph at the Nile. However, the government declined to pay for its transportation and it was not brought here until 1877 when Sir William Wilson offered contributions to shipping costs along with £15,000 donated by public conscription. The needle's seaborne journey proved hazardous when the specially constructed vessel designed for the purpose nearly foundered and six lives were lost before her crew abandoned ship. It was discovered drifting a four days later and salvage costs added another £2,000 to the eventual bill. It was placed here on 12 September 1878 and the names of sailors lost during its transportation are recorded on a bronze plaque on the mounting stone. Decorative bronze adornments were added at the obelisk's base along with an Egyptian sphinx on its eastern side.

Greenwich contains a number of nautical sites including the National Maritime Museum and the clipper ship *Cutty Sark*, kept in dry dock close to the riverbank. The former Royal Naval Hospital for Seamen is the most relevant site for Nelson and eventually became the Royal Naval College. It is a large complex of baroque buildings constructed in palatial style to the designs of Sir Christopher Wren (1632–1723) and Nicholas Hawksmoor (1661–1736) and has appeared in many historical films. Along with treating sick and wounded seamen, this complex once housed navy pensioners unable to care for themselves due to age or disability. They began arriving here in 1705 and 2,710 pensioners were living here by 1814 with the Royal Navy maintaining their presence until 1869.

Nelson visited the hospital in 1797 seeking medical advice for the treatment of the stump of his right arm which became extremely painful throughout his later life at various times. He stayed in the official residence of his old friend Captain Locker, who was acting Lieutenant Governor for the hospital at that time. It was here that he posed for the artist Lemuel Abbott who drew preliminary sketches before painting his famous portraits of Nelson. He returned on 9 September 1805 for a dinner at The Ship Tavern that once stood near the riverbank where Nelson and Admiral Sir Sidney Smith were celebrated as guests of honour.

In the aftermath of Trafalgar, Nelson's body was brought here on 23 December 1805. It was briefly placed in what is now known as the Nelson Room, which is occasionally opened to the public and boasts a replica of his statue in Trafalgar Square. He had been placed in a coffin made from wood taken from the mainmast of *l'Orient*, which was recovered after the Battle of the Nile. Shortly after the body was brought ashore at the hospital's landing stage, this first coffin was contained within a larger lead coffin before being set upon a catafalque in the Painted Hall where the vast array of paintings that gave the hall its name were draped in black cloth for this event. Its magnificent ceiling is painted with the Triumph of the Protestant Monarchy by Sir James Thornhill. The hospital has two domed towers and the Painted Hall lies under the tower on the right hand side when viewed from the riverbank.

Nelson lay in state here from 5 to 7 January 1806 and the first mourner was HRH the Princess of Wales during a private visit with the doors opened to the public over the following days. At least 60,000 people came to pay their respects and the press of the crowds was so alarming that Lord Hood (the Hospital Governor) turned many away and requested further soldiers to guard the Painted Hall fearing injuries in the press or even a riot amidst scenes of hysterical public grief. On 8 January, Nelson's body was carried onto a barge and rowed upriver in funeral procession along the Thames before being entombed the following day (see Chapter 6). The Painted Hall was used as the National Gallery of Naval Art from 1824 until its transfer to the nearby National Maritime Museum (see Chapter 8) but some naval relics remain including two black memorial flagstones with gold lettering set into its floor, one dedicated to the 'Immortal Memory' of Nelson and the other commemorating Vice Admiral Collingwood.

Outside, visitors should take particular note of the pediment within the triangular architrave above the columns upon the King William Building, which depicts Nelson's battles and death. This was sculpted by Benjamin West and measures 12ft x 15ft/3.6m x 4.5m and looks down upon the King William Courtyard in the centre of the complex. The Admiral's House (Governor's Residence at the northern end of King Charles Court) is where Nelson was hosted by Captain Locker. This is private but occasionally opens to the public during the annual Open House London Weekend in September. A bust of Admiral Hardy by William Behnes stands in the Old Chapel that was sculpted shortly after Hardy's death in 1839 with its plinth recording his achievements and great friendship with Nelson. Entry to the grounds and chapel are free but a charge is levied for access to the Painted Hall. For details about opening hours see – www.ornc.org/plan-a-visit/

Portsmouth

Sadly a considerable portion of old Portsmouth was destroyed during the Second World War, which included buildings associated with Nelson. Many of those that survive stand within the Naval Base incorporating the former dockyard area. These include the Royal Naval Museum and The Ropery that were used as storehouses to meet the demands of maintaining a huge fleet, which increased from 272 to 949 ships over the period 1702–1805. The Royal Naval Academy (built 1733) now acts as an officers' mess and many of the officers' houses along Long Row and Short Row existed prior to 1805 with most dating to the expansion of the docks between 1776 and 1783. Admiralty House (built 1787) also remains and 'was the grandest of the Royal Dockyard commissioner's houses on account of the frequent visits to it by King George III'. All of these buildings can be seen but only some are open to the public – see Chapter 8 for details about the dockyard and its museums.

In Portsmouth itself, the Landport Gate (built 1760) that Nelson would have been driven through in his carriage can be seen and the house that his tailor Melchisedek Meredith originally occupied 72–73 High Street still exists. Nelson ordered many uniforms from here but Meredith eventually went out of business and the famous Gieves & Hawkes Naval Outfitters took his building over in 1852 but currently operate out of No1 Saville Row (London) still producing army and navy uniforms.

Nearly all the public houses from the Georgian period were lost during the war or have been demolished. Only the former Dolphin Hotel at 41 High Street and the George Hotel 100 yds/91m from the docks at 84 Queen Street can trace their origins back as far as Nelson's time. Nelson may well have used the latter due to its close proximity to the docks but it should not be confused with 'The George' where he is definitely known to have stayed. This hotel was bombed and destroyed in 1941 but once stood on High Street.

Nelson arrived at The George on 14 September 1805 and attended meetings at the dockyard the following morning but returned to confer with George Rose (President of the Board of Trade) and George Canning (Navy Treasurer). His fame was so great by this time that Nelson was hounded by hordes of admirers when they caught sight of him, which slowed his progress through the town. People shouted loud huzzas, often approached to shake his hand and even knelt before him to pray for his safety. Ship's captains' usually embarked from the Sally Port at the end of High Street but Nelson left quietly by the back entrance to avoid the crowds, hoping to reach HMS *Victory* swiftly.

Visitors can trace his route by beginning at Penny Street roughly 100yds/91m north of the turning into Pembroke Road, where the George Hotel once stood. Walk along Penny Street and turn into Pembroke Road (known as Green Row in 1805). The Garrison Chapel is visible while walking along this road and a statue of Nelson stands alongside it. Walk past the old red-brick guardhouse (erected 1833) on the right-hand side before moving onto the path running alongside Governor's Green and at the end of this path are the remains of eighteenth-century coastal defences. The large mound on the left was part of the King's Bastion and numerous onlookers stood upon it watching Nelson's progress in 1805. He paused many times to speak with well-wishers as his small entourage politely but firmly cleared a path for him. Below the ramparts and to the right of the bastion is a brick-lined archway leading into a narrow tunnel. This runs under the old defences and visitors are now treading in Nelson's footsteps as it is known he walked through it. This tunnel was only recently reopened to the public.

It emerges before a bridge crossing a moat into the remains of the Spur Redoubt and this modern span is called 'Nelson's Bridge,' which should be crossed before turning left into the ruins where a narrow passage leads through the wall that once acted as this fort's sally port. Nelson went through this to step directly onto the beach but this part of his route is now blocked by a car park. Therefore, turn right and walk along the wall through some widely spaced railings and approach the sea wall. Here walkers are standing near to where Nelson embarked and will be able to see the easternmost point of the Isle of Wight (St Helen's) on a clear day. HMS *Victory* lay at anchorage here in 1805.

Captain Hardy stood beside Nelson as he prepared to board his ship's barge preparing to row out to his command. Cheering people thronged the shoreline in spite of his efforts to leave discreetly and as Nelson raised his hat to them he murmured to his friend 'I had their huzzas before – I have their hearts now' before boarding the boat. It was extremely rare for anyone other than royalty to receive public adulation on this scale during the Georgian period. Many believed Nelson was the only man capable of thwarting an invasion and this expectation must have weighed heavily upon him as bringing the French fleet to battle would be costly in lives regardless of its outcome. He would soon fight the decisive sea battle of the Napoleonic Wars and had taken his last steps on English soil.

Case Study: HMS *Victory*

For those who wish to learn more about Nelson, HMS *Victory* is undoubtedly the most rewarding and important location to visit. She is one of very few surviving warships from the age of sail and it was in vessels like this that Nelson learned his profession from a very early age. A 104-gun First Rate ship of the line with three decks, she remained in active service for over 50 years and is one of the most famous fighting ships in the world. Admiral Lord St Vincent called her 'by far the handiest [ship] I ever set my foot on, sailing remarkably fast and being of easy draft of water'. One reason this vessel has survived for so long is that she was laid down in 1759 but only floated out from dry dock six years afterwards, unlike many contemporary vessels due to Britain's desperate need for warships. This meant HMS *Victory*'s timbers were fully seasoned when she took to sea, which helped enormously with preservation.

The ship is displayed in Portsmouth's historic dockyard and forms part of a series of nautical museums and other men-of-war exhibited there. For information about travelling to Portsmouth and building HMS *Victory* at Chatham Docks see Chapter 8 but for specific details about booking advance tickets or guided tours see – www.historicdockyard.co.uk/site-attractions/hms-victory

HMS *Victory*'s exterior has been painted in the black and yellow chequered pattern favoured by Nelson so that she closely resembles her 1805 appearance, with restoration and preservation being ongoing

It is difficult to think of a better Nelson-related site than HMS Victory.

processes onboard. Visitors are permitted access to most of the ship, being allowed to tour the upper decks, all three gun decks, orlop deck and hold. They are not allowed to climb the rigging for obvious safety reasons and the upper masts, yards and upper rigging have been removed for restoration. Hopefully the ship will be restored to her fully-rigged appearance before 2030, although time estimates vary.

It is difficult to fully describe the incredible array of naval exhibits that can be seen onboard and walking the upper decks where fierce fighting took place in 1805 is an awe-inspiring experience for those interested in war at sea. Visitors should take particular notice of the engraved brass plaque set into the quarterdeck that records 'Here Nelson fell 21st Oct. 1805' after being mortally wounded by an enemy sharpshooter firing down at him from one of the fighting tops of the *Redoubtable*.

The furnishing of the officers' cabins at the rear of the ship give an good impression of the conditions that Nelson and Captain Hardy lived and worked in but are thought to be slightly more elegant than those they knew as some features were modernized in the Victorian period. Visitors should pay special attention to the dining cabin where officers from other ships were hosted and Nelson is thought to have briefed his sea captains before Trafalgar. This room is used for official Royal Navy dinners and other functions to this day due to its famous associations.

The three gun decks provide an insight into how the ordinary seamen lived in far more spartan conditions than their officers endured and observers will see how the head room reduces progressively the deeper one descends into the ship, which speaks volumes about living in these confined quarters let alone fighting here during a battle. Indeed, when one considers that this was a large ship for the period, living and fighting conditions on smaller vessels (sloops, brigs and frigates for example) must have been even more cramped with the large number of men required to sail and fight in them.

Combat was this ship's primary role so every available space was used for cannon with even officer's sleeping quarters containing guns and the senior officers' living quarters had removable dividing walls that would be stowed away before battle to allow more space for them to be used. *Victory* was originally a 100-gun ship but mounted 104 guns at Trafalgar in a variety of calibres including 12pdr, 24pdr and 32pdr cannon and it took 623 men to man all of them. Two large carronades, notorious for their devastating effect during close-quarters combat, added to *Victory*'s awesome firepower but it is unlikely that any of those currently displayed saw action in 1805. Although many hail from the Napoleonic Wars, the cannon used at Trafalgar were removed in 1806 and replaced in 1808.

Although guided tours are available for HMS *Victory* volunteers are often stationed throughout the ship and are happy to answer questions. Indeed, although cabins and equipment are often labelled, their use is not always apparent and such expert knowledge is often appreciated by visitors as there are a host of cabins and storage rooms designed to accommodate, cater and provide for a crew of 800 men (821 at Trafalgar). The fact that stores were kept to feed this number of men for up to six months gives visitors some idea of how complicated it was to stow and preserve such an amount of food (mostly dried) and fresh water.

The mortally-wounded Nelson was carried down to the orlop deck for treatment as battle raged above, where he died in extreme pain leaning against one of the ship's wooden knees (curved supporting brace set against a ship's hull). This scene was immortalised in many paintings but some historians now believe it more likely that he was laid flat upon the deck for treatment and the exact location is under dispute. Nevertheless, a carved wreath picked out in gold leaf was placed here in 1900 and visitors standing in this lantern lit area are certainly extremely close to the point where Nelson died. As such, the orlop deck is a highly emotive place for an admirer of Nelson to visit.

HMS *Victory* continued to be used by the Royal Navy well after 1805 but was eventually placed in dry dock in 1922 and the public was granted permission to board and view the ship on 17 July 1928 by King George V. She was damaged by a German bomb in 1941 and requires regular maintenance and annual treatment against insect infection for its conservation. A considerable amount of eighteenth-century timber has been replaced but the bulk of the lower and orlop decks are original. Furthermore, in 1887 severe rot was discovered in the wooden lower masts and these were replaced with lighter, hollow iron masts from the frigate HMS *Shah* (built 1870) and the figurehead is also a replica of the 1805 original. HMS *Victory* is an iconic ship and usable wooden fragments were sold for the creation of memorabilia with one of their best sources being the Staithe Gallery in Wells-next-the-Sea that houses pieces of the 'HMS *Victory* Oak and Copper Collection' (hand-crafted items made from reclaimed material from Nelson's flagship) – see www.thestaithe-gallery. co.uk

Incredibly, HMS *Victory* is not only a commissioned warship but is the flagship of the First Sea Lord, which is why she is permitted to fly the White Ensign in dry dock. The ship retains a full time crew of seventeen and the Royal Navy hold events here that often involve 'toasting Nelson's immortal memory.' The tradition of flying Nelson's signal 'England Expects' from the ships masts on Trafalgar Day (21 October) also began here in 1899 and continues to this day.

Many are unaware that Emperor Napoleon I admired Nelson and had a bust of him placed in the Tuileries Palace during the Peace of Amiens to recall his victories. While the Franco-Spanish defeat at Trafalgar was deeply frustrating for Napoleon, he was impressed by Nelson's famous signal 'England expects that every man should do his duty' and decided his navy should emulate it, ordering French ships to inscribe the line '*La France compte que chacun fera son devoir*' (France expects that everyone will do his duty) in prominent positions. This was a remarkable tribute for an enemy to pay to a gallant and respected foe.

Chapter 2

Marching with Wellington

Field Marshal Sir Arthur Wellesley, Duke of Wellington, is arguably Britain's most accomplished general with John Churchill, Duke of Marlborough (1650–1722) and Field Marshal Bernard Montgomery (1887–1976) being the other main contenders for this title. Wellington took a keen interest in every aspect of soldiering and his approach to campaigning was marked by meticulous preparation and careful calculation of the odds of success or failure on the battlefield. He campaigned in Europe and India but really made his reputation in the Iberian Peninsula fighting against some of the best French generals of the age. The Battle of Waterloo was his ultimate triumph where the Allies inflicted a final decisive defeat on Napoleon himself. While his political career was less impressive, his fame as a commander gained Wellington enormous respect and he was known as the 'father of the country' during the Victorian period. His achievements were celebrated by monuments across the country and his residences have become places of pilgrimage for Wellington devotees where much can be learned about the 'Great Duke' today.

Sepoy General

Born in 1769, Arthur was the fourth son of Garrett Wesley, First Earl of Mornington, who taught music at Trinity College in Dublin. He was educated at Eton, Brussels and Angers but showed little promise for any subject other than music and was overshadowed by the educational attainments of his brothers. In 1787 he received a commission in the army with his mother remarking disparagingly that he was 'food for powder and nothing more'. After the death of his father, his elder brother Richard decided to change the family surname from Wesley back to Wellesley, which was the English West Country spelling in the county the family hailed from and sounded more aristocratic. Arthur's brothers entered politics but, while he was elected as a Member of Parliament several times, he made the decision to concentrate on learning his profession and symbolically burned his violin to put childish interests behind him. It is less well known that he also gave up gambling at the same time.

Ever since the English Civil War, the British establishment had feared rebellion from within the army and therefore prized an officer's loyalty above all else, paying them so little that only men with private means, who therefore had a stake in the country and made unlikely revolutionaries, could cope financially in the service. Officers could only make money through buying or selling their commissions and Arthur was able to purchase his way up the ranks quickly due to this. By 1793 he was Colonel of the 33rd Foot and fought in the Duke of York's ill-fated Netherlands campaign where he learned 'what one ought not to do, and that is always something', as he later remarked.

In 1797 he was sent to India and spent most of the long sea voyage there reading earnestly about his profession in a way that most other officers failed to do at this time. Some aspects of campaigning were held in poor esteem by his fellow officers but Arthur tried to learn about everything. Accordingly he made a particular study of army logistics which was dismissed as tedious work better suited to non-commissioned officers by many of his contemporaries but his studies paid off handsomely in India when the armies he led had to convey vast numbers of men, servants, munitions, food and water for long distances and over difficult terrain.

Marquis Richard Wellesley was appointed Governor-General of India 1797 and obtained the command of a division for his brother through his influence in 1799. During the invasion of Mysore, Wellesley participated in the Siege of Seringapatam where Tippoo Sultan was killed during the storming of the city's defences and was appointed Governor of Mysore after the fall of the city. He subsequently fought the warlord Doondiah Waugh in 1799–1800 in what amounted to a guerrilla war at some stages but eventually defeated him in open battle. By 1802 he had been promoted to major general and during the Second Mahratta War won important victories at Argaum and Assaye in 1803. At the Battle of Assaye in particular, Wellesley learned useful lessons about reconnaissance and interpreting the lay of the land prior to battle and the campaign earned him a knighthood.

Wellesley dwelt upon what he had learned in India and wrote 'rapid movement cannot be made without good cattle, well driven and well taken care of', recognizing the necessity of employing vast numbers of baggage animals to carry an army's equipment, food and water in such a climate. Huge numbers of camp followers were also required to keep an army clothed, fed and supplied, with between six and ten people in non-combatant roles like wagon drivers, water carriers or cooks necessary to keep one fighting soldier in the field. The amount of administration required for campaigning on the Indian Subcontinent was daunting but Wellesley was undeterred by hard work and took great pains to ensure that mundane but important tasks he delegated were carried out efficiently. His careful planning undoubtedly contributed to his success in India but on one occasion even he almost met with disaster when a river unexpectedly broke its banks behind his advance, cutting off his communications. His army nearly ate all their supplies during the ten days it took for the flood to subside and Wellesley ruefully recorded 'How true it is, that in military operations, time is everything'.

Napoleon famously described Wellesley as a 'Sepoy General',[1] dismissing him as a commander who was only capable of fighting colonial campaigns, which was a common prejudice among European officers at the time. Many incorrectly believed that those who served in colonial conflicts were used to lax standards of discipline due to the climate and fought against 'native' opponents who were easily outmatched. The truth was that many of Wellesley's Indian adversaries were well equipped with modern weaponry, his army was often badly outnumbered, communication routes were poor and moving over rough terrain in a difficult climate was immensely challenging. Wellesley faced odds of six to one at Assaye against the Mahrattas who employed European officers and had superior artillery to the British, so it is unsurprising that he considered it among his greatest triumphs.

By this time Wellesley took his career extremely seriously and presented a cool, impassive demeanour to the world, demonstrating a sense of purpose and showing that he was not to be trifled with. He discouraged over-familiarity with anyone he considered beneath his social status and rarely showed his true feelings in public. This won him few friends but his achievements and no-nonsense attitude gained him respect in military circles.

Wellesley returned to England in 1805 and married Catherine Pakenham. She was Lord Longford's daughter and her family initially denied the pair permission to marry until Wellesley had risen within his profession but Arthur pledged himself to her nonetheless. He honoured his promise to her but found they had little in common after his long absence abroad and their marriage was not a happy one. Indeed, Wellesley kept mistresses throughout his life but had the decency to be discreet during these affairs.

Although he was appointed Chief Secretary for Ireland from 1807 to 1809, he was given permission to join the expedition to Copenhagen in 1807 during his tenure. He defeated Danish militia at the Battle of Kiöge and subsequently witnessed the devastating bombardment of Copenhagen that forced the Danes to submit and yield up their fleet to the British. The number of civilian casualties this neutral city suffered appalled Wellesley and convinced him to

1. A 'Sepoy' was an Indian private soldier.

avoid the bombardment of urban areas or street fighting whenever possible in future.

1808 saw Wellesley promoted to lieutenant general and he was sent to Portugal, beginning a series of campaigns that made him a household name in Britain. His army landed at Mondego Bay where he commenced a swift and aggressive campaign, defeating General Delaborde at Roliça and General Junot at Vimeiro. However, he was replaced in command just as he repulsed the final French attack and was denied permission to pursue the fleeing army, which could have inflicted a total defeat upon the enemy. His successor General Dalrymple subsequently agreed to overly-generous peace terms at the armistice and Wellesley's endorsement of the Convention of Cintra allowed the enemy to return to France but led to his recall to face an official inquiry. This investigation ended the active careers of his superiors (Dalrymple and Burrard) but Wellesley's careful testimony and political connections ensured he received another command.

He returned to the Peninsula in 1809 at a time when the British had been forced from Spain and Portugal was threatened with invasion. General Soult invaded northern Portugal but Wellesley defeated his army at Porto in a daring surprise assault over the River Douro. Soult was forced to abandon his artillery and baggage and retreated into the mountains where pursuing British forces and Portuguese guerrilla actions came close to trapping his entire army. Wellesley had thwarted the second French invasion of Portugal in return for surprisingly few casualties but Parliament considered his attack across the Douro reckless and made their displeasure known. Ultimately, Britain only had one small army to send so his superiors wanted its commander to avoid taking unnecessary risks with it. Having learned this, Wellesley wrote 'I knew that if I ever lost five hundred men without the clearest necessity, I should be brought upon my knees to the bar of the House of Commons.'

Wellesley found that lessons he had learned about guerrilla warfare in India were applicable in a conflict where many civilians had taken up arms against the French and which was marred by atrocities and reprisals. Guerrilla bands lacked discipline and could easily turn upon the British so he took care to pay for supplies, especially in areas where provisions were scarce, and punish any excesses committed by his troops. By July 1809 he felt confident enough to march over the frontier and defeated the French at the Battle of Talavera on 27–28 July in conjunction with General Cuesta's Spanish army. This victory over forces commanded by King Joseph (Napoleon's elder brother) and Marshal Jourdan earned him the title Viscount Wellington but he found it difficult to co-operate with his Spanish allies and the British withdrew into Portugal.

Wellington considered the border fortresses were inadequate to prevent a third invasion of Portugal and began to build fortifications that became known as the Lines of Torres Vedras. These were three lines of 108 redoubts (small forts) mounting 447 cannon between them and linked by defensive ditches and other obstacles with their ultimate goal being the protection of Lisbon (the Portuguese capital). British and Portuguese engineers, sappers and labourers began this mammoth task in 1809 (the longest line was 29 miles wide) but they were still under construction when General Massena invaded in July 1810.

After the northern border fortresses fell, the British retreated before the invading French army and conducted a scorched-earth policy to deny the enemy supplies, which was costly for rural Portugal. Wellington repulsed French attacks at the Battle of Busaco but continued to withdraw until reaching the lines. The French were confounded by these fortifications blocking their advance and Massena turned angrily upon Portuguese officers in his staff, demanding to know why they had not warned him. They protested that no one could have predicted Wellington's building these forts but he retorted '*Que Diable!* Wellington didn't make these mountains!'[2] The French remained before the lines for two months and probed Wellington's defences but Massena then retreated. He was pursued back into Spain by the British but fought the frontier Battle of Fuentes de Oñoro on 3–5 May 1811, which ended in stalemate but effectively dashed French hopes of invading Portugal again.

Wellington set about securing Portugal by methodically recapturing the frontier fortresses so that his rear would be secure when the British advanced into Spain. His Portuguese soldiers became increasingly effective under General Beresford's direction and eventually formed almost half his army. By 1812 Wellington felt strong enough to cross the frontier, winning a major victory over Marshal Marmont's army at Salamanca in July and occupying Madrid the following month. His attempt to besiege Burgos that autumn was over-optimistic and he was obliged to withdraw over the frontier but this was typical of his adaptable approach that he summed up by writing 'The French planned their campaigns just as you might make a splendid piece of harness; it looks very well until it gets broken and then you are done for. Now I make my campaigns of ropes. If anything went wrong, I tied a knot and went on.'

British offensive operations resumed early the next year and Wellington brought King Joseph and Marshal Jourdan to battle at Vitoria on 21 June 1813, where the French suffered a decisive defeat and began to withdraw from Spain.

---

2. They were built upon tall, steep hills rather than mountains but these were significant obstacles and Massena's exaggeration is understandable.

Marshal Soult fought an excellent defensive campaign to delay Wellington but the British advance was inexorable and they crossed the Pyrenees into Southern France in 1814. The Battle of Toulouse was the last major action of the Peninsular War, beginning on 10 April, but the fighting halted when the participants received news of the Emperor Napoleon's abdication four days before.

The war had made Wellington's reputation and the army he had forged there over six years of warfare was one of the best Britain ever put into the field. Commanders like Hill, Picton, Graham and Pakenham learned their trade under Wellington's leadership and his use of British infantry in particular made them respected throughout the world. Although he is often quoted as calling his men 'the scum of the earth', this is regularly taken out of context and rarely accompanied by the qualifying remark that runs 'but you can hardly conceive such a set brought together, and it really is wonderful that we should have made them the fine fellows they are'.

Wellington was capable of over-management as a general, seldom trusting subordinates and riding constantly over the battlefield to ensure orders were carried out to the letter but such methods were effective and he never lost a battle or risked lives without cause. Although he was never loved like the more flamboyant figures of his age such as Nelson or Napoleon, he was held in enormous regard by all ranks of the British Army. If an officer let him down, his cold anger was said to be terrible but the army knew they could depend upon him to act in their interests and deliver victory, with many considering him the nation's finest commander even before Waterloo.

The return of Napoleon in 1815 came as an unpleasant shock to the allied powers that had ousted him and the Seventh Coalition was rapidly formed to crush him and raised huge forces to do so. Wellington was appointed to command a multinational army in Belgium alongside the Prussian army commanded by Marshal Gebhard Blücher. Nevertheless, Napoleon seized the initiative, knowing that the apparently safer option of fighting a defensive campaign would eventually see France overwhelmed by Allied armies totalling almost a million men. Napoleon's strategy caught the Allies off guard as he crossed the Belgian frontier and split Wellington and Blücher's armies apart, hoping they would retreat away from each other along their supply lines so he could defeat each in turn.

While Wellington fought Marshal Ney to a standstill at the Battle of Quatre Bras, the Prussian defeat at Ligny meant both armies had to retreat and Napoleon was able to concentrate superior numbers against the Anglo-Allied army at Waterloo. Blücher promised to march to Wellington's assistance who agreed to stand firm until the Prussians reinforced him in return. He selected a long ridgeline to defend, occupying large farmhouses as strongpoints before it to break up French attacks and placing his infantry on its reverse slopes to reduce the effects of French cannon fire. Although the French inflicted dreadful casualties upon the Anglo-Allied army, it clung stubbornly to its position and repulsed Napoleon's last assault with his Imperial Guard just as the French right wing began to crumble as the Prussians arrived in force. The French army was routed and left all its artillery on the battlefield in one of the most decisive victories in modern warfare.

Although Napoleon tried to rally France to fight a defensive campaign as the Allies invaded, he was forced to abdicate for a second time and was

Wellington writing his Waterloo Dispatch describing the battle that ensured his fame.

exiled to the island of Saint Helena in the South Atlantic, where he died in 1821. Waterloo ended the Napoleonic Wars and the part Wellington played in Napoleon's downfall ensured him a place in history and the gratitude of the British establishment. He played a diplomatic role in the negotiations at Vienna (before and after Waterloo) that decided upon the division of territory and power in Europe after years of conflict. The Congress of Vienna in 1814–15 made rulings on many subjects but it is interesting in the light of current concerns that Wellington was among those who pressed for the abolition of slavery and was a signatory of the final act that outlawed this vile trade in human lives as unworthy of Christian states on 9 June 1815.

Wellington was made Commander-in-Chief of the Army in 1827, a position he held until his death, but had fought his last battle. Resuming his political career in earnest, he served in several Conservative governments and was Prime Minister from 1828 to 1830. However, his reactionary opposition to social reform in a nation where inequalities were rife saw his popularity wane for a time. In combination with his failure to intervene in important European disputes and ill-judged decision to fight a duel while in office, this led many to judge him as a fine soldier but a poor politician.

Nevertheless, he was still seen as one of the best generals that Britain had ever produced and a grateful country honoured him with a full state funeral and burial in St Paul's Cathedral when he died in 1852 (see Chapter 6). Many tributes were paid to the Great Duke but perhaps the simple words of Private Wheeler of the 51st Regiment of Foot are among the most poignant 'If England should require … her Army again … let me have old Nosey to Command … we should always be … well supplied with rations … we should be sure to give the enemy a damned good thrashing. What can a soldier desire more?'

Southern Ireland

Considering the extent of Wellington's fame and numerous studies examining his life, it is strange that his precise date of birth and its location remain obscure. The problem is that contemporary accounts disagree, with some saying he was born in the middle of the Irish Sea on a ship sailing from England to Ireland but it is more likely that he was born in Dublin or County Meath. The year of 1769 is not contested but the day of his birth was either in late April or early May that year with most records claiming 1 May as the date. Since he celebrated that day as his birthday it is probably correct.

A famously arrogant remark about his birth in Ireland is also incorrectly attributed to Wellington, making him unpopular in the land of his birth. In fact the Irish patriot Daniel O'Connell actually made the infamous comment in 1844 during a court case. Asked about whether Wellington was an Irishman, he responded 'The poor old Duke! What shall I say of him? To be sure he was born in Ireland, but being born in a stable to not make a man a horse. No he is not an Irishman.' Most historians believe that Wellington considered himself as British rather than Anglo-Irish but he spoke positively about the Irish on numerous occasions. For example, he thought highly of the Irish soldiers who fought under his command and said as much, along with fighting a duel with a member of his own political party over Catholic emancipation (the right to vote) which was an important issue in Ireland.

Perhaps the best location to visit in the Irish capital of Dublin is Phoenix Park, which is the location of the vast Wellington Obelisk – described in detail in Chapter 5. However, Mornington House was built around 1762 and Garrett Wesley bought the lease from the Earl of Antrim and took up residence in this elegant former townhouse. The Dublin Tourist Office has placed a circular plaque on its frontage reading 'Birthplace of the 1st Duke of Wellington (1769-1852) son of the Earl of Mornington.' Used by the Irish Land Commission during the late nineteenth and early twentieth century, it is now attached to two neighbouring Georgian houses and used as a hotel. It still boasts its original Doric doorway and some fine Georgian plasterwork can still be seen in the interior. Its address is The Merrion Hotel, 24 Upper Merrion Street, Dublin 2, Ireland, D02 KF79. See – www.merrionhotel.com

Dangan Castle near Summerhill, County Meath is the other contender for Wellington's birthplace, and was a large Georgian house rather than an actual castle. When Garrett Wesley became Viscount of Dangan Castle in 1760, he lavished time and money upon it and continued to do so when made Earl of Mornington. The house and grounds became a beautiful setting for his musical pursuits and a fine home for his family but his spendthrift ways endangered the family's fortune. Eventually the Earl's overspending forced him to mortgage his Irish estates and transfer his family to London to avoid his creditors.

The family sold Dangan Castle in 1793 to Captain Thomas Burrowes who leased it to Roger O'Connor in 1809. Ironically, O'Connor was an Irish nationalist who considered it 'a suitable residence in which to entertain Napoleon' but was foiled in this plan when the Emperor failed to defeat the British. During his occupancy, the house caught fire, with insurance fraud being the suspected cause of this arson, but Francisco Burdett O'Connor (Roger's son) admitted he fired it accidentally while casting bullets years afterwards. The house was abandoned in 1817 and fell into ruin but its outer shell remains, still displaying an impressive five-bay two-storey frontage with moulded cornices and parapet. The ruins and grounds were advertised for sale in 2013 but its long-term future is uncertain.

Dangan Castle is not open to the public but visitors are rarely turned away as long as they treat this private land respectfully. It is located close to the village of Summerhill (County Meath) near the intersection of the R156 and R158. It is almost impossible to reach the house by public transport alone with the nearest town being Trim, which can be reached on bus routes from Dublin. It is 4 miles/6.5km from Trim and visitors can walk (1.5 hours) or cycle (30 minutes) along the R158 to get there. Most will prefer to drive the 27 miles/44km from Dublin via the R109–R148–R158 (1 hour) After leaving the R158, visitors will need to navigate narrow country lanes and the house is difficult to see until close by as it is obscured by woods. Dangan Castle lacks a full address or postcode to assist satnav use so visiting this house has become the mark of a truly dedicated Wellington enthusiast.

Wellington's London

There are many relevant memorials, museums and statues commemorating Wellington or the Napoleonic Wars in Britain's capital and Apsley House stands in central London close to Marble Arch, the Hyde Park Screen and the Achilles statue that all have connections with Wellington – see Chapter 5. This area is particularly congested by traffic with the busy thoroughfares of Knightsbridge, Piccadilly, Park Lane, Constitution Hill and Grosvenor Place converging at Hyde Park Corner. Although parking is available, it is in great demand and visitors may be better advised to use the London Underground network or travel there by foot, taxi or bus. The Underground stations of Marble Arch (Central Line) and Hyde Park Corner (Piccadilly Line) are very close and most visitors will find the Underground the cheapest and most convenient form of travel in the city.

Case Study: Apsley House – *Map 1*

Apsley House contains a treasure trove of objects that once belonged to Wellington or his family and the house was remodelled on his instructions. Although the 7th Duke donated the house and its contents to the nation, the Wellesley family still retain private rooms here. It was built between 1771 and 1778 by the architect Robert Adam for Lord Apsley (whom the house is named after) opposite the toll houses of the main turnpike entrance into central London at that time. Accordingly it was called No. 1

London since it was the first major house on the edge of the capital and is still referred to by that name. Marquis Richard Wellesley purchased the house in 1807 and Wellington bought the lease from his brother in 1817. He engaged architect Benjamin Dean Wyatt to enlarge and improve Apsley House and had the entire building faced in Bath stonework, along with adding a two-storey extension and making internal modifications. Most of this work was carried out from 1828 to 1830 while the Duke (as Prime Minister) resided at 10 Downing Street. After the Napoleonic Wars, Wellington divided his time between three main residences, which were Apsley House, Stratfield Saye and Walmer Castle. He used Apsley as a town house while occupied by his military or parliamentary duties and for socialising in the capital.

Wellington became Prime Minister during a turbulent time in politics and although his nickname of the 'Iron Duke' appeared in London newspapers in June 1830 referring to his iron resolve, it soon took on different meaning. Wellington opposed reform thinking it encouraged potential revolution and this made him unpopular and ensuing riots witnessed stones and bricks being hurled through the windows of Apsley House. As historian Julian Bryant recorded 'Wellington installed iron shutters and high iron railings to protect his town house, and it is thought that this may have led to his enduring nickname, the Iron Duke.' Eventually, Wellington was forced to give his reluctant support to help pass the 1832 Reform Bill but entertained serious reservations about it nonetheless.

Efforts were made to restore the house to its appearance during the time of the 1st Duke but, as its collection of artefacts numbers over 3,000 paintings, busts, swords, standards, prints and other works of art, only a selected few are described here. One of the finest of these exhibits is a colossal marble statue known as 'Napoleon as Mars the Peacemaker.' Napoleon commissioned Antonio Canova to create this while he was First Consul but it was not delivered to Paris until 1811. It portrays him as the Roman God Mars holding a gilded figure of Nike (Greek Goddess of Victory) upon an orb in his right hand while holding a metal staff in his left. A sword and scabbard are draped around a tree stump in the background and the figure is naked but for a cloak draped over one shoulder. Napoleon was more embarrassed than flattered by this tall, muscular and perfectly proportioned figure that represented him and refused to display it in the Louvre. Canova tried to buy his masterpiece after the wars but Britain's Prince Regent purchased it as a gift for Wellington in 1816, paying 66,000 francs (£191,000 in today's money). As it stands 11.3ft/3.45m tall, the statue was placed in the well of the principal staircase and a brick pillar was set under the floor beneath it to support its weight.

Of the many paintings displayed from Wellington's time, 'Chelsea Pensioners Reading the Waterloo Dispatch' by David Wilkie is worthy of particular attention as the Duke personally commissioned it in 1816. Wilkie drew many of the figures it depicts from real-life subjects to make it as authentic as possible and the painting currently hangs in the Piccadilly Drawing Room. There are a host of other military paintings, statuettes and busts including depictions of Marshal Blücher, Napoleon, Marshal Soult and Lord Uxbridge (of Waterloo fame) but one of the most interesting is Sir William Allan's 'The Battle of Waterloo' that Wellington bought in 1843. This shows the battlefield from the French point of view with Napoleon in the foreground watching the final attack of his Imperial Guard. Wellington and his staff are visible upon the ridge of Mont St Jean above awaiting the assault and the Duke was impressed by this painting's authenticity, commenting 'Good, not too much smoke,' during his first viewing.

The Waterloo Gallery stretches across the full width of one side of the house and incorporates an innovative ceiling with skylights designed to filter controlled light onto the paintings hung upon its walls. Lady Arbuthnot thought the Duke spoiled this effect by decorating the walls in yellow damask, which diminished their impact in her opinion. This colour was highly fashionable during the Regency period but the 2nd Duke soon redecorated with red wallpaper after his father's demise. The 1st Duke hung 130 paintings here but only 70 are usually displayed today, with many examples selected from the Spanish Royal Collection including masterpieces by Goya, Velázquez, Rubens and Van Dyck. This collection is largely composed of works recovered from the baggage train of King Joseph during the French retreat after the Battle of Vitoria 1813 and was given to the Duke by King Ferdinand VII of Spain.

The addition of the main gallery and state dining room elevated this aristocratic house to palatial status and Wellington received foreign princes, politicians and other dignitaries here but another motive for its construction was to celebrate his greatest victory in magnificent style at the Waterloo Banquet, which became an annual event until his death. To this end the Waterloo Gallery is decorated with extensive gilding, chandeliers, silk hangings and mirrored shutters that can be pulled across the windows during evening events. It is capable of seating eighty-five

A colossal statue was originally placed on the Wellington Arch.

guests and it was here that he famously hosted senior officers who had fought at Waterloo and entertained King George IV and William IV on separate anniversaries.

The Waterloo Shield and pair of Standard Candelabra were given to Wellington in 1822 by merchants and bankers of the City of London and, while usually kept on display in the museum section, they were regularly used at the Waterloo Banquets. They are made of silver and silver-gilt and the shield was modelled on that of Achilles by Thomas Stothard with Wellington depicted in the centre and scenes of his Peninsula battles represented at the edges. The candelabra are decorated in similar style with arms placed at the base, Napoleonic soldiers reclining against the stem and the Goddess of Victory surmounting them. A large silver/silver-gilt centrepiece was given to Wellington by the Portuguese Regency Council in 1816 as part of a 1,000-piece gilded service set and was also used during these anniversary events. It commemorates the victory of Britain, Portugal and Spain over the French invaders and is usually kept in the State Dining Room.

The museum area on the ground floor contains a number of porcelain collections. Although the Prussian, Saxon and Austrian Services are stunning examples of exquisite Regency-period work, the Egyptian Service is generally considered the finest on display. This was given to the Empress Josephine by Napoleon when he divorced her but she refused to accept it, which is one reason why it resides here today. All of these collections contain pictorially decorated plates, cups and dining implements and portray various scenes including some drawn from the campaigns of Wellington and Napoleon. Other exhibits in the museum include field marshal's batons, French Eagle standards (Victorian rather than Napoleonic) and a collection of swords. Prominent among this display are those worn by Wellington and Napoleon at Waterloo and the sword carried by Tippoo Sultan during the Siege of Seringapatam.

The descriptions above represent a fraction of the exhibits at Apsley House and enthusiasts will be immensely impressed by what is on display here. For satnav purposes, the full address is 149 Piccadilly, Hyde Park Corner, London, W1J 7NT. The museum and rooms that are open to the public are run by English Heritage so for up to date ticket prices, booking tours and parking details see – www.english-heritage.org.uk/visit/places/apsley-house/ Optional hand-held audio guides are included in the entry fee and the museum shop stocks learning packs and guidebooks.

Wellington's Mounting Blocks

The Athenaeum Club in Pall Mall (central London) is one of England's oldest and most respected gentleman's clubs and former members include Sir Winston Churchill, Charles Dickens and Sir Arthur Conan Doyle among others. The Great Duke was a member and regular visitor who consequently ordered a pair of mounting stones or blocks placed outside the entrance to assist riders to mount or dismount from their horses. They were particularly useful during his later years when horse-riding became more challenging to him. They are easy to miss but have stood there for nearly two centuries and boast a bronze plaque that reads 'This Horse-Block was erected by desire of the Duke of Wellington, 1830'.

Stratfield Saye House

In 1814 Parliament voted to purchase a ducal palace for Wellington in return for his military service and his requirements were that it should be within easy reach of London and boast an estate big enough for his field sports (foxhunting, shooting and fishing). Eventually he chose the house of Stratfield Saye in Hampshire, which was bought as a gift from the nation to the Duke costing £263,000 (around £16 million in today's money). The Duke initially wanted to drastically extend the house with a rather elaborate vision of a 'Waterloo Palace' in mind. He abandoned these plans as too expensive in 1821, which was fortunate as most considered the house sufficiently well-appointed in splendid grounds already. Stratfield Saye was begun by Sir William Pitt in 1630 and extended by Lord Rivers in the eighteenth century and Wellington went on to make structural improvements, adding a further story to each wing (1846), building a portico (1820) and constructing a large conservatory (1838).

Kitty loved the house and grounds but by this time their marriage had deteriorated to the extent that each occupied a separate wing of the house and used servants to carry messages across the 656ft/200m between their rooms when they wished to communicate. Wellington's military and parliamentary duties also meant that he saw little of his sons until they were adults but the birth of nephews and nieces delighted him and he spent considerable time in their company as he got older.

Stratfield Saye was the Duke's country house and he used it as a base for riding to hounds, shooting and fishing, living life as a country gentleman while in residence. Although a capable rider, the Duke was supposedly a 'wild shot' and a dangerous companion for his fellow shooters. There are accounts of the Duke accidentally peppering hunting dogs, gamekeepers and even rural bystanders with bird-shot. No serious injuries are recorded but it is interesting to note that he shared this failing with men who are regularly compared to him, as Nelson was reputedly excitable while out hunting, often firing from the hip with his shotgun, and Napoleon blinded Marshal Massena in one eye with a careless shot.

Visitors often complained the house was cold and as Wellington began to feel the elements in his later years, he installed early forms of central heating, soundproofing for most bedrooms and water closets to make it more comfortable. Even so, he did his best to dissuade Queen Victoria from visiting commenting that Stratfield Saye was 'not fit for the reception of the queen and her court', but when she visited in 1845, the Queen found her stay agreeable writing 'Stratfieldsaye is a low & not very large house, but warm & comfortable & with a good deal of room in it'.

Today the house is full of artefacts that once belonged to Wellington or his family. He brought back many items from campaign or bought during his political appointments in Europe but the house also contains gifts from King Frederick Wilhelm III of Prussia, Tsar Alexander I and Prince Blücher among others. These include paintings or busts of the various dukes and family members and numerous military paintings of scenes in the Iberian Peninsula, India and Belgium. The collection boasts items captured in King Joseph's baggage train (overtaken during the pursuit after Vitoria) and technical drawings submitted by various architects demonstrating what 'Waterloo Palace' may have looked like if the Duke's project had gone ahead.

The two most intriguing objects at Stratfield Saye are Copenhagen's grave and the carriage used during Wellington's state funeral. Copenhagen was the Duke's most famous horse and was chestnut brown with two white heels, 15 hands high and possessed a muscular, compact frame. Sired by Meteor (stallion and racehorse) and Lady Catherine (mare), Copenhagen competed as a racehorse but only won twice and retired aged 4. He was shipped to Spain for Sir Charles Vane but, when Vane was assigned elsewhere, Copenhagen was bought by an officer on Wellington's behalf in 1812. Wellington employed a stable of eight horses on campaign and used his mounts selectively depending on the kind of terrain he expected to encounter and matching that with the horses' fitness, speed, stamina and other factors. They were all fine mounts but Copenhagen swiftly became his favourite and the Duke once said 'There have been many faster horses, no doubt, but for bottom and endurance I never saw his fellow'.

Wellington often rode Copenhagen while campaigning in Spain and Southern France (1812–14) but rode him all day at Waterloo. During this defensive battle, Wellington constantly cantered along the ridge of Mount

St Jean to ensure his orders were carried out and was constantly fired upon. So many of Wellington's staff officers were killed or wounded as they rode with him that it is remarkable that neither man or horse suffered a scratch during the 17 hours the Duke remained in the saddle (he was seldom able to dismount). As night fell, the exhausted Wellington rode back to Waterloo village and patted Copenhagen affectionately on the rump after dismounting. The horse had endured terrible sights, smells and noises all day and returned this gesture with a savage kick that would have killed or crippled his master had it landed.

Wellington continued to use Copenhagen in London and rode him to 10 Downing Street when he became Prime Minister but his old warhorse was aging and he left him at Stratfield Saye in a state of semi-retirement in 1828. He died in 1836 aged 28 and was buried with full military honours in the garden but the Duke flew into a rage when he saw that one of Copenhagen's hooves had been removed as a souvenir, probably by one of the servants. Fearful of the Duke's anger, the guilty party swiftly returned the hoof and the 2nd Duke later had it made into an ink stand.

When the skeleton of Napoleon's famous horse Marengo (captured after Waterloo) was put on display, Wellington was asked if Copenhagen could be disinterred and placed alongside him but the Duke had forgotten the precise location of the grave and was unenthusiastic about the idea anyway. The current headstone was placed in the approximate location of the grave by the 2nd Duke after his father's death. It is regularly featured in guided tours and its inscription reads 'Here lies Copenhagen the Charger ridden by the Duke of Wellington the entire day at The Battle of Waterloo. Born 1808. Died 1836. *God's humbler instrument through meaner clay, Should share the glory of that glorious day.'*

Wellington received a full state funeral (see Chapter 6) and the huge carriage that bore him to St Paul's Cathedral was returned to Stratfield Saye and is currently displayed in its stables. The Duke's death came as a surprise to the establishment and preparations for his funeral were made very quickly so it is remarkable that this fine work was completed in only 18 days by the Department of Practical Arts, which used six foundries and over 100 men to complete the task but was only finished minutes before it was actually used.

The main frame and six large wheels of the carriage are made of solid bronze reputedly cast from French cannon captured at Waterloo. The carriage is 27ft/8.2m long, 11ft/3.4m wide and 17ft/5.1m high. The names of Assaye and Waterloo are given prominence at front along with the Wellesley family crest and motto *Virtutis Fortuna Comes* ('Fortune is the Companion of Virtue'). A panoply of weapons and armour were displayed around the funeral bier at the centre of the carriage and were donated by the Royal Armouries. These include halberds, standards, muskets, cuirasses (breastplates) and cavalry helmets. The polearms and flags made the carriage too tall to pass under the Temple Bar archway between Horse Guards and St Paul's Cathedral so a mechanism was installed to lower or raise them when required.

Wellington's body was contained inside several coffins and placed on the large wooden bier in the centre of the carriage. This was covered by a velvet pall embroidered in silver with the Wellesley family crest, field marshal's batons and the words *Blessed are the dead which die in the Lord*. The sheer size and weight of this carriage (12 tons) are staggering and observers will not be surprised to learn that twelve black brewery dray horses were required to draw it during the funeral procession in three ranks abreast. Even so, the carriage had difficulty negotiating the route and required the help of dozens of sailors using ropes to free it on several occasions.

The 8th Duke opened the house to the public in 2003 and great efforts have been made to return rooms to how they appeared during the 1st Duke's residence here. One change is that Wellington disliked showing paintings of himself and hung few portraits here but many fine images of him are now on display and a monument topped by his statue has been placed at the main entrance to the grounds.

Stratfield Saye can be reached by car using the M4–M3 from London on a journey that takes 1.5 hours. Its full address is Wellington Estates, The Estate Office, Stratfield Saye, Hampshire, RG7 2BT but the house's isolated location means that it is almost impossible to reach by public transport alone. The nearest railway stations are at Reading (8 miles/12.8km away) and Basingstoke (10 miles/16km away) and there are no bus routes here, with an expensive taxi ride being the only other option. It is only open to the public for a few weekends every year during Easter and August and visits must be pre-booked and conducted in the company of a tour guide – see www.wellington.co.uk/stratfield-saye-house/

Walmer Castle

Built by Henry VIII as one of a line of coastal fortresses in 1539–40 in the county of Kent, Walmer Castle defended a section of an area that would be an ideal landing place for an invading army as the nine-mile-long Goodwin Sands form a natural breakwater and anchorage here. The castle became the official residence of the Lord Warden of the Cinque Ports who headed a mercantile federation of the ports of Dover, Hastings, New Romney, Hythe and Sandwich. It was a position of considerable power and held by Prime Minister William Pitt and the Duke of Wellington.

Drivers should take the A2 to Walmer from London but be aware that there are tolls charged along this route. A slightly longer route is via the M25–M2, goes through Dover and takes just over two hours. Trains run from London St Pancras and Victoria to Walmer village that has its own station and journeys last 2–3 hours. There is a coach service from London Victoria to Dover and regular bus services are available from Dover to Walmer. The full address is Walmer Castle, Kingsdown Road, Deal, Kent, CT14 7LJ and the property is run by English Heritage. For opening times and admission fees see – http:// www.english-heritage.org.uk/visit/places/walmer-castle-and-gardens/

William Pitt became Lord Warden in 1792 and used Walmer as his anti-French invasion headquarters, spending significant time here from 1802 to 1805. The castle was armed with cannon capable of firing on approaching ships and would have caused an invading force considerable difficulty acting in conjunction with the nearby forts at Deal and Sandown but Pitt considered its landward defences so old-fashioned that he concentrated on beautifying the grounds, even filling the deep moat with trees and plants, knowing that it would not withstand an infantry assault for long. Had the enemy landed in force, Walmer would probably have been abandoned with its guns spiked or removed if there was time. Pitt paid far greater attention to drilling the local Cinque Port volunteers and maintaining the army garrison and military hospital in nearby Deal.

Pitt's former rooms have recently been restored with his bedchamber and library returned to their appearance during his time, although the dining room where he held informal meetings with cabinet ministers and senior military officers is maintained in an early twentieth-century style. Following a conference here, it was agreed to send a clandestine mission to France in 1803 and Royalist General Jean-Charles Pichegru and his followers embarked from the beach before the castle for France. They hoped to overthrow or assassinate Napoleon but this mission ended in abject failure with its leading conspirators guillotined or imprisoned.

On 15 October 1805 the American inventor Robert Fulton demonstrated an experimental explosive device suspended from a buoy and ignited by clockwork timer in the ocean before the castle. Observers watching from the gun terraces saw this device sink the brig *Dorothea* in the bay and the force of its explosion shattered some of the castle windows. Pitt and Nelson judged this device highly effective but both died within months of this demonstration and the Admiralty decided against buying this new weapon.

Wellington usually came to live at Walmer between August and November every year and once called it 'The most charming marine residence I have ever seen. The Queen herself has nothing to be compared with it.' He was created Lord Warden in 1829 and used rooms on the castle's south-west side. In 1934–5 Lady Reading had these rooms' masonry restored to their appearance during his occupation and some of the possessions Wellington kept here were donated by the Wellesley family. His former bedroom enjoys ocean views and contains his writing desk, campaign bed and the armchair he died in. Most officers dispensed with such beds after returning from the wars but incessant campaigning made Wellington so accustomed to their use that he still used one. When Lady Mary Salisbury voiced her concerns over this, saying that the bed was far too narrow to be comfortable, the Duke dryly replied 'When it is time to turn over it is time to turn out'.

Many exhibits relating to Wellington are displayed in the south-west bastion and a pair of his boots is a focal exhibit. The Duke considered the Hessian boots that were fashionable at that time to be uncomfortable and had a bespoke pair made to his requirements by George Hoby in the early nineteenth century. These dispensed with the V-shaped cut and tassel below the knee and were cut lower at the back to increase comfort while riding, which also allowed riders to wear pantaloons (trousers) rather than breeches. They inspired the design of 'Wellington Boots' that became fashionable from 1820 to 1840 but the name was also adopted for the famous waterproof rubber boots made by Hiram Hutchinson in 1852, which were ideal for farmers or gardeners and widely used in the trenches during the First World War.

Walmer remained an active fortress until 1815 and eight 32pdr cannon still stand on the north-east and south-east bastions today but Wellington considered it obsolete and declined the Royal Artillery's offer of new guns in 1829, commenting 'the percussion and recoil would probably shake down the old masonry'. The sea-facing bastions' parapets were lowered to improve the view for those relaxing on the terraces during the Duke's tenure as the protection they once provided was no longer required, providing a clear sign that Walmer was now a stately home rather than a fortress.

On the morning of 14 September 1852 James Kendall (the Duke's valet) found Wellington was unable to rise from his camp bed. The Duke was carried to a nearby armchair and William Hulke (the apothecary) suggested an ammonia stimulant and offered him a cup of tea, to which he replied 'Yes, if you please.' These were his last words as the Duke lapsed into unconsciousness and he died at 3:30pm. Once death was confirmed, the room was cleared and hung with black crepe with the Duke's body placed in a coffin upon a bier in the centre. While his magnificent funeral was being prepared in London,

Wellington lay at Walmer Castle and over 9,000 people visited to pay their respects. One of his death masks and a cast of his hands made shortly after death are exhibited in his former dressing room.

Walmer Castle contains a host of original items relating to Pitt and Wellington including busts, paintings, prints and furniture. Sadly English Heritage prohibits internal photography but visitors will enjoy this incredible site, which is set within sumptuous grounds and enjoys stunning views of the ocean and coastline. It is pleasing to think that Britain's greatest general lived out his twilight years in such a fine residence.

Chapter 3

Defending Great Britain

The last successful invasion of Britain by a foreign power took place in 1066 when William, Duke of Normandy landed his army on the south coast, defeated the Saxon King Harold Godwinson at the Battle of Hastings and was eventually crowned King of England. Since that time there have been incursions in support of internal claimants of the throne and rebellions but the English Channel proved too formidable a barrier for most continental enemies to cross. The last full-scale invasion attempt was by the Spanish Armada in 1588, which was thwarted during sea battles with the English fleet and by inclement weather, with no serious landings taking place.

The French Revolution terrified the British establishment with the nobility violently overthrown by the middle and working classes and dispossessed. The execution of the French king and the creation of what conservatives saw as a dangerous secular form of government intent on destroying the old order, led to the Revolutionary Wars. Although Napoleon did much to lessen revolutionary excesses, this failed to placate the British who feared his skill on the battlefield and felt threatened by the rapidly expanding French First Empire. The British refused to consider peace terms until the French relinquished their territorial gains and restored the balance of European power. They were particularly concerned that Holland, a maritime nation lying close to British shores, had fallen under French control.

Napoleon saw Britain as an implacable foe that funded his enemies and interfered in French concerns across the globe with its powerful navy. He realized that seeking favourable peace terms from such a traditional, monarchist state was futile and Britain would only be subdued by military force. Overcoming the Royal Navy was Napoleon's greatest problem but he considered the combined fleets of France and Spain capable of achieving this, at least to the extent of gaining control of the English Channel long enough for his army to be ferried across. He was confident of defeating British forces on land and believed his continental enemies would lose heart if Britain surrendered, commenting 'Let us be masters of the Channel for six hours and we are masters of the world'. So the French began building flotillas of flat-bottomed boats as troop transports and massed an army of over 160,000 men at Boulogne to invade.

The threat of French invasion was very real throughout the Napoleonic Wars as France lay so close to England's south coast (20 miles/33km at its nearest point) and some features can be seen with the naked eye on a clear day. Diarist Thomas Pattenden scrutinized the French coast by telescope on 1 July 1805 and wrote 'Could see this evening through my glass the rows of tents on the hills on both sides of Boulogne; they appeared to extend to great length'. Hostile military preparations were clearly underway in France and many Britons, especially wealthy investors who could vote and therefore had influence, welcomed the construction of Martello towers and other defences.

The common belief that Trafalgar ended British fears of invasion is misleading. Napoleon had already marched his army inland against Austrian and Russian forces at the time of Nelson's victory but only postponed his plans to defeat Britain rather than abandoned them. The evidence for this is demonstrated by France's extensive shipbuilding programme after 1805 and Napoleon's attempts to seize the Danish and Portuguese fleets in 1807, which the British took drastic steps to prevent. Although the threat of a full-scale French invasion diminished as the Royal Navy maintained its supremacy at sea and Napoleon suffered reverses in Spain and Russia, French privateers posed a threat to British merchant shipping right up until the last year of the war. The War of 1812 against the United States of America (fought from 1812 to 1815) also saw an increased naval threat from the US Navy and American privateers. Coastal fortifications could assist British ships at sea or resist large-scale raids so the British continued to build them and substantial remnants can be seen on Britain's coast today.

British Defensive Strategy

Plans to defend the British Isles were bold, progressive and spared little expense, which was unusual for a wartime government, and demonstrated how serious the fear of invasion was. Even when the county militias were added to the regular army, Britain would be lucky to put 130,000 men into the field. This small army was clearly inadequate to defend the entire coastline so building fortifications to defend likely invasion points was an obvious solution. Theoretically these forts would delay an invader long enough for the army to concentrate and repel the invasion or mount a defensive campaign focussed on protecting London.

The port city of Dover was the most advantageous point for an invader to attack, capture and land troops at but already possessed substantial defences, although the government planned to improve them. Their primary concern was defending potential landing points along the south and east coasts of England that could allow an invader to gain a foothold on British soil. The south coast was considered more vulnerable due to its close proximity to France and possessed beaches between Folkestone and Dymchurch, Rye and Hastings, Pevensey Bay and Eastbourne that all needed protection. On the east coast, the areas under greatest threat were Hollesley Bay, those beaches between the Deben and Orwell rivers and between Harwich and Clacton-on-Sea.

'Star fortresses' pioneered by the great French military engineer Vauban were considered the forefront of military defensive technology in the eighteenth century but they were large, costly and too many were needed to defend such long stretches of coastline. Therefore, the government decided to build lines of small 'bombproof' gun towers along the beaches, which became known as Martello towers. They would have small garrisons, be armed with at least one large piece of ordnance and were designed to provided mutual fire support with neighbouring towers in their defensive chain. Three large circular redoubts were also built as headquarters to coordinate defensive strategy with the lines of towers, fielding a substantial number of guns and larger garrisons to support or reinforce them. For further details on Martello towers see Chapter 4.

England already possessed many castles and fortifications from earlier times and, although most were militarily obsolete, the government selected those whose defences could be adapted and rearmed for modern warfare. These would be incorporated into a general defensive plan for the coastlines concerned that were also linked to existing army garrisons and new innovations such as the Royal Military Canal.

The Western Heights – *Map 5*

The port city of Dover is the most obvious invasion point in England for a continental force as it is only 30 miles/48km from the French port of Calais. Dover Castle has been maintained here since Norman times with British rulers considering its possession vital for national security and calling it 'the key to England'. The British updated the castle's defences to withstand a modern bombardment during this period but no longer considered the aging fortress strong enough to defend Dover alone. The city lies within a valley overlooked by two large hills and artillery on these spurs can command both Dover and its harbour. The castle stands upon the eastern hill and it was decided to fortify its western counterpart during the American War of Independence as the British were also at war with France, Spain and Holland who were easily capable of raiding English shores. They began constructing earthworks in 1779 but this slowed and finally halted as the threat diminished. Work resumed between 1789 and 1795 and the government decided to build a permanent fortress on the site in 1804.

While the fortifications commanded the harbour, military strategists considered a direct naval assault upon the docks unlikely due to British naval supremacy at sea. They believed an attacker would land forces nearby to assail Dover from the land before entering the port itself, so the majority of the new fort's gun emplacements would face inland, based on the likelihood of French forces landing between Folkestone and Romney Marsh. Extensive barracks were constructed for a large garrison so that the French would have to capture Dover before marching on London or risk having a substantial enemy force behind them.

Captain William Ford RE drew up plans to fortify the area in 1803 largely based on Vauban's principles but incorporated designs of other Royal Engineer officers for specific areas. The largest fort would be the 'Citadel' placed at the highest point of the Western Heights, which would be connected to outlying bastions and the 'Drop Redoubt', which would be a strong and almost independent fort in itself. Building took place from 1804–14 and cost £236,305 (£125 million today) but these vast defensive works are surprisingly obscure in England and historian John Peverly commented 'Unknown to most people, there exists on the hills to the west of the town and port of Dover a fortification which was considered at the beginning of the [twentieth] century to be the strongest and most elaborate of the country'.

The parts of the Western Heights open to the public can only be explored on foot and it is possible to gain good views of both fortresses and the brick-lined ditches connecting them and the bastions from adjacent footpaths. Information panels in the area reveal twelve main points of interest but those most relevant to the Georgian period are the Citadel, Grand Shaft and Drop Redoubt.

The Citadel was a large star-shaped fortress surrounded by deep dry moats, which were 'unrevetted' in 1806 but had been strengthened with brick by 1814. The star shape of the walls these surround was designed to allow the garrison to bring heavy firepower to bear against besiegers who would have to dig trenches towards the fort to get their guns close enough to bombard it. It stands roughly 100ft/30.48m higher than the Drop Redoubt with a large parade ground surrounded by barracks, magazines and storerooms. A well was dug 420ft/128m deep into the hill to provide a permanent source of water for the garrison. The Citadel had three loopholed guardhouses and its initial armament consisted of forty-three 18pdr cannon and thirty-one carronades.

Construction of the North Centre Bastion and other outworks began in 1809 but they and the Citadel were unfinished when work stopped in 1814 and they were only completed in the 1860s. The army left the structure in the 1950s and the site was given to HM Prison Service in 1956 and used as a Young Offenders Institution for many years. Its most recent use was as the Dover Immigration Removal Centre but the freehold was offered for sale in 2018 and the Citadel's future is uncertain. It is currently closed to the public but can be seen and photographed from adjacent footpaths.

The Grand Shaft is open to the public and is a remarkable example of military architecture. It was designed by Brigadier General William Twiss, Commanding Engineer of the Southern District, and provided a quick and secure way for troops to march from the heights into Dover or to the docks. In addition to improving communication with other parts of the city defences, Twiss thought it 'may eventually be useful in sending reinforcements to troops employed in the defence of the beach and town or in affording them a secure retreat'.

The Grand Shaft Barracks were built in 1803 with accommodation for 1,200 men along with a military hospital. The barracks were demolished in 1965 but their parade ground still exists and the great stairwell's upper entrance was deliberately placed nearby where, as John Peverley writes in *Dover's Hidden Fortress*, '59 steps descend to the bottom of a circular bowl excavated in the top of the cliff. From here three spiral staircases each of 140 steps descend around a vertical, circular brick faced shaft, open at the top. At the bottom it is connected to Snargate Street by a horizontal tunnel emerging from the foot of the cliff.' These three staircases allowed large numbers of troops to descend simultaneously if marching three or four abreast and windows set into the sides of the central shaft give light and ventilation. Work began on this structure in 1804 and it was ready for use by 1807 but only fully completed in 1809. It is the only triple spiral staircase in Great Britain but two double spiral staircases (almost as rare) were built in the Citadel leading down to its well room and sally port.

Visitors climbing these stairs will swiftly appreciate that their width and height would allow troops to move very quickly to threatened areas, which had obvious benefits to Dover's defenders. A demonstration of how large they are was provided by Mr Leith of Walmer who rode a horse up one of the stairwells for a bet in 1812. The amount he won in this wager is unrecorded but the army only permitted this feat because he owned the land the barracks were built upon. The lower entrance of the Grand Shaft emerges onto the A20, which is the main coastal road leading into Dover. There is parking at the nearby marina and visitors can climb to the Western Heights using the shaft for a

The near-impregnable Drop Redoubt on the Western Heights in Dover.

small fee and leaflets and site maps are also available here. For opening times see – www.doverwesternheights.org/

The Drop Redoubt is a very interesting fortification. Standing on the lip of its dry moat today, it is easy to imagine an enemy officer's dismay upon seeing the scale of this work and realizing how difficult and costly it would be to assault. It is formidable in its own right but would be almost impregnable when combined with the mightier Citadel that could offer supporting fire from its superior position.

It was designed in 1784 by Sir Thomas Hyde Page RE who initially named it the Eastern Redoubt and it was built in a pentagonal shape surrounded by a deep (40ft/12m) brick-lined moat. Four caponiers extend into the dry moat, allowing defenders more firing points along its length, but these were added in Victorian times and altered the fort's appearance somewhat. Its only entrance lay above the moat and was reached by a light bridge over the moat that could pivot downward against the fortress wall. If the bridge was lowered in this fashion, attackers storming the fort would be forced to enter the moat and climb the fort's walls with ladders but it was more likely that they would bombard the Drop Redoubt into submission or blockade it as they would lose many men in such an assault.

The Drop Redoubt was armed with twelve 24pdr smoothbore cannon and two carronades with emplacements set all around the summit of the structure. The 24pdrs were intended for long-range use but could also be used to fire on infantry assaulting the structure with case shot. The carronades and musket fire could also turn the fort's moats into a lethal killing ground if French infantry entered them and tried to climb up to the gun platforms.

There was accommodation for 200 men in five bombproof brick-vaulted casemates on top of the redoubt but these are oddly exposed to fire from some quarters, explaining why they were covered with earth for greater protection from mortar and howitzer shells. The redoubt can be viewed from nearby footpaths and visitors can enter the moats to look up at it from close quarters but the fort itself is usually closed to visitors. However, internal tours can be booked to see the gun platforms, magazine and barracks on top of the redoubt along with the largely Victorian inner passageways and rooms.

The Drop Redoubt was extensively modified and rearmed during the Victorian period and anti-aircraft guns were placed on its gun platforms during the Second World War. These were vital as the south-east of England was known as 'Hellfire Corner' during the First and Second World Wars, being subjected to repeated air attacks. Commandos were also secretly stationed in the redoubt and tasked with sabotaging the docks if they seemed likely to fall into German hands.

Lines or ditches were dug into the hillsides to delay the progress of attackers and provide killing grounds for the guns of the fortifications on the Western Heights. These were hewn into the chalk, lined with brick and designed to be easy to enter but difficult to emerge from. These were begun in 1804 but only partially completed by the end of the Napoleonic Wars, being finished in the 1860s. The north lines run between the citadel and the Drop Redoubt and the south lines from the Citadel to Old Folkestone Road and both can be seen from footpaths running along the heights.

It is easy to travel from London to Dover by car, coach or train and there are regular ferry services running from Calais and other French ports into the harbour. To drive from London take the A2–M2 and join the A256 to reach the central Dover but use the A20 to approach the Western Heights directly. Turn left at the first A20 roundabout on the outskirts of Dover and follow the South Military Road to the heights. This turns into the North Military Road and signs direct drivers to a car park on the right, which is located at the north entrance of the Western Heights. Regular buses and coaches are available from Victoria Coach Station arriving in Dover town centre. Here the 62 bus can be taken to the north entrance or travellers can walk to the site, which is less than a mile away. Trains run from London Victoria, St Pancras and Charing Cross railway stations to Dover Priory Station, which is about half a mile (15–20 minutes' walk) from the Western Heights.

Today English Heritage owns the Drop Redoubt and Dover City Council own the Grand Shaft. The Western Heights Preservation Society help run the Western Heights and hold regular activities, re-enactments and fundraising activities here. They also provide internal tours of the Drop Redoubt (usually monthly) and details of these can be found on www.doverwesternheights.org/

The Royal Military Canal

British strategic planners considered the peninsula between Hythe and Hastings particularly vulnerable if the French landed on the south coast. Frustratingly, this was a long stretch of coastline to protect with the Romney and Walland marshlands behind it meaning that large areas were impossible to build upon. A potential solution was to open floodgates to inundate the surrounding area, which might prevent an enemy army moving inland. The Rochester Conference of 21 October 1804 approved the proposal of building Martello towers and their defensive system (see Chapter 4) but also revealed that the idea of flooding the marshes was redundant. Adopting this strategy would damage farmland, kill livestock and disrupt civilian and military activity in the area, which was unacceptable in the event of a false alarm. Furthermore, it would take ten days to completely flood this region, which was ample time for an enemy commander to interfere with flooding operations or force his way inland before they took effect.

Lieutenant Colonel John Brown of the Royal Staff Corps of Field Engineers is generally credited with the idea of constructing a military canal to overcome this dilemma. If his proposals were adopted, it would virtually cut off the peninsula and turn it into an island for defensive purposes. The idea was approved by the Prime Minister and Duke of York (Commander-in-Chief of the Army) on 26 September and they appointed John Rennie as consultant engineer. The Prime Minister was so enthusiastic about the project that he personally persuaded local landowners to sell or lease land for its construction. Excavation began at Seabrook village near Hythe in Kent on 30 October 1804 and eventually extended to Cliff End near Hastings. By May the next year, only six miles had been dug so Rennie and most of the civilian contractors were dismissed and the project returned to the Quarter Master General's Department.

Brown planned for the canal to be 40ft/12m wide at the bottom, tapering out to 60ft/18m wide at water surface level. It would eventually be 9ft/2.74m deep and 28 miles/45km long. Civilian navvies dug the canal while soldiers built ramparts and batteries with over 1,500 men eventually working on its construction. The canal was built in two sections, which were linked by the rivers Rother and Brede and a military road was built on its inland side, protected by earth banks made from the soil dug out of the canal. This road allowed troops, supplies and guns to be transported quickly to areas under attack and moveable wooden bridges were constructed to allow troops to cross to the other side when necessary.

Small two-gun batteries of 12pdr or 18pdr guns were established at regular 500-yard intervals along the canal's length and its route was 'staggered' in places to allow artillery to fire directly along stretches of the waterway if the enemy attempted to cross. Sluices were built to control the water level and the canal was incorporated into the Martello tower defensive system with towers 22–27 and 30 built in positions to support its defence.

The Royal Military Canal was completed in April 1809 at the cost of £234,000 (roughly £10 million in today's money), exceeding the initial estimate by £34,000. At first its construction was welcomed and the *Sussex Weekly Advertiser* proclaimed that it was 'one of the greatest military works in this or any other kingdom!' adding that its construction would benefit waterborne trade when the war ended. However, once the war was over, many criticized the government's 'excessive spending' on fortifying the coastline for an invasion that never came. In his book *Rural Rides*, William Cobbett wrote scathingly about Martello towers but also singled out the canal, remarking 'Here is a canal made for the length of 30 miles to keep out the French. Those armies who had so often crossed the Rhine and the Danube were to be kept back by a canal 30 feet wide at most!' The canal was actually double that width and under that length but it was true that Napoleon's armies had regularly crossed great European rivers and this man-made obstacle was not as formidable.

Military historians can only speculate over how long this waterway might have delayed a French army but the most important factor was how well it was defended by the troops manning it. If sufficient infantry manned its ramparts supported by well-supplied artillery batteries, the canal would probably have caused the French considerable difficulties. The morale of the troops was also a crucial factor and the Battle of Wavre in 1815 provides an interesting comparison. Here a determined force of 15,000 Prussians under General Thielmann held off Marshal Grouchy's 33,000 men by defending the small River Dyle. The Dyle was swollen by recent rains and far narrower than the canal but Thielmann delayed Grouchy significantly, whose troops were badly needed at Waterloo (fought on the same day). Ultimately, the canal was never put to the test but its defensive capabilities should not be lightly dismissed.

From 1809 the canal was used to ferry troops along the south coast, which cut the time of their journey between Rye and Hythe in half. Transporting troops using the canal between Dover and Hastings was also quicker and the journey from Dover to Rye was shortened from three days when marching to a single day via narrow boats. As canal historian P. Vine commented 'The sight of 500 troops in their redcoats being speedily carried in five barges each drawn by a pair of horses from the Royal Wagon Train across Romney Marsh at 5 miles an hour, must have aroused as great an interest as did the passing of the first steam trains.'

Government hopes that tolls for using the canal and military road would pay for their construction proved ill-founded but the canal was useful for deterring smuggling on the south coast, which had become endemic. Companies used narrowboats to transport goods along the canal for a time but the increasing use of railways damaged this trade and it ended on the Royal Military Canal in 1877. The military used the canal once more during the Second World War, recognizing its potential to combat paratrooper landings that were inevitable if the Germans attempted to invade. Pillboxes and barbed-wire impediments were built along the canal, often where Napoleonic batteries had been placed, and many can still be seen today.

The memorial to the navvies who dug the Royal Military Canal.

Today the entire length of this defensive work can be walked by public footpaths running alongside the canal. Some of its route can be followed by car using the B2067 or A259 from Hythe to Hastings but the canal frequently flows through isolated farmland and its length cannot be followed entirely by road. There is picturesque countryside along the canal banks in many areas but the best vantage points are the beginning of the canal at Seabrook, central Hythe (it runs through this town) and the village of Appledore in Kent. The centre of Hythe is particularly informative as interpretative history panels are located at points along the canal's banks providing details of its construction and what this meant for the locals who called it 'Mr Pitt's Ditch'. There are also two sets of modern sculptures depicting soldiers of the Royal Staff Corps who supervised and built military defences along the canal and another to the civilian navvies (manual construction workers) who dug the waterway itself with information panels placed between each set of statues.

Circular Redoubts – *Map 5*

Delegates at the Rochester Conference agreed that Martello tower chains would act as the first line of defence for threatened coastlines but required additional strongpoints to support them and co-ordinate regional defence. Accordingly, they agreed to build three large circular redoubts at Eastbourne, Dymchurch and Harwich. A redoubt is an enclosed fort designed to act in support of larger fortifications or guard features such as roads or bridges either independently or as part of a series of redoubts. They varied enormously in size and ranged from simple earthworks to more permanent structures built in brick or faced with stone. The word redoubt originally meant 'place of retreat' and various kinds were used from medieval times onward but particularly during the English Civil War.

The three circular redoubts built between 1804 and 1812 were designed as permanent structures and constructed in brick and stone. They would offer direct fire support to nearby Martello towers and could resupply threatened areas of the line with men, arms and munitions if necessary. If a line of Martellos fell, they would act as a place of refuge for their retreating garrisons and contained enough supplies to withstand a siege for a considerable time. All three mounted ten heavy guns and their circular construction meant they could fire in a full 360-degree circle and were essentially control points for co-ordinating the defence of their respective areas.

Construction began at Eastbourne in 1805 and its redoubt was built from over three million bricks with stone-faced gun embrasures. It was finished in 1807 and presented a low profile to warships at sea and 'Everything about the Redoubt was built to be bomb proof, from the great earth mound that surrounded it, to the single filled cavities throughout the building. This fortress was constructed to absorb enemy fire whilst being able to dish out a considerable amount of its own through 10 huge cannon.'

An earth glacis (slope) raised around the redoubt was designed to deflect shot over the structure and partially conceal it from the view of enemy artillerymen. The redoubt was 224ft/68m in diameter and surrounded by a dry moat 30ft/9.14m deep. A 'drop bridge' spanned the 20ft/6m brick-lined ditch that swung downwards on a pivot to lie against the fortress wall if it came under attack from the land. The bridge led directly onto the fort's roof where there were firing positions for eleven guns, although only ten 24pdr cannon were ever deployed. Firing steps enabled the garrison to fire muskets at enemy infantry attempting to climb the glacis or enter the moat around the structure. The fort actually fired upon a French ship that approached too closely in 1812 but two shots were enough to persuade this vessel to alter its course.

A main double stairway ran down into the circular parade ground in the centre of the redoubt. This was exposed to plunging shellfire so three spiral stairwells were sunk into the roof for use by gunners if the fort came under attack. Twenty-four casemates (bombproof vaulted chambers) were built around a circular parade ground in the centre of the redoubt with small storerooms between them. These provided accommodation for officers and men, stores, magazines and a cookhouse.

The garrison's full strength was 350 men but this meant each barrack room had to accommodate 15 soldiers who had to switch beds according to shift times so conditions were cramped and unhygienic. Therefore, it was rare for more than 250 men to be stationed here unless the fort was threatened with attack and only 150 of these were soldiers, with others in civilian support roles. Tents could be pitched in the parade ground for additional accommodation and this area was designed to amplify sound so orders shouted by officers and NCOs were more audible during parades or over the sound of gunfire.

Until recently many of the casemates were used for exhibitions and original features could be seen at Eastbourne including hearths and ventilation shafts, which were largely retained even during modernization. Original features can still be seen at Eastbourne including hearths and ventilation shafts, which were largely retained even during modernization. Wooden tanks were used to supply water for serving the guns but some became contaminated with seawater at high tide making their contents unsuitable for drinking. The redoubt remained in use for the rest of the nineteenth century and was used during the First and Second World Wars.

Eastbourne can be reached by road from London with key approach roads including the A27, A22 and A259. Follow the signs for the seafront to Eastbourne Redoubt, Royal Parade, Eastbourne, BN22 7AQ. There are regular trains from London Victoria, Brighton or Hastings and the redoubt is 20 minutes' walk from Eastbourne Railway Station. In early 2023 the redoubt was closed to the public, although it can still be photographed externally. The future of this structure is currently under discussion by local authorities and if this site opens again it will be listed on – https://www.visiteastbourne.com/things-to-do/atttractions/museums-and-galleries

Dymchurch Redoubt was built along very similar lines to Eastbourne between 1804 and 1812, being 224ft/68m in diameter with twenty-four casements surrounding a circular parade ground. It is situated at the top of a shingle beach on the edge of the Hythe Ranges and was intended to guard sluices used for draining Romney Marshes and support towers guarding the area between Hythe and Rye. Dymchurch deployed ten 24pdr cannon and remained in operation during the Victorian period. During the First World War it was used primarily as a barracks but was extensively updated during the Second World War with modern guns and pillboxes added to its gun positions. The fort was used as an observation post and an Emergency Coastal Battery and given to the coastguard after the war. Today it is closed to the public and owned by the Ministry of Defence with its future in some doubt.

Case Study: Harwich Redoubt – *Map 5*

The small town of Harwich stands on a peninsula projecting out into the estuary of the rivers Stour and Orwell, which is an excellent defensive position with even the most vulnerable approaches from the south and east presenting a challenge to an attacker. Although the nearby city of Ipswich enjoyed more trade, Harwich was the largest safe haven for ships on the east coast evading storms or enemy vessels between the Thames and Humber estuary. It was for these reasons that Henry VIII decided to fortify Harwich and began a major shipyard here.

Further fortifications were added between 1600 and 1700 but were almost obsolete by 1780. The need for modernization during the Napoleonic Wars added urgency as the harbour was important for Royal Navy operations in the North Sea (often called the German Sea until the First World War) but also conveyed great advantages to an invader if it fell into enemy hands. Possession of Harwich would give Napoleon a safe anchorage where troops could disembark that was equipped with shipyards to construct or repair vessels. It would make an excellent base of operations and was only three days' march from London (80 miles/128km).

Numerous proposals for a strong, permanent fortification capable of fighting in conjunction with the fort on Landguard Point were entertained but eventually a circular redoubt mounting ten guns was chosen. Construction began in 1807 with bricks brought by barge from the London area. The redoubt was set upon granite foundations (10ft/ 3m deep), its outer walls were built of brick and varied between 3–8ft/ 0.9–2.4m thick. It was finished in 1810 and cost just under £60,000, which was roughly treble the estimated cost.

Harwich Redoubt is slightly smaller than its sister fortifications at Dymchurch and Eastbourne, being 200ft/60.96m in diameter, and is encircled by a 30ft/9m dry moat that is 20ft/6m deep. Entry was gained over a drawbridge that could once be partly raised but is now permanently fixed in position. Visitors crossing the bridge will see graffiti carved into the sides of the brick entrance that was mostly written by bored sentries and is predominantly soldiers' initials and dates. To enter the fort today, visitors cross the bridge, emerging straight onto the gun platform. There are ten gun positions here that are named after local families, landmarks, streets, shipbuilders and notable local individuals. Most of the artillery storerooms on the gun platform are Victorian but the iron railing preventing people from approaching the sheer 20ft/6m drop onto the parade ground was present in the early nineteenth century.

A large variety of armament is displayed on the gun positions dating from Napoleonic times to the Second World War. It mounted ten 24pdr cannon in 1810 that were placed on traversable wooden carriages to fire through stone-lined embrasures in the parapet. The gun that conforms closest to them is the 12pdr English cannon on the Queen Street platform. It is mounted on a wooden carriage with wheels that run along an iron rail set into the floor of this position. This allows the gun to be manoeuvred from left to right and its chassis also allows the gun to be pushed forward so that its muzzle emerges from the embrasure immediately before firing. The cannon's violent recoil after firing slid it backwards along the carriage towards its loading position.

Most of the gun platforms still retain iron brackets on their walls so that artillery equipment could be stored here such as rammers, wormers, swabs and buckets of water. There were also five joists (winches) allowing ammunition to be hoisted up to the gun decks from below. Other Napoleonic guns displayed here include two 12pdr carronades and three 4pdr, 11.5pdr and 24pdr cannon mounted on naval carriages.

Three staircases descend into the redoubt to its lower levels. Here eighteen casemates housing the garrison's accommodation, stores and magazines surround its circular parade ground, which is 85ft/25m wide. Three hundred men could be housed in these bombproof casemates when the garrison was at full strength and they are built with vaulted roofs to support the weight of the guns above them. A sally port allows access into the dry moat at this level and a 20ft/6m-deep well stands in the centre of the parade ground that once provided fresh water for servicing the guns when in action and as the garrison's drinking water.

The casemates are all named and it is worth noting that the powder magazines are placed on the seaward-facing side. Their depth and positioning theoretically meant that warships firing from the estuary at this fort were likely to overshoot these rooms, either missing the redoubt entirely or hitting latrines on the other side. Some magazines have been restored to their original appearance and were designed with a sharp turn at the entrance to prevent fire from enemy shells landing in the parade ground from igniting the gunpowder within. Niches with glass windows are set in the walls for lanterns so that gunners could still see by their light while limiting the risk of them causing an accidental explosion.

There are exhibitions detailing the redoubt's martial history over two centuries and the gaol, kitchen and barracks rooms have all been restored to their appearance at various time periods. An exhibition examining the restoration work that began in 1969 is particularly noteworthy and shows the enormous amount of work required by volunteers to repair this once dilapidated fortress.

From London drivers should follow the A13–A12–A120 to reach Harwich. Trains run from London Liverpool Station to Manningtree then Harwich Town. Felixstowe also offers a good point of access via foot ferry (see Chapter 4). Today the Harwich Society runs the redoubt, which is located opposite 42a, Main Road, Harwich, CO12 3LT. For up to date entry fees, opening hours and group tours see – www.harwich-society.co.uk

To appreciate the defences, visitors can try approaching Harwich using the daytime foot ferries running between Felixstowe-Harwich or Felixstowe-Shotley. French ships would have approached along the route they take through this estuary and would already have come under fire from Landguard Fort on the Felixstowe side on their approach. Harwich circular redoubt is barely visible from sea level with only its parapets showing on the hillsides and the first sign of its presence would probably be the smoke as its guns fired on ships entering the estuary. Its low profile means that returning fire from ship level effectively required very skilled gunnery indeed. Ships would then come under fire from the Martellos on Shotley Peninsula, which also had supporting artillery batteries nearby and further batteries were placed upon Beacon Hill near the redoubt and in the region of Landguard Fort, with as many as 300 cannon trained on the estuary. Most naval commanders would deem this position too strong to attack and land troops further up the coast to assail it from the land. With a garrison of 2,000 men in Harwich alone, this would still be a formidable operation to undertake.

Dungeness Bastion – *Map 5*

The headland of Dungeness is sparsely populated and jokingly referred to as 'Britain's only desert' today with shingle and scrubland extending an unusually long way inland. It was an isolated place during the early nineteenth century and its surrounding waters are deep, allowing ships to approach closely and put troops ashore although the strong currents here are highly dangerous to swimmers. A semaphore station was erected here so that other parts of the region could be warned of enemy activity but its defences were primarily intended to delay an invader's advance inland with the Royal Military Canal designed to cut this Peninsula off.

Work to construct the bastion began in 1798 with an octagonal earth redoubt (705ft/215m in diameter) equipped with counterscarps and glacis surrounded by four artillery batteries. It was armed with 24pdr cannon but considered vulnerable to infantry assaults so the earthwork was reinforced with brick and an 11ft/3.5m high wall that was loopholed for musketry was added in 1803. The triangular-shaped batteries deployed four or five 24pdr cannon each and covered the shingle beaches and anchorage with small barracks, guardhouses and magazines for three officers and up to thirty men each. The batteries were all placed within two miles of the redoubt where their garrisons could retreat if hard pressed.

Drivers should approach Dungeness from Hythe or Rye via the A259 but the headland itself is low and easily to navigate as so few buildings have been constructed here, with structures higher than a single storey prohibited. Indeed, the area is famous for its unusual dwellings built from railway sleepers and other makeshift materials. Buses routes run from Hythe (No. 102) and Rye (Nos. 102/293 or 11) but services to this lonely spot are limited and visitors will have to walk onto the headland after alighting near the Pilot public house. The remains of the redoubt stand a few hundred yards behind the two lighthouses on the point and the musketry wall is visible from some distance, overlooked by a number of Royal Naval Shore Signal Service (RNSSS) cottages. The batteries are in varying states of preservation with

No. 2 Battery (eventually upgraded as an independent fort) classified as an Ancient Scheduled Monument. For detailed information on the forts see – www.theromneymarsh.net/militaryheritage

Modified Fortresses

Following centuries of warfare, Britain possessed an abundance of castles and forts built prior to 1792. Most were totally obsolete but the government sent military engineers to decide whether some could be adapted to withstand early nineteenth-century artillery and assess their capability of deploying modern cannon effectively. Those on the coast were given priority and, although they would not be as effective as modern forts, some could fire in support of naval actions near the coast, cover landing beaches or deter raids. A few would be even more effective if their positioning allowed them to be incorporated into the new defensive system with the support of Martello towers. Dover Castle provides a good example of this kind of work with its perimeter walls strengthened to withstand artillery fire and earthworks thrown up to deflect cannon shot over its outer walls. New gun platforms were constructed to deploy modern cannon but strategists predicted that new works on the opposing Western Heights would take the brunt of enemy assaults, if the town was attacked with Dover Castle acting in their support.

Henry VIII's artillery forts were a logical choice for modernization as they were built to counter invasion and designed as gun platforms, albeit for sixteenth-century cannon. One of these was Sandgate Castle which was directly incorporated into the new defensive system with a Martello constructed within it and supporting towers on either flank built within cannon range (see Chapter 4). Others were simply rearmed with only minor structural alterations to gun platforms and embrasures. Deal and Walmer Castles are good examples of this approach and deemed capable of firing at ships at sea or troops coming ashore but were unlikely to withstand a land assault for long with almost no effort made to update Walmer's landward protection (see Chapter 2).

Dartmouth Castle, which dates back to the fifteenth century but was modified many times since, had a modern battery added to its defences as it was perfectly positioned to defend the mouth of the River Dart on the south Devonshire coast. It provides an excellent example of a Napoleonic artillery battery subsequently adapted during the Victorian period, see – www.english-heritage.org.uk/visit/places/dartmouth-castle/ Even more modern strongholds like Landguard Fort (Felixstowe) were simply rearmed with minimal structural alterations as it was thought it would fall to the first escalade from the land and modernization was time-consuming and costly.

Thames and Medway Defences

Fort Pitt was named after the Prime Minister and built between 1805 and 1819 as part of the defences protecting the River Thames and River Medway. The 'Pool of London' was a huge port and vital for British trade and shipyards in this area were necessary for building and maintaining the Royal Navy's ships. Situated on the boundary between Chatham and Rochester in Kent, it formed part of a defensive ring protecting Chatham Dockyard that included other forts. Fort Pitt's defences included a brick-lined 15ft/4.6m trench with bastions at each corner, a central blockhouse and gun embrasures. It was never used as an active fortress but wounded were brought back from Waterloo and were treated here. The blockhouse and other facilities have been demolished but the barracks are currently used as a school and there is no public access at the time of writing.

Fort Amherst was begun during the American War of Independence but hugely expanded during the late eighteenth and early nineteenth centuries as one of the largest forts in this area. It was also part of the same defensive ring and protected Chatham Dockyard from landward attacks, being strengthened by the addition of two barriers (Spur and Prince William's batteries) on the highest point that overlooks Chatham. A large guardhouse and a bridge were added and the fort eventually presented almost two miles of gun positions and ramparts with its barracks and storerooms protected underground. One of its primary purposes was to store ammunition and Amherst's Grand Magazine held a vast amount of powder, musket balls and various forms of cannon shot. See – www.fortamherst.com/history/ for details of tours and the regular Napoleonic re-enactments held here.

Two fortresses were built on opposing banks of the Thames almost opposite each other to prevent a naval force sailing upriver and attacking London itself as the Dutch had done in the seventeenth century. Tilbury Fort stands on the northern bank and had become a formidable work by the seventeenth century but was modernized with the addition of heavy guns and magazines in the 1700s. Its stores could hold over 20,000 barrels of gunpowder and it was considered an important defence for England's greatest river in the period 1793–1815. For opening times and other details, see – www.english-heritage.org.uk/visit/places/tilbury-fort/history/ New Tavern Fort was constructed on the south bank between 1780 and 1783 but extended and improved during the 1790s with new buildings such as an officers' mess, magazines and stables. It was also provided with furnaces to provide the devastatingly effective heated shot for anti-ship actions in the Thames. For visitor's information, see – www. discovergravesham.co.uk/new-tavern-fort.html

South and South-west England

Although Portsmouth and Plymouth were and remain the foremost naval bases in England, the British declined to seriously update their fortifications during this period. This was because the Royal Navy became so strong during the Napoleonic Wars that their famous 'wooden walls' were thought capable of defending these ports without support from the land as their harbours and anchorages invariably held a strong naval presence. It was also logical that the French would select London as their primary objective and, if they attacked from the land, it would be because the capital had already fallen and that probably would have ended hostilities in any case.

However, work was carried out to modernize the medieval Round Tower at Portsmouth and Southsea Castle (one of Henry VIII's artillery forts) was updated with its sea-facing walls elevated and thickened. Southsea's gun platforms were strengthened so they could deploy heavier cannon, garrison accommodation was enlarged, a covered way built to protect the gunners and a new battery constructed that projected outside the original walls. Southsea was well positioned to defend the harbour entrance and could offer some fire support into parts of the Royal Navy's famous Spithead anchorage between Portsmouth and the Isle of Wight. It was later used as a military prison and updated for use in the Second World War. For visitor's details see – www. southseacastle.co.uk

Case Study: Berry Head Fort – *Map 8*

Although it was considered unlikely that the French would attempt to land so far to the south-west, Torbay (Devonshire) was an important Royal Navy anchorage and the beaches here were suitable for a hostile landing. As works had already begun there in 1780–3, they would provide an ideal foundation for improvements and major work began on the headland of Berry Head in 1794 under the direction of Lieutenant Colonel Alexander Mercer. It was an ideal place for a fortification as it overlooked the entire bay and the western approaches of the English Channel. A large half-moon battery was established in the main (North) fort as the fortress's main armament and as it stood upon tall cliffs (200ft/60m high) it was almost impregnable to a direct assault from the ocean.

The half-moon battery was the only position with cannon placed to fire directly out to sea, with the guns of its protecting forts facing inland to defend it from a land assault. The army had wanted to build two outlying redoubts to defend the main fort but this was considered too expensive and only the 'South Fort' was constructed 1,476ft/450m south of the North Fort with Hardy's Battery placed where the other redoubt would have been and provided with only minimal defences.

Work on the North Fort began in 1795 and it was operational before 1800 but only completed in 1809. Its defences were formidable: 'The major landward defence was formed by a stone-revetted earthen rampart with a parapet fronted by a wide dry moat strung across the neck of the headland. The dry moat, which is revetted on the landward side by a battered stone wall, is nearly 7 metres (22.9ft) in width and is accompanied by an inner rampart wall over 5 metres (16.4ft) high of roughly coursed squared Devonian limestone topped by a parapet pierced by multiple splayed gun embrasures. A single western entrance to the fort was approached by a drawbridge' (Berry Head Fort and Battery and Hardy's Head Battery' - http://historicengland. org.uk/listing/the-list/list-entry/1017322). Its parapet had eighteen cannon embrasures and musketry walls were placed to the north-west but most have disappeared due to adjacent quarrying.

The South Fort is a virtually independent fort rather than an outwork, with embrasures for nineteen cannon and entry by a drawbridge on the seaward side, covered by the North Fort's guns. It had a garrison of 150 militia and was surrounded by a dry moat with its flank protected by sheer cliffs dropping to the sea. The remains of a guard house are just beyond the entrance along with a well-preserved powder magazine, which has a stone reinforced doorway and walls 4ft/1.2m thick. Its curved roof was designed to contain an accidental explosion and ventilation slits were made in its walls to prevent gunpowder becoming damp.

A semaphore signalling station was established on Berry Head in 1794 that not only allowed communication with its nearby stations but was part of a system allowing coded intelligence to be sent from Land's End in South-west England to Edinburgh's Calton Hill (Scotland). This relied upon line of sight, using flags and discs, and was a major step forward in military intelligence and would have been a great advantage for co-ordinating the British defence if an invasion had occurred. A full-sized replica pole and equipment was placed here in 2015.

The Guard House of the North Fort lies directly beyond its main entrance and now contains its heritage centre with cannon on naval carriages placed before it and on some of the ramparts' gun platforms. The fort's garrison comprised 500–600 militiamen who were largely replaced by regular troops as training purposes began to dominate the garrison's duties after 1805. Little remains of the half-moon battery that lay beyond the landward defences. It replaced a similar 1780s structure and stood upon a wide terrace protected by a low semi-circular wall that gives this type of fortification its name. It once fielded twelve 42pdr cannon mounted on platforms constructed of wood and stone.

An artillery store and large powder magazine still stand in the main fort built circa 1780 but were adapted to support a Napoleonic battery. In 1906 a coastguard lookout station was placed inside the magazine but it has an interesting feature beside it: 'a coursed limestone rubble sentry box … It is an octagonal building of ingenious design which allowed the four sentries to remain in contact with one another through apertures placed in the partition walls' ('Berry Head Fort and Battery and Hardy's Head Battery' - http://historicengland.org.uk/listing/the-list/list-entry/1017322). This gave guards considerable protection against the elements on this windswept headland as they kept watch on the fort's ocean approaches.

On 24 July 1815 HMS *Bellerophon* anchored in Torbay with the Emperor Napoleon I aboard. For nine days the warship lay under the guns of Berry Head while the government debated over what to do with their guest who had requested exile but was subject to British law if he came ashore. Attempts at secrecy proved futile and hundreds of sightseers rowed out into the bay to catch a glimpse of him with Napoleon appearing on deck to raise his hat to observers. This alarmed the authorities so HMS *Bellerophon* sailed to Plymouth to avoid public attention but soon returned and anchored in nearby Saint Mary's Bay where its presence was less obvious. On 7 August 1815, Napoleon was transferred to HMS *Northumberland* and sailed into exile on Saint Helena, so his last sight of England may have been Berry Head.

The nearest town to Berry Head is Brixham and drivers from London should take the M25–M4 to Bristol, follow the M4 to Exeter, the A380 to Paignton and finally the A3079–A3022 to Brixham. Driving through the town, take Berry Head Road to reach the car park before the fort. The nearest railway station is Paignton and trains run here from Paddington Station in London. There are regular bus services from Paignton to Brixham (Nos 12 or 23) but it is over a mile's walk from Brixham to

Berry Head and there are no buses so hiring a taxi may be advisable. Entry to the forts is free and for details see – https://www.countryside-trust.org.uk/berryhead/bh-things-to-do/visitor-centre-bh   The   nearby Brixham Heritage Museum, see – www.brixhamheritage.org.uk exhibits archaeological evidence from 1794–1832 discovered on Berry Head along with displays examining garrison life for what must be the most interesting Napoleonic fortress in the South-west.

Chapter 4

Martello Towers

Martello towers are the most famous of all British Napoleonic fortifications and are worthy of detailed study. This chapter focuses on those built along the south and east coasts of England since that area lay under the greatest threat but also covers examples from the Channel Islands along with Scotland and Ireland. Great faith was placed in their defensive capabilities and the Duke of Wellington claimed 'There is no better way of defending a coast than by Martello towers. They require no expense to keep them up when once built.' However, his opinion was not universally shared, with some politicians criticizing their enormous cost once the war was over, pointing out that they never fired a shot in anger. Yet it is interesting to speculate about the criticism the government would have faced if a French invasion had been mounted and their preparations were inadequate. Furthermore, all defensive works are built with deterrence in mind and the towers affected enemy planning, with French and American privateers deterred from mounting raids due to their presence alone.

Although the Martellos were never put to the test during the Napoleonic Wars, they would have presented formidable obstacles to an invader. Evidence of this was provided in Victorian times when the British Army destroyed a few towers with more sophisticated guns than they were designed to counter, being amazed at how much punishment they withstood. Twentieth-century councils also demolished towers with internal explosive charges during building projects and discovered how difficult they were to destroy, with three or more attempts required to bring them down. Anticipating the kind of stubborn resistance they expected, French strategic planners nicknamed them 'Bulldogs' but ultimately historians can only speculate over how effective Martello towers would have been.

Of the 103 towers built on the English coast only forty-three survive today and many go unnoticed by tourists due to their modern appearance or are often mistaken for relics from another age. Some retain something approaching their original appearance but the fact that many were adapted during the Second World War or have been converted as private residences adds further confusion. A few have been restored to their original state and armament with visitors able to explore inside but all are visible reminders of how the British strove to create strong coastal defences when threatened with invasion during the early nineteenth century.

The Channel Islands Towers

The towers built on the Channel Islands of Jersey and Guernsey were modelled on Mediterranean medieval watchtowers built to counter corsairs and invasion attempts and were one inspiration for the Martello tower design. General Conway (Jersey's governor) recognized the islands' need for modern fortifications when France sided with the American rebels in 1778 as the French knew British privateers operated out of the Channel Islands and had wanted to seize the islands for their own for some time. Conway personally helped design a series of towers and construction began under Captain Bassett RE with the project spurred on by an invasion in 1781 when the French landed virtually unopposed and were only defeated after reaching Saint Helier (Jersey's capital).

Twenty-three round towers were built between 1778 and 1801 to defend potential landing sites but they lacked the sloping walls (batter) of the Martello tower design and were constructed with ashlar walling blocks rather than brick. Most were pierced with loopholes for musket fire and their primary weapon was mounted on a gun deck on the roof. They usually had machicolated galleries projecting out from their parapets to shield soldiers using muskets and allow them to fire at a sharp downward angle at anyone assaulting the tower's entrance. This was a doorway set high up on the first floor and reached by a ladder that could be withdrawn if the tower was threatened with infantry attacks.

Towers were usually two storeys high and internal movement was enabled by ladders or trapdoors rather than a permanent stairway in order to slow attackers who gained entry. The lack of a strong supporting central pillar dictated what kind of weapon was placed on the gun platform above, with most deploying light mortars or carronades intended to target light boats bringing infantry ashore. Some were equipped with heavier guns such as 18pdr or 24pdr cannon capable of firing out to sea and circular tower design meant guns could rotate in a 360° arc on a traversing wooden carriage. Towers built after 1804 resembled the elliptical towers then being constructed on England's south coast but were smaller than their English counterparts with thinner walls that were slightly angled to deflect enemy cannon shot. Only six were built on the islands between 1804 and 1814 and were intended to act in support of artillery batteries placed around them, also providing a strongpoint for artillerymen to withdraw to if overrun.

Today many of these towers can still be seen on the Channel Islands, although some were destroyed during the German occupation of 1940–5. The Germans fortified the islands heavily and some towers were adapted with features such as concrete observations posts while others were converted for use as private residences after the war. The Royal Engineers learned many lessons about tower construction in the Channel Islands that proved useful in England, Scotland and Ireland.

English Towers

Captain William Ford RE was not the first to propose the idea of constructing bombproof gun towers along the English coast to provide converging fire on landing beaches but his suggestions were the first to be adopted. One of his inspirations was the strong resistance an enemy tower put up at Mortella Point against two British warships on the Corsican coast in 1794. It withstood a two-day bombardment from vessels deploying 74 and 32 guns respectively and inflicted considerable damage in return before catching fire, when its garrison abandoned the fortification. Upon entering the Mortella tower, British officers were surprised to discover that it was only armed with two 18pdr and one 6pdr cannon and took care to disable the structure before leaving. The Martello towers were named after this fort but experts disagree over why the spelling differs, with some thinking it was misspelt in early accounts of the action and others believing that soldiers mispronounced it.

The Duke of York, Commander-in-Chief of the Army, supported Ford's proposals and General William Twiss was put in charge of the project. The Prime Minister ordered government surveys and began negotiations to purchase the land for this gigantic construction project that began in 1804. Towers numbered 1 to 74 were planned for England's south coast and twenty-nine towers on the east coast named in alphabetical order (the first twenty-six were A–Z with the other final three designated AA, BB and CC). The estimated cost was £2,000 per tower but the government paid over £3,000 for many with the most expensive (Seaford Tower) priced at £18,000 according to the Board of Ordnance when the project neared completion in 1812. Bill Clements writes in *Towers of Strength* that the 'cost of construction of the English towers was about £350,000, including … the three circular redoubts and … a further £150,000 for the towers in Ireland. The total spent in providing these defences exceeded £500,000, an enormous sum at the time when … the total expenditure of the British government in 1811 was only £82 million.' The British had never spent so much on fortifying their coastline, demonstrating how much the establishment feared a French invasion.

South Coast – *Map 5*

There are regular train services running from London to towns along this coastline such as Dover, Folkestone, Hastings and Eastbourne and there are regular coastal bus services. However, it is far better to explore this coastline by car or cycle if visitors wish to see large sections of the former defensive line rather than individual towers and the following description is primarily intended for drivers.

The defensive system was designed to cover beaches and river estuaries west of Dover, starting with Tower 1 at Folkestone in Kent and ending at Tower 74 in Sussex. Many towers were destroyed during Victorian artillery exercises, demolished by local building projects and one was even bombed during enemy action in the Second World War (Pevensey Bay). Twenty-five towers still stand along this coast and Folkestone is an ideal place to begin viewing them, where Towers 1, 2 and 3 are strung out in a defensive line on either side of Wear Bay Road. Set above the cliffs on rising land, No. 1 looks down on the others and all three could fire out to sea, down at the beaches or act in support of each other. Towers 1 and 2 are private residences and all three can be seen from each other's positions, though houses and trees obscure them to an extent.

Tower 3 is located on the East Cliffs above Folkestone harbour and stands out starkly against the grass of the golf course it is placed upon. During the Second World War it was used as an observation post and its gun platform was modified for this purpose with bunkers added nearby below the tower and on the cliff, which can still be seen. Shepway District Council used it as a heritage centre but the tower suffered from vandalism and was eventually closed to the public. Hopefully it will be restored and reopened soon.

On the opposite (western) side of Folkestone Harbour, visitors will find Tower 4 at the end of The Leas, which runs along the top of the cliffs, at the end of a long line of Victorian and Edwardian hotels. This tower enjoyed a commanding position at this height to fire into Folkestone roads at approaching ships or support Tower 5 but the structure itself is completely overgrown by vegetation and is inaccessible. Tower 5 is within easy walking distance of Tower 4 but enclosed within the private grounds of a school. It is in excellent condition but it is unlikely that visitors will get permission to view it.

Sandgate village lies west of Folkestone and several towers are located here. The first was built within Sandgate Castle, one of Henry VIII's artillery forts built in 1539–40 that lies above the beach. This is the only tower without a number as it was referred to by the castle's name and its incongruous setting in the centre of this sixteenth-century fort is unfortunate as it was designed to be militarily functional rather than photogenic. It was placed here to cover the beach and lies so close to the ocean that the fort's original sea wall was swept away during storms in the twentieth century. It is best photographed from the beach but is currently a private house that is closed to the public.

From the centre of Sandgate, take the Military Road, passing exits to Gough Road and Bybrook Field, until reaching a signposted public footpath on the left. Footpaths lead up into the woods from here and by walking uphill and bypassing a Second World War pillbox, visitors will eventually find Tower 6. It is enclosed within a circular, brick-lined ditch 20ft/6m deep surrounded by chain link fencing. The tower is neglected but good photographs can be taken of it depending upon the time of year because it is often covered by ivy and other vegetation. The tower once enjoyed commanding views but these are now obscured by trees, although visitors will be able to gain some impression of its original line of fire.

A series of towers run in a line from this point but are difficult to gain access to for photographic purposes. Follow the coastal Seabrook Road running from Sandgate to Hythe and take the turning marked Hospital Hill. Take the first exit on the left (Sandy Lane) and Tower 7 can be seen from a distance from the military cemetery on the left within the woods. The army currently use it for storage and, as it lies within Shorncliffe Barracks, it cannot be approached any closer than this point. Retrace the route to Hospital Hill, continue along this road and Tower 8 stands on the left-hand side of this road and has been converted into a private residence.

Hythe is the next coastal town and the Military Canal (see Chapter 3) begins halfway along The Esplanade between Hythe and Sandgate just off Princes Parade. It flows through the town and was designed to be defended in conjunction with the Martello towers. Enter Hythe and approach the seafront where three towers are located, the first being Tower 13, which has been converted into a private residence at the end of West Parade. Look south-west from Tower 13 and two towers can be seen, which are particularly photogenic as they stand closer together than the usual 600 yards/548m that separated most of them. Originally they formed part of a longer defensive chain and the remains of Tower 19 lie somewhere beyond them but are completely inaccessible as they lie on an active military firing range. Although Towers 14 and 15 can be photographed from the beach, the area is closely monitored by security and visitors should be very wary indeed if the red flag is flown, indicating the ranges are being used. This crucial area was well defended in the 1800s with Dymchurch circular redoubt (see Chapter 3) and Fort Sutherland also located on the Hythe Ranges.

Following the Dymchurch Road (A259), Dymchurch Redoubt can be seen on the left but it is unwise to pause for long to take photos as this is an active military installation and stopping will draw attention from the military police. Follow the A259 into Dymchurch and Tower 23 stands at the start of this village on the roadside close to the beach, which has been converted into a house and is in good condition. Continue into Dymchurch centre along the High Street, to see Towers 24 and 25 in the centre. Tower 25 stands in the car park and is in good condition and can be approached closely but is empty and inaccessible. Tower 24 is one of the most important Martellos as it has been restored – see this chapter's first Case Study.

After Dymchurch, there is a long gap in the defensive line but the intervening coastline used to boast three further towers that are now long gone but the Dungeness Bastion can still be seen (see Chapter 3). Follow the A259 to Rye where Tower 28 stands on the west bank of the River Rother where its gun covered the river mouth and Rye Harbour. It is now empty and derelict but is worth photographing nonetheless. Continue along the A259 to Winchelsea where Tower 30 seems to have been placed at an unusual point two miles inland. It was located here to cover the River Brede (a tributary of the Rother) and is now a private home that can be approached via the appropriately-named Martello Close and is in good condition.

None of the towers in the Hastings area have survived so another gap now appears in the original defensive line. The next tower is at Normans Bay just beyond Bexhill and lies just over a mile from the small Normans Bay railway platform on the East Coastway Line for East Sussex. This stop has no station and allows holidaymakers to reach the surrounding static caravan sites but the train service is irregular so check railway timetables carefully if planning to alight here. Tower 55 can be reached by following the coast road to the south-west standing virtually upon the beach and has been converted as a residence or holiday let but is currently unoccupied.

Proceeding along the A259, there are a number of towers at Pevensey Bay. Tower 60 is on Millward Road and Tower 61 is on Leyland Road to the north-east of the town and both are private residences. Tower 62 lies on Grey Tower Caravan Park on Grey Tower Road. It appears to be used for storage and this holiday park is named after it. All of these towers are in built-up areas and can be difficult to find without entering these road names into a satnav. Towers 64 and 66 are easier to find with both located near the Sovereign Harbour in Eastbourne. 64 lies very close to the beach and drivers can park nearby but it is currently unoccupied and in dilapidated condition. Tower 66 at Langley Point lies beside the harbour entrance and had a concrete machine-gun post added to its platform in 1940. It was used by HM Coastguard after the war but is now unoccupied. Looking along the coast from this point, it is possible to see Eastbourne circular redoubt (see Chapter 3).

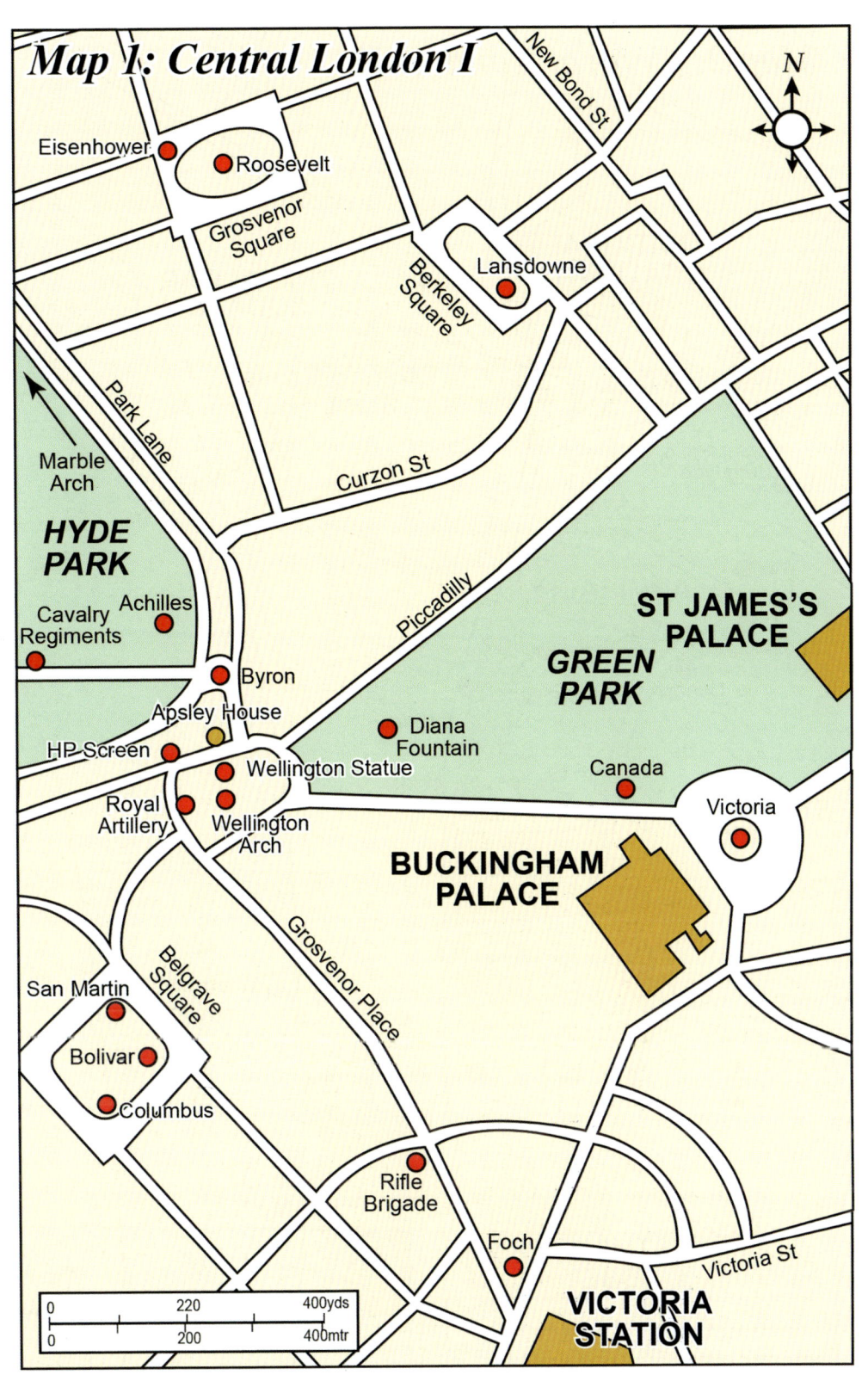

Map 1: Central London I

N

Eisenhower
Roosevelt

Grosvenor Square

New Bond St

Berkeley Square

Lansdowne

Park Lane

Curzon St

Marble Arch

HYDE PARK

Piccadilly

ST JAMES'S PALACE

GREEN PARK

Achilles
Cavalry Regiments

Byron

Apsley House

HP Screen

Diana Fountain

Canada

Victoria

Wellington Statue

Royal Artillery

Wellington Arch

BUCKINGHAM PALACE

San Martin

Belgrave Square

Grosvenor Place

Bolivar

Columbus

Rifle Brigade

Foch

Victoria St

VICTORIA STATION

| 0 | 220 | 400yds |
| 0 | 200 | 400mtr |

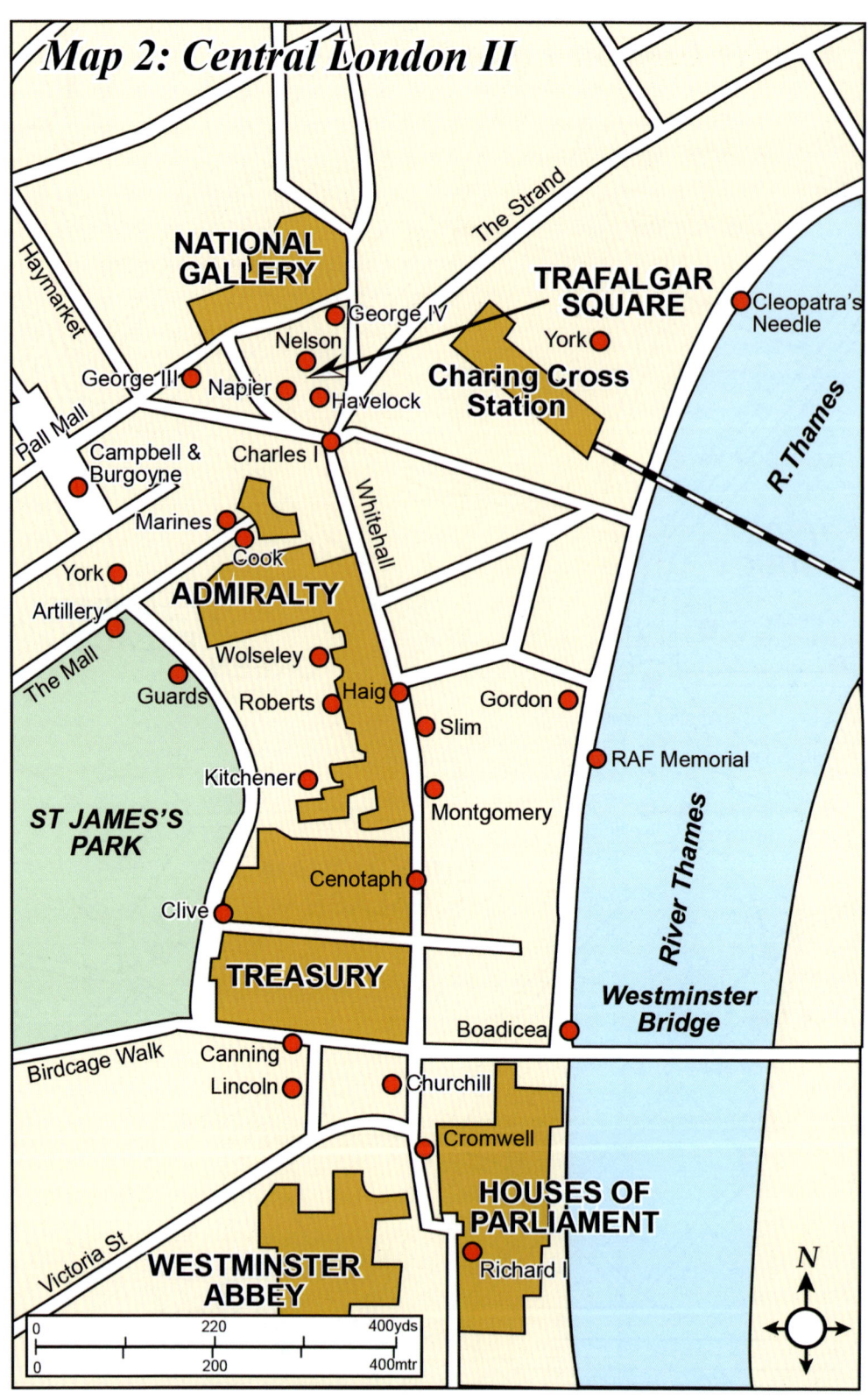

Map 2: Central London II

NATIONAL GALLERY

Haymarket

The Strand

TRAFALGAR SQUARE

Cleopatra's Needle

George IV

Nelson

York

Charing Cross Station

George III

Napier

Pall Mall

Havelock

R.Thames

Campbell & Burgoyne

Charles I

Marines

Whitehall

Cook

York

ADMIRALTY

Artillery

The Mall

Wolseley

Guards

Roberts

Haig

Gordon

Slim

RAF Memorial

Kitchener

Montgomery

River Thames

ST JAMES'S PARK

Cenotaph

Clive

TREASURY

Boadicea

Westminster Bridge

Birdcage Walk

Canning

Lincoln

Churchill

Cromwell

HOUSES OF PARLIAMENT

Victoria St

WESTMINSTER ABBEY

Richard I

N

0   220   400yds

0   200   400mtr

Map 3: Saint Paul's Cathedral

N

The Cathedral Floor

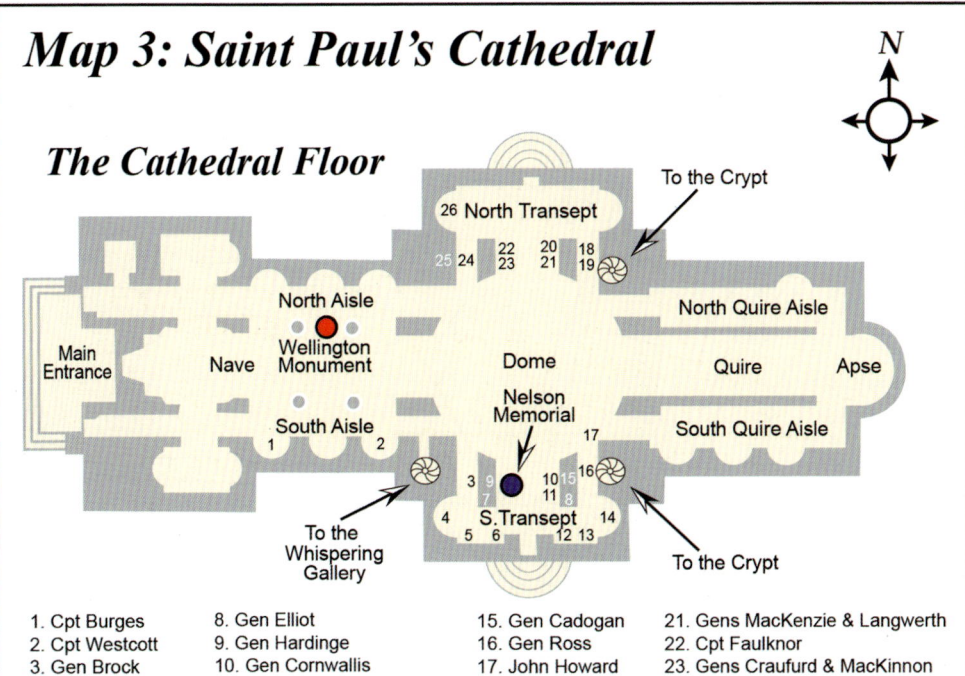

To the Crypt

26 North Transept

25 24   22 23   20 21   18 19

North Aisle

Main Entrance

Nave

Wellington Monument

North Quire Aisle

Dome

Quire

Apse

Nelson Memorial

South Aisle

South Quire Aisle

1   2   17

3 9   10 15 16
7   11   8

To the Whispering Gallery

4   S.Transept   14
5   6   12 13

To the Crypt

1. Cpt Burges	8. Gen Elliot	15. Gen Cadogan	21. Gens MacKenzie & Langwerth
2. Cpt Westcott	9. Gen Hardinge	16. Gen Ross	22. Cpt Faulknor
3. Gen Brock	10. Gen Cornwallis	17. John Howard	23. Gens Craufurd & MacKinnon
4. Gen Abercromby	11. Cpt Miller	18. Gen Bowes	24. Gen Myers
5. Gen Moore	12. Gens Pakenham & Gibbs	19. Gen Marchant	25. Gen Houghton
6. Gen Gillespie	13. Adm Collingwood	20. Gen Dundas	26. Gen Picton
7. Cpt Hoste	14. Adm Lord Howe		

The Crypt

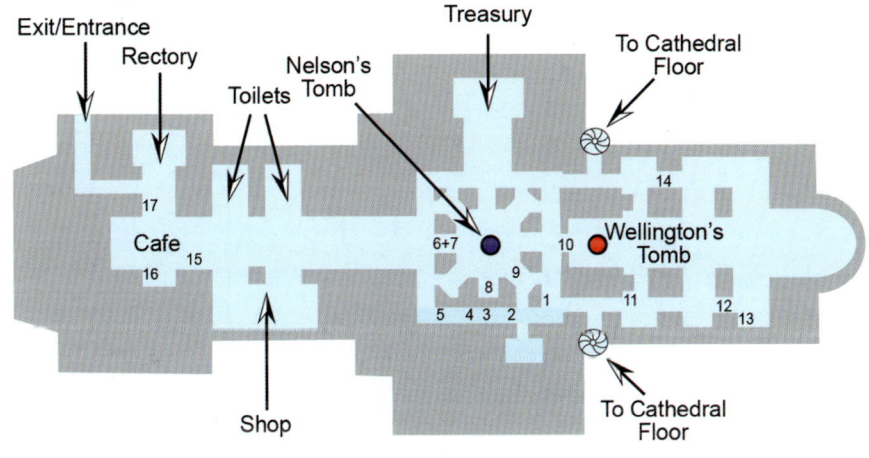

Treasury

Exit/Entrance

To Cathedral Floor

Rectory

Nelson's Tomb

Toilets

17

Cafe

15

16

6+7

10

Wellington's Tomb

14

9

8

1

11

12 13

5 4 3 2

Shop

To Cathedral Floor

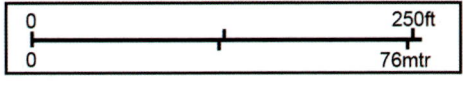

1. Rev. Nelson & family	6. Cpt Cooke	10. Col Gurwood	14. Sir Orchardson
2. Gen W. Napier	7. Cpt Duff	11. Cpt McNab & Picton	15. Adm Jervis (Earl St Vincent)
3. Adm Lord Rodney	8. Adm Collingwood	12. War Correspondents	16. Gen Ponsonby
4. Adm Malcolm	9. Adm Codrington	13. Sir Christopher Wren	17. Cpts Mosse & Riou
5. Gen J. Napier			

0		250ft
0		76mtr

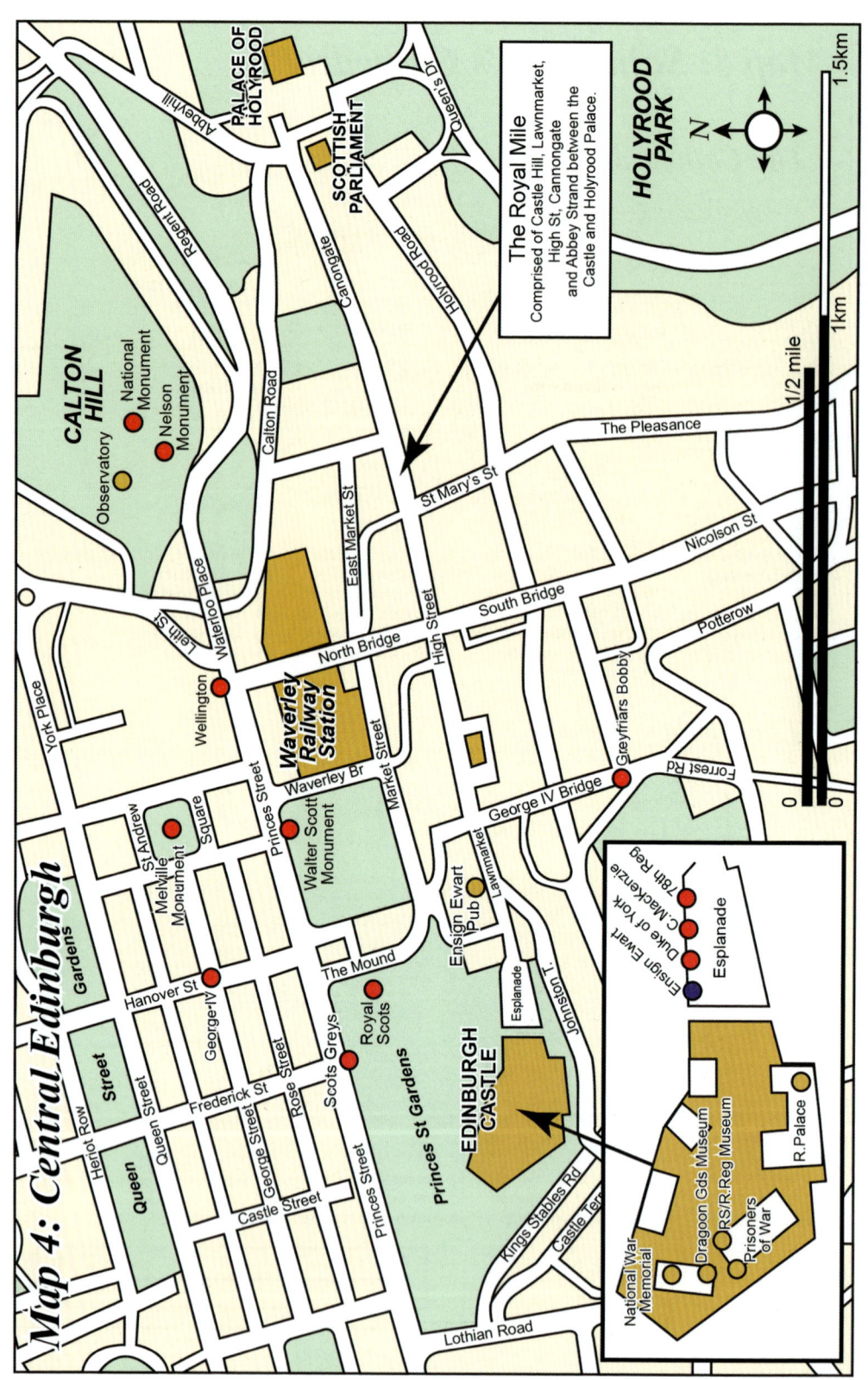

Map 4: Central Edinburgh

The Royal Mile
Comprised of Castle Hill, Lawnmarket, High St, Cannongate, and Abbey Strand between the Castle and Holyrood Palace.

HOLYROOD PARK

N

PALACE OF HOLYROOD

SCOTTISH PARLIAMENT

CALTON HILL

Observatory
National Monument
Nelson Monument

Abbeyhill

Regent Road

Canongate

Holyrood Road

Queen's Dr

1.5km
1km
1/2 mile

The Pleasance

Calton Road

East Market St

St Mary's St

Nicolson St

York Place

Waterloo Place

Leith St

Wellington

St Andrew Square

Melville Monument

Princes Street

Walter Scott Monument

Waverley Railway Station

Waverley Br

North Bridge

High Street

South Bridge

Market Street

Potterow

Greyfriars Bobby

George IV Bridge

Forrest Rd

Gardens

Hanover St

George IV

Queen Street

Heriot Row

Frederick St

George Street

Castle Street

Rose Street

Scots Greys

Princes Street

The Mound

Royal Scots

Ensign Ewart Pub

Lawnmarket

Esplanade

Johnston T.

EDINBURGH CASTLE

Princes St Gardens

Kings Stables Rd

Castle Ter

Lothian Road

Edinburgh Castle inset

Ensign Ewart
Duke of York
C. Mackenzie
78th Reg

Esplanade

National War Memorial

Dragoon Gds Museum

RS/R.Reg Museum

Prisoners of War

R. Palace

Map 5: Surviving Martello Towers

ENGLAND

SUFFOLK

Aldeburgh
CC
AA
Z
W
Y
V
X
IPSWICH
T-U
Q
L-M
P
Felixstowe
H. Redoubt
Harwich
K
Walton-on-the-Naze
ESSEX
A
E-F
C D
Clacton-on-Sea
Brightingsea

CHELMSFORD

LONDON

MAIDSTONE

Western
Heights
Dover
1 - 9
13-15
Folkestone
19
Hythe
23
24
Dymchurch
Rye 25
KENT
30
28
E.SUSSEX
55
Hastings
EB
Redoubt
64
62
60-61 Bexhill
Seaford 73
66
Eastbourne
74

Dungeness Bastion

- Martello Towers
- Redoubts/Bastions
- Cities & Towns

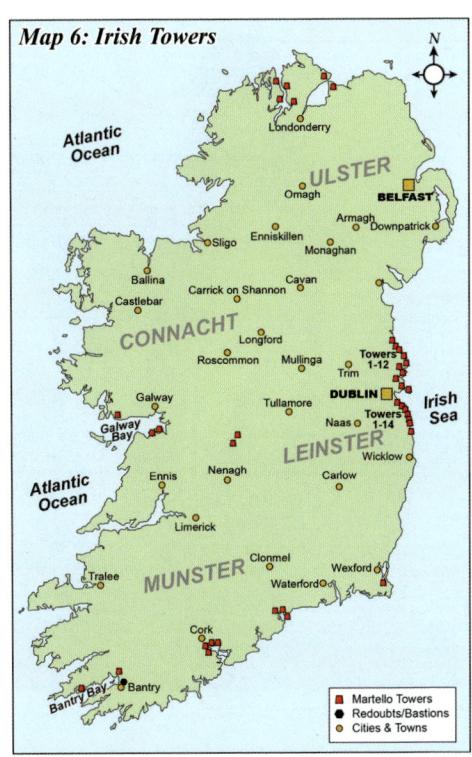

Map 6: Irish Towers

Atlantic
Ocean

Londonderry
ULSTER
Omagh
BELFAST
Armagh
Downpatrick
Sligo
Enniskillen
Monaghan
Ballina
Cavan
Castlebar
Carrick on Shannon
CONNACHT
Longford
Roscommon
Mullinga
Towers
1-12
Trim
Galway
Tullamore
DUBLIN
Galway Bay
Naas
Towers
1-14
Irish
Sea
Wicklow
LEINSTER
Atlantic
Ocean
Ennis
Nenagh
Carlow
Limerick
Clonmel
Wexford
Tralee
MUNSTER
Waterford
Cork
Bantry Bay
Bantry

- Martello Towers
- Redoubts/Bastions
- Cities & Towns

Map 7: Invasions of Ireland

Bompart & Tone

Napper Tandy

Londonderry
ULSTER
Humbert
Omagh
BELFAST
Ballycastle
Enniskillen
Downpatrick
Killala
Armagh
Ballina
Monaghan
Sligo
Cavan
Carrick on Shannon
CASTLEBAR
CONNACHT
BALLINAMUCK
Longford
Roscommon
Mullinga
Trim
DUBLIN
Galway
Tullamore
Naas
Irish
Sea
Galway
Bay
Wicklow
LEINSTER
Atlantic
Ocean
Ennis
Nenagh
Carlow
Limerick
Enniscorthy
Clonmel
VINEGAR
HILL
Waterford
Wexford
MUNSTER
Tralee
Cork
Bantry Bay
Bantry
Morard de Gallis & Hoche

- French Invasions
- Battles and main clashes
- Cities & Towns

Map 8: Museums & Heritage Centres

ORKNEY
ISLANDS
Lerwick
Kirkwall
SHETLAND
ISLANDS
100km
30   60miles

WESTERN
ISLES
Stornoway
Inverness
Aberdeen
SCOTLAND
Dundee
ATLANTIC
OCEAN
Dalmeny
House
Glasgow
EDINBURGH
Dumfries
Newcastle
NORTHERN
IRELAND
Carlisle
Sligo
BELFAST
ISLE OF
MAN
Middlesbrough
Northallerton
Dundalk
Dangan
Castle
IRISH
SEA
ISLE OF
ANGLESEY
Beverley
Leeds
Castlebar
Galway
DUBLIN
Plas
Newydd
Liverpool
Lincoln
IRELAND
Caernarfon
Nottingham
Leicester
Burnham
Thorpe
Shrewsbury
Norwich
Great
Yarmouth
Limerick
WALES
ENGLAND
Ipswich
Enniscorthy
Harwich
Fishguard
Wexford
LONDON
Cork
Chatham
Carmarthen
Monmouth
Oxford
CARDIFF
Bristol
Walmer
Dover
Hythe
Exeter
Dorchester
Stratfield Saye
Portsmouth
Brixham
ISLE OF
WIGHT
Truro
ENGLISH CHANNEL
CHANNEL
ISLANDS
St Helier
FRANCE

- Capital Cities and towns with important Napoleonic associations included in this guidebook
- Towns & Cities
- Stately Homes & Heritage Sites

Napoleon I, Emperor of the French, whose ambitions threatened British interests – Ernest Crofts

The bust of Nelson above the tombstones of his parents.

The former Wrestler's Inn in Great Yarmouth, where Nelson stayed with Lady Hamilton.

The Norfolk Pillar in Great Yarmouth commemorating Nelson's victories.

A First Rate, three-decked ship of the line possessed devastating firepower.

One of HMS Victory's gun-decks.

The entire ship is a treasure trove of Royal Navy artefacts.

Walking in Nelson's footsteps is an unforgettable experience.

The stern of HMS Victory.

The tunnel entrance that Nelson walked through in Portsmouth before joining his final command.

Arthur Wellesley, Duke of Wellington, Britain's greatest commander – Sir Thomas Lawrence.

Apsley House (No. 1 London), the Duke of Wellington's London residence.

The Duke was given a giant statue of his greatest enemy to adorn his home.

The drawing room of Apsley House.

A more modest-sized statue of Wellington than its predecessor stands opposite Apsley House today.

Wellington's mounting blocks outside the Athenaeum Club in Pall Mall.

The Duke had Walmer Castle's parapets lowered, marking the transition from fortress to stately home.

Wellington lived out his final years at Walmer Castle.

Bombproof brick–vaulted casemates at the summit of the Drop Redoubt.

The Grand Shaft stairway allowing swift access to Dover and its harbour.

A section of the Royal Military Canal.

The circular redoubt at Harwich.

Harwich Redoubt's gun embrasures over its brick-lined dry ditch.

A long gun on a traversing wooden carriage at Dartmouth Castle.

Flanked by the ocean, the South Fort's defences at Berry Head are impressive.

The gunpowder store in the South Fort.

The North Fort's magazine and four-way sentry box.

The entrance to the North Fort.

Two Martello towers at Hythe on the south coast of England.

It is an easy drive or walk along the seafront to see the redoubt but Tower 73 is located just half a mile (10 minutes' walk) from Eastbourne Pier. Known locally as the Wish Tower, its moat and glacis remain and it is in good condition. It is cared for by a trust called the Wish Tower Friends, who are planning further restoration projects and hope to re-open soon now that the Covid-19 pandemic threat is reduced. This is one of the few towers that can be viewed internally in a condition that is similar to its appearance during the Napoleonic Wars. For details about restoration and opening hours see – www. wishtower.org.uk

The strategic positioning of the final tower at Seaford is mysterious as it lies over 11 miles/17.7km from Tower 73 with a large headland between them so it could not have co-operated easily with neighbouring towers. Tower 74 was restored by Lewes District Council in 1979 and is now houses a well-established local history museum. Set within a brick-lined moat, it is entered over a permanent bridge that replaced the original 1800s drawbridge. A Napoleonic cannon has been placed upon a revolving wooden carriage on its gun platform and the museum offers displays, tours and research services. For further details see –webmaster@seafordmuseum.co.uk

Tower Construction

Towers on the south coast required around 500,000 bricks to build but their east coast counterparts needed 700,000 or more and were constructed by civilian contractors under the direction of officers of the Royal Engineers. The cement joining their bricks together was an experimental solution mixed with lime, ash and hot tallow forming a hard but supple glue-like substance. This was subjected to cannon fire during tests at Woolwich and proved highly resistant to roundshot, especially when walls were slightly inclined to reduce a shot's impact. It also made the towers more structurally sound so when a tower near St Osyth (Essex) subsided by several feet, it was easily righted by excavation on its opposite side. Most structures would have suffered catastrophic damage under these circumstances but 'though the fabric must have sustained a great degree of percussion, no crack or fissure appears in the brickwork', as *The Times* reported in February 1811.

While they conformed to the same general design, southern towers were roughly elliptical in shape with eastern towers being 'cam shaped'. Towers of particular strategic importance were surrounded by brick-lined moats and equipped with drawbridges to their entrances. These spans were raised by chains from the tower and an inclined slope (glacis) was constructed before the moat to deflect enemy shot. Most were 40ft/12m high with entry gained via a door set into the wall on the landward-facing side of the structure, opening onto the tower's first floor and was set 20ft/6m above ground floor level. Doorways had a chute directly beneath them, allowing the tower's ladder to be drawn inside so attackers would need some kind of equipment to scale the wall and enter, which would be made even more difficult by the garrison firing muskets or dropping grenades[1] on them.

The first floor provided accommodation for an officer and twenty-four men, and muskets were stored here in a rack around the thick central pillar. This column bore the weight of the tower's main armament above and ran from roof to cellar. A trapdoor in the first floor permitted access to the cellar with a winch and pulley used to raise barrels of powder and shot to the gun deck. Ammunition for the gun(s) was stored in the cellar, which usually had a dividing wall with a glass-shielded recess for a lantern, enabling gunners to use its light but prevent the accidental ignition of gunpowder stored within.

On the third level was the *terreplein*, commonly known as the gun deck or gun platform and reached by a single stair in southern towers while two stairwells were used in many east-coast towers. The gun platform had a 6ft/1.8m parapet running around it to shield artillerymen from enemy fire while they served the cannon. Recesses for storing gunners' equipment, powder barrels and ammunition were cut into the parapet and a piping system funnelled rainwater down into a cistern within the tower as water was important for the garrison to drink and to operate their gun(s), providing a supplement to water already stored below. Fire was always a risk so flues were added with chimney outlets on the roof but since they might restrict guns traversing in action, the chimneys could be swiftly removed if the tower came under attack.

East Coast – *Map 5*

Essex and Suffolk possess rugged, beautiful and unspoilt coastlines that are highly photogenic and less built upon than the south coast. Their relative isolation means that their towers are better preserved, with seventeen of the original twenty-nine still standing, but the disadvantage of this is that they are even more difficult to reach by those lacking vehicular transport. There are railway stations at Clacton-on-Sea and Felixstowe (with connections from mainline stations at Ipswich or Colchester) that allow access to two vantage points along this line of Martello towers. Coastal bus services are regular but the land is often broken by river estuaries where bus routes often halt and

---

1. Georgian-period grenades were primitive and temperamental but well suited for defending static fortifications.

Case Study: Dymchurch – *Map 5*

Tower 24 at Dymchurch has been lovingly restored to a condition close to how it would have appeared in the early nineteenth century, making it an excellent tower to visit. Exploring a Martello internally allows visitors to gain an impression of just how strong the towers are, with thick walls and a sturdy central pillar, along with gauging how much ammunition and equipment could be stowed in storage areas. When entering this small fort, it becomes immediately apparent how difficult this would be if the ladder were withdrawn as the entrance is 12ft/4m high, which would delay attackers while they procured ladders, ropes or other means of scaling the structure. Today a permanent metal staircase has been erected to assist entry and allow visitors a better view of the tower's exterior as they climb it.

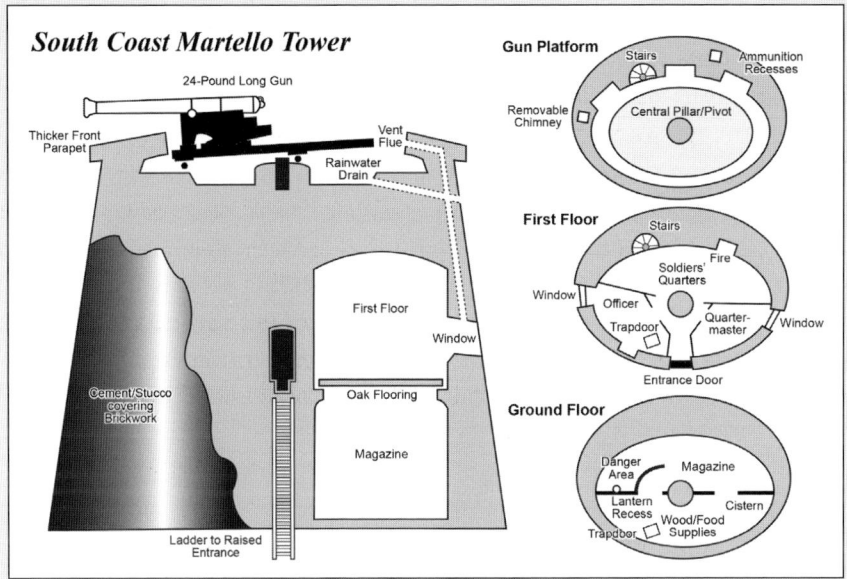

When observing the tower from various distances, visitors will note that little can be seen of the 24pdr cannon on the gun deck other than its muzzle, which would only be in this position immediately before it fired. This meant that a large section of the parapet would have to be battered down by gunfire before the cannon could be hit and put out of action. Obviously this would be no easy task while the gun was returning enemy fire, especially in combination with the fire from other towers in its defensive line.

Most rooms have been whitewashed in British Army fashion and visitors can observe the size of the rooms, fireplaces, windows, ventilation shafts and other features that would have affected living conditions for the small garrison. Good discipline would have been necessary to ensure cleanliness was maintained if a full complement of men were living here in these confined and cramped quarters, which is why Martellos were only fully manned if an attack was thought to be imminent. Replica Georgian-period beds and other military paraphernalia have been added to the rooms and a rack of India Pattern flintlock muskets (commonly known as the Brown Bess) has been placed around the central pillar.

The ground floor provides a surprisingly large space for storing gunpowder barrels, various forms of cannon shot, artillery equipment and food supplies in what seems a far smaller structure from the outside. The water cistern is also located here and its contents would have been vital to defenders fighting a prolonged action but especially if they were cut off from resupply as thirst would become a problem far sooner than hunger for the garrison and water was necessary to sponge out the cannon's barrel during the firing process. One of the most interesting features is the glass-shielded recess that allowed gunners to use a lantern or candle for light while reducing the chances of an accidental explosion.

Access to the gun deck is via a narrow stairway and the roof area is very revealing but disabled visitors may find negotiating it very difficult. On the roof, visitors can see the height and thickness of the parapet designed to shield the gunners as they operated the 24pdr cannon along with large shot and equipment lockers that are housed within it. Iron rings have also been sunk into the parapet and other areas to allow gunners to haul on ropes and rotate the gun on its wooden carriage. The size of both gun and carriage make it immediately apparent why a gun crew of 10–14 men was required for efficient use, although it was technically possible for only two men to operate it if their fellow artillerymen were incapacitated (although the rate of fire would be greatly slowed). Theoretically a 24pdr could fire roundshot to well over a mile but targets were usually engaged at lesser ranges during this period. Visitors will note that this tower still possesses fine views, although modern housing in Dymchurch reduces its line of sight inland to some extent. Keeping in mind that Tower 24 was one of a chain of gun towers capable of mutual fire support, visitors will soon appreciate how formidable Martello towers would have been to an invading force.

Tower 24 was bought by English Heritage and restored in 1969 and is located at High Street, Dymchurch, Romney Marsh, Kent, TN29 0NU. For details see – www.english-heritage.org.uk/visit/places/dymchurch-martello-tower/ Information is also available from the Friends of Martello24 society and the Cinque Port Volunteers hold regular re-enactments here see – http://theromneymarsh.net/martello24.

are sometimes difficult to circumnavigate when travelling by cycle or on foot as bridges are often some way inland. The case study on Felixstowe provides some hints for those confined to public transport, cycle or travelling on foot to follow based upon a stay of a few days in the area.

One of the first east-coast constructions was Tower A that overlooks the estuary of the River Colne, Brightlingsea Creek and the east side of Mersea Island. The River Blackwater's estuary is within sight, although beyond the range of Tower A's guns, and this chain of towers was placed here to defend these areas in conjunction with nearby fortresses. It was modified during the Second World War and currently houses an aviation museum run by the East Essex Aviation Society. Its displays concentrate on the Second World War with some exhibits on the Napoleonic Wars and the tower's construction with re-enactments sometimes held here. See – www.facebook.com/EastEssexAviationSociety

Tower B was almost certainly swept away by the ocean judging by the nature of the coast between St Osyth Point and the next tower in the line, Tower C, can be reached by driving east along Point Clear Road before taking the B1027 and following signposts to Jaywick. It contains an arts, heritage and community venue that displays visual and digital artwork and is run by Bishop's Park College and the Friends of Jaywick Tower. An additional room and a sunroof have been added to the gun platform but one of the front emplacements has a nineteenth-century gun mounted on a traversing wooden carriage within it and some information about the tower's history is exhibited here. See – The Promenade, Belsize Avenue, Jaywick, Clacton-on-Sea CO15 2LF. For up to date opening hours – www.explore-essex.com/places-to-go/find-whats-near-me/jaywick-martello-tower

Tower D can be seen from Tower C and both are part of the local Martello Towers Trail with outdoor information panels conveying information about the towers and the Napoleonic Wars. It is just under two miles away (35 minutes' walk) and stands at the edge of the golf course before the beach. It is unused but closed to the public, although it is worth a photograph, being relatively unaltered when compared to other towers in this area.

The next tower is 2.2 miles/3.5km from Tower D (45 minutes' walk) but a nine-minute drive along the coast road (Golf Green Road) and then West Road before the Clacton seafront area. If driving, turn right onto Hastings Avenue and the tower is located on the edge of the beach in Hastings Avenue car park, just beyond Clacton-on-Sea RNLI Lifeboat Station. Tower E has suffered over the years with most of its stucco gone or crumbling, revealing the brickwork underneath. It has been used as a water tower but is now empty and unoccupied.

Tower F is half a mile away and reached by returning to West Road and turning right at the point where this roadway becomes Marine Road. Continue along the seafront passing Clacton Pier and the tower is on the left. This tower is set within a deep moat with a wartime observation point built upon it but is in good condition and used by the Coast Guard. Tower K is 9 miles/14km away and located in Walton-on-the-Naze and is the last of the Essex towers. It stands near the marina on Walton Mere just off Arthur Ransome Way. This tower is in reasonable condition but unused and can be approached closely for photographic purposes.

Tower L stands on the Shotley Peninsula in Suffolk and is 23 miles/37km from Tower K. Follow the coastline to Harwich but note that the ferry there only carries foot passengers and cycles. Drivers are obliged to circumnavigate the Stour River, travelling via Manningtree, and approach Ipswich on the B1080. This peninsula has few roads and turning onto the B1456 will allow drivers to reach the area where towers L and M are located near the confluence of the Stour and Orwell rivers. For further details on Towers L–Y, see the Case Study on Felixstowe in this chapter.

The last two towers are located in a remote area along the Suffolk coastline. Tower AA is within walking distance of the Bawdsey towers (see Case Study) but Ipswich is the nearest city if visitors are not tracing the coastline from that point. When driving from Ipswich follow the A1214 to the A12 then A1152 until reaching Alderton village. Take the B1083 from Alderton to Bawdsey village, turning left off the main street onto Red Farm Lane, which eventually becomes Beach Lane, and the tower is located at its end. Tower AA can be hired as a holiday home by the nearby Buckanay Farm, Alderton, Woodbridge IP12 3FB. For details see – www.uniquehomestays.com/self-catering/uk/suffolk/woodbridge/found-tower/ It stands in an isolated and unspoilt location on the Deben Peninsula and the towers at Bawdsey are only 2 miles/3.2km miles away. It is an ideal place for a Martello enthusiast to stay and has been sympathetically converted to a holiday home with only a sunroof on the gun deck marring its external appearance.

Aldeburgh is the last and most unusual tower upon this coastline and lies just over 9 miles/14km from Tower AA but the necessity of circumventing the Alde River means that the journey is likely to be more like 20 miles/32km. Standing at the end of the Orford Ness peninsula, it was placed here to defend the lower reaches of the River Alde and drivers can reach it from Tower Z using the B1083 then A1094 or B1083–A12–B1083.

Tower CC is a quatrefoil design, which makes it the equivalent of four normal towers in size and it is far larger than any of the other surviving examples, with almost a million bricks used in its construction. Originally it deployed four

A view of the Deben estuary showing two remaining towers.

24pdr cannon on traversing carriages, which would have made it formidable to bombard from a distance let alone storm with infantry and it could respond with considerable firepower. It has been bought by The Landmark Trust, extensively renovated and can be rented as a holiday home that was recently covered in Channel 4's *Extraordinary Escapes* travel documentary with Sandy Toksvig. It is the last and most northerly tower to be built on the east coast and details about staying here can be found on – www.landmarktrust.org.uk/search-and-book/properties/martello-tower-9317/#Overview

Case Study: Felixstowe – *Map 5*

Felixstowe is right in the middle of the east coast defensive line so it makes an ideal base for exploring sections of it. The town has a railway station and this study is based on the concept of staying in Felixstowe for a long weekend and walking or cycling to the towers making use of the foot-ferries. This 'Martello march' is meant to be a pleasant experience rather than a Napoleonic route march though so keep in mind that regular buses run along Felixstowe seafront in addition to taxis if members of your party tire. Two towers lie close to the centre but the remains of Tower R are often overlooked as it was incorporated into the former Bartlett Hospital just above Undercliff Road East near the Cliff Gardens on the seafront.

It has been extensively modified with the insertion of a large entranceway and was used as a boiler room by the hospital that closed in 2006 and now performs a similar service for a series of flats.

Tower Q is located on the hill above the seafront near Felixstowe Pier. From Undercliff Road West (B1082) turn onto South Hill, walk uphill along this road and the tower is on the left-hand side. It has been converted into a private house and medieval-style crenelations have been added to the roof. It once enjoyed a considerable vantage point on this hill and is still contained within the remains of its moat, although this has been partially removed for vehicular access. A pair of iron gates blocks the driveway of this private dwelling with the words 'The Q Tower' emblazoned in white upon it.

Return to Undercliff Road West and walk or cycle west to the roundabout before travelling half a mile down Langer Road. Take the left hand turning into Orford Road and go right, walking along the seafront to where Tower P stands in open ground but is surrounded by houses. Once used by HM Coastguard, it has been extensively restored with a large viewing platform placed on its gun deck and is manned by volunteers of the National Coastwatch Institution, see – www.coastwatch-felixstowe. co.uk This is an interesting tower and an area nearby is being turned into 'Martello Park' by a local developer with restaurants and other features in the process of construction at the time of writing. Five interpretation boards stand on the path before Tower P, detailing its history from the Regency and Victorian periods up to its use in the First and Second World Wars. It saw service during the Cold War and an underground nuclear radiation fallout shelter, built to protect RAF personnel, is located nearby but is closed to the public. The local council plan to convert Tower P into a museum, which would be marvellous for enthusiasts, although its current use is a valued one.

The previous three towers can easily be viewed within a day but visitors may also wish to continue along the front to see Landguard Fortress on the point if they have time (see Chapter 3). Travellers can walk or cycle along the seafront or take Langer Road, turning into Carr Road and then Point Road before reaching the fort. On the riverbank close to Landguard Fort is a landing point for the foot-ferry that also takes bicycles. A kiosk nearby sells tickets and services run to Harwich and the Shotley Peninsula with fares and times available on – www. harwichhabourferry.com Visitors can use the ferry to travel to Harwich circular redoubt (see Chapter 3) or view the Martello towers at Shotley and the ferry travels along the route French warships might have taken to attack Harwich and its harbour.

Travellers visiting Shotley must go to Harwich first then on to Shotley Marina. Although partly obscured by trees, which would not have been the case in the early nineteenth century, the two Martellos at Shotley stand out starkly to ferry passengers. The opposite is true of Landguard Fort and Harwich redoubt, which both enjoy deliberately low profiles to protect them from enemy gunfire. The redoubt is difficult to spot even using binoculars or spyglasses but lies to the left of the church tower above Harwich and its flag often gives its location away.

Alighting on Shotley Peninsula, visitors will see Tower M above the trees behind the Marina. It can be approached but only over broken and rough ground and is set within woodland, which is also true of its neighbour, and visitors should take care when attempting this. Tower L is in very poor condition and a large water tower added to its platform has partially caused this with cracks visible on its facade and the structure appears to lean slightly. Tower L is situated to the south-west of Tower M and in similarly dilapidated state. It was also used as a water tower and both appear on the Buildings at Risk Register. They were ideally placed to defend the openings of the rivers Orwell and Stour and could have levelled a heavy enfilading fire against vessels approaching Harwich Harbour. They were supported by artillery batteries that lay between them and were improved with brickwork defences in Victorian times and called Shotley Point Battery.

The last towers are best viewed on a separate day's outing to the north of the town. It is a pleasant walk or cycle ride along the seafront from Felixstowe Pier to Felixstowe Ferry Golf Club but travellers should keep in mind that some areas of shingle beach need to be crossed where bikes are best walked. Local buses only travel about half this distance but taxis are available in the centre if visitors want to save time.

The golf course before the village of Felixstowe Ferry is beautiful and has a causeway, seawall and beach running alongside. Photographers will find the towers here highly photogenic but Tower T is the course's crowning feature with the ocean to its front and is further enhanced by the River Deben that sweeps out into the estuary beyond it. The estuary contains numerous sandbanks that are sometimes used by basking seals and Bawdsley Manor (built 1886) stands on the low cliffs overlooking the river where another Martello tower formerly stood, helping to cover the estuary in conjunction with Towers T and U.

Tower T lies on the eastern edge of the golf course and can be approached using the causeway above the beach. The club use it for storage and a crude doorway has been cut into the back of this tower to improve access but has been barred by an iron gate. It can be approached but observers should be aware that the golf course is in regular use and inattentive photographers risk being struck by golf balls if they wander onto the greens in its vicinity. Continue along the causeway into Felixstowe Ferry village to see Tower U on the left of the path on the Deben's south bank. It is in good condition but is a private residence so visitors should be tactful if photographing it.

Another foot-ferry is located here that allows passengers to cross the Deben, see – www.felixstowe.org.uk/things-to-do/attractions/felixstowe-ferry/ After crossing the Deben, walkers can reach the next towers by taking the footpath running along the coast before Bawdsley Manor but coastal erosion means it is sometimes closed to the public. An alternative route is to follow Ferry Road to the north-east and try to keep parallel with the coastline. This road lacks pavements for most of its length so cycling is preferable to walking and it is 2.7 miles/4.3km (11 minutes' cycle ride) to East Lane Car Park near Tower Z. Walking takes longer but there is a bridleway on the right hand side of Ferry Road that permits walkers to rejoin the coastal path and approach the towers from the south, reducing the distance considerably. Cyclists should be aware that this short cut is sometimes deeply rutted and crossed by deep drainage ditches along the low cliffs at the coast that will slow their progress.

Tower W stands on Bawdsey Cliffs and three more Martello towers can be seen looking north from its location. It is in good condition, appears unused and boulders have recently been placed here to protect the point it stands upon from coastal erosion, which is obviously necessary judging from the number of trees and even a Second World War pillbox that have been claimed by the sea in the vicinity. The other towers can be reached by walking along a raised causeway running behind the shingle beach with stagnant water pools (filled by spring tides) between the beach and causeway.

Tower X lies along the causeway and is now a private residence. It is a very modern conversion into private residence and a number of its former chimneys had been removed from the roof and placed at the tower's foot during the author's last visit. Tower Y is derelict, unoccupied and inaccessible with its parapet visibly crumbling in places. However, it is placed within wheat fields and is photogenic, being in an almost original state with minor additions made during the Second World War.

To reach the final tower in this line (Tower Z) walk to the end of the causeway and enter Shingle Street village or join the paths leading onto the beach from the causeway and approach over the shingle. The tower stands on the southern edge of this small village and has been converted into a private house with sunroofs on its summit and a broad wooden stairway added. The four towers are placed 600yds/548.6m apart (standard separation distance for covering beaches) demonstrating how much ground a defensive chain could dominate. Theoretically, a ship at sea could be fired upon by fifteen towers simultaneously when spaced in this manner, although no lines were ever made that long. They were capable of delivering considerable firepower against ships standing out at sea or troops coming ashore in small boats and a frontal assault on this beach would be exposed and likely to suffer heavy casualties. However, the distance dividing these towers presents a challenge to photographers as they can be captured in the same photo but the most distant tower is usually indistinct with most lenses unable to replicate what the human eye can see under these circumstances.

Tower Armament

South-coast towers were usually equipped with one long gun, mounted on a traversing wooden platform but some had an additional 5.5in howitzer (firing shells rather than solid shot) in its support. Most primary weapons were 24pdr cannon but 18pdrs were occasionally used and traversing carriages allowed them to rotate around a 360-degree arc to meet attacks coming from all around the tower with a scale of degrees often scored upon parapets to assist gun direction and rangefinding. Carriages were constructed from oak with iron fittings and small metal wheels that ran along an iron rail.

Armament was different on the east coast because the towers were larger and deployed more guns on a trefoil-shaped (three-leafed) platform covered by a cam-shaped parapet. Typically, a 24pdr long gun was placed so it could fire out to sea as a tower's main armament with two 5.5in howitzers or two 24pdr carronades in support. Carronades fired a variety of shot and were devastating at close quarters (particularly against infantry) but lacked the range of a long gun. They would be used against infantry landing or advancing along a beach and to defend the tower against their attempts to escalade or storm it. Garrisons relied on their long gun for more distant targets like warships or landing barges. Occasionally two 24pdr long guns were deployed but, as they were covered by carronades to their rear, could only traverse in 180-degree arcs.

With three cannon and twin staircases, east-coast towers possessed more firepower and could bring ammunition up to their guns more swiftly than their south coast equivalents. The amount of munitions stored in their magazines varied but the following list was considered appropriate – 100 roundshot (solid iron cannon balls), 20 case-shot (the equivalent of naval grapeshot), 280 shells of various types, 80 hand grenades, 380 flannel cartridges, 120 bursters, half a ton of gunpowder and 11lb of slow match.

Ireland – *Map 6*

It is generally accepted that only the cam and elliptical-shaped towers on the English coasts can be classified as true Martellos but Scottish and Irish towers also helped defend British shores during this period (Southern Ireland gained independence in 1922). French Republican governments of the 1790s thought the Irish would welcome their military intervention due to widespread civil unrest there with both Protestant and Catholic groups calling for independence at this time. They hoped rebels would join the French cause and this proved to be the case during General Humbert's invasion in 1798 (see Chapter 7). Since the seventeenth century, British governments considered Ireland as 'England's back door' in strategic terms and the events of 1796–8 convinced them to fortify Ireland's coastline.

Long stretches of the Irish coastline could be used as landing sites by the French with the west coast being particularly vulnerable and defending them would be expensive so British strategists concentrated their efforts on protecting Ireland's two largest cities (Dublin and Cork) along with potential anchorages for an enemy fleet such as Bantry Bay, Galway Bay, Lough Foyle and Lough Swilly. Fifty towers were eventually built with construction from 1804 to 1806, seeing the first towers completed in a rush as the Great Rebellion of 1798 had alarmed authorities and added urgency. Twenty-six towers were placed in two chains to the north and south of Dublin and predominantly built using rubble masonry and granite ashlar with some brickwork employed. Their design was reminiscent of Mediterranean towers but they were weaker than English Martello towers as they lacked the new lime mortar cement.

Most towers were two storeys high with the ground floor containing the magazine and stores while the first floor provided accommodation and many were equipped with machicolations above their entrances for musketry in similar fashion to towers in the Channel Islands. Virtually all of them lacked a strong central pillar to support the weight of the main weapon (usually 2.5 tons or more) on the gun deck with their armament usually being an 18pdr or 24pdr long gun, mortar or carronade.

As relations with the United States deteriorated, tower-building resumed from 1810 to 1815 as the British anticipated American raids along the Irish coast. These new towers were made from ashlar stone blocks and some employed internal stairwells while others continued to rely on ladders for the garrison's movement between floors. A number lacked sufficient room to accommodate a garrison, leading to interesting features like additional barrack rooms built alongside the tower that were often loopholed for musketry. Overall, their design was varied and erratic, which explains why military historians do not classify them as Martellos. This was also true of the three circular redoubts built to protect Bantry Bay Harbour as they lacked the casemates that were a defining feature of their English counterparts and are therefore classified as a different fortification.

The last towers built in Ireland defended the approaches to Cork Harbour but these lacked the typical 'batter' effect of sloping walls on the instructions of Lieutenant Colonel Fenwick who thought the erosive threat of Ireland's inclement weather more threatening than their supposed resistance to cannon fire, writing 'Walls in this country should be made perpendicular and not sloping, there is no advantage that I know in the latter mode, and it certainly may expose them more to the effect of driving Rain'.

After the Napoleonic Wars, the army gradually abandoned the towers as they became militarily obsolete and some were taken over by the Coastguard. Two were even attacked by Irish insurgents during the late nineteenth century and one was briefly seized by the IRA in 1922. Many have been demolished or succumbed to coastal erosion but a few are open to the public. The vast majority of the Dublin towers have been converted into residences and are private property but Tower 11 has been restored and currently houses the James Joyce Museum. This famous Irish author set the opening chapter of Ulysses, his greatest novel, in this tower that stands above the cliffs and possesses magnificent ocean views. It is situated 8.6 miles/14km from the centre of Dublin at Sandycove Point, Dún Laoghaire, Dublin, A96 FX33. Entry is free and it contains exhibitions on Joyce's work, see – https://joycetower.ie

Tower 7 at Tara Hill has also been restored with a 24pdr cannon mounted on its gun platform and is contained inside a partial moat with glacis. Its guardroom has been restored along with additional garrison accommodation at the foot of the structure. Located 300yds/274m from the sea, this tower enjoys incredible views of Killiney Bay and the Sugar Loaf and Wicklow mountains. See – https://www.facebook.com/martellotower7. For a general description of the remaining Irish towers located beyond the Dublin area, see – https://martellotowers.co.uk/ireland

Scotland

Only three towers were built in Scotland and were mainly intended to counter raids by French or American privateers. The Royal Navy relied heavily on Russia and Scandinavia for wood supplies and it was thought that convoys might be attacked and Britain needed secure naval bases this far north. The Board of Ordnance approved construction of a tower at Leith (Edinburgh's port) in 1807 on offshore rocks where it would defend the harbour entrance and anchorage. However, its builders had supply difficulties and the tower was completed years after the Napoleonic Wars and was never armed. It became known as Tally Toor Tower and its circular construction differed from the classic Martello tower design. Today the port has expanded out into what were Leith Roads and the tower is incorporated into the breakwater and docks and is in dilapidated condition. Because of security measures, it cannot be approached closely by the public and can only be photographed from a distance.

Alarmed by the increasing success of the US Navy, the Secretary of the Baltic Association persuaded the Admiralty to fortify Long Hope Sound on Hoy (Orkney Islands) as British merchant ships often assembled offshore near this point where privateers might attack them. Accordingly, the construction of two towers and an eight-gun battery began in 1813 with the towers placed on the headlands either side of the sound. Their design was similar to England's south-coast towers but they employed sandstone ashlar rather than brick in their construction. Known as the Crockness and Hackness towers, they were armed with 24pdr long cannon and their supporting battery was placed 200yds/182.8m before Hackness tower with its guns equipped with traversing wooden platforms. Hostilities ended in 1815 well before their completion but they were rearmed and garrisoned during the Victorian period and Hackness saw use as a RN signal station and Crockness had radar equipment installed during the Second World War. Crockness lies on private land today but Hackness tower is run by Historic Scotland and is open to the public with a visitors centre, see – www.historicenviornment.scot/visit-a-place/places/hackness-martello-tower-and-battery/

The Invasion That Never Was

With the benefit of hindsight, was there ever a realistic chance of Napoleon invading England? He imposed his Continental System to close European ports to British trade but knew Britain would only be defeated with military force. Could his navy have held the Channel open long enough for his army to cross in the face of British naval supremacy? Defeat at Trafalgar failed to stop Napoleon from increasing the size of the French Navy and this strongly implies that he never abandoned his invasion plans. Marshal Soult participated in high-level strategic planning at Boulogne and must have had a good idea of the Emperor's true intentions but was evasive on this subject to the end of his days. When asked about whether Napoleon seriously meant to invade he invariably replied 'Ah, Monsieur, that is the great question,' and declined to comment any further.

The huge amounts of money the British government spent on fortifying coastlines reveals that the invasion threat was taken seriously and historians should never underestimate the fear of the influential landed classes who stood to lose a great deal if England was occupied by France. It is also true that Napoleon must have been delighted when he learned his enemies were spending millions of pounds on static defences when this money could have been spent on offensive operations against France. However, it is difficult to calculate the effect these fortifications had on French foreign policy as they were a considerable deterrent for a potential invader hoping to land on British shores after a hazardous crossing. Ultimately, historians will never know if Napoleon truly intended to invade but British attempts to thwart him resulted in the construction of an incredible range of fortifications, which enthusiasts can study and enjoy today.

Chapter 5

Monuments and Statues

S tatues and monuments are essentially tributes raised to commemorate the lives, sacrifices and achievements of individuals or groups of people. Many provide fine examples of a sculptor's artwork with accompanying dedications giving some insight into how people felt about their subject matter at the time of their creation, especially as considerable time and money were devoted to their construction. Public examples provide a visible reminder of how individuals or organizations were regarded in the past and statues are popular with historians due to their often photogenic appearance. The selection of pertinent examples for this chapter was a difficult task due to the great number of monuments in Britain, so the author has chosen from those he has personally seen in combination with their relevance to this historical period.

While commemoration is the main purpose of most monuments, statues are also designed to celebrate the life and achievements of an individual in the hope that they will inspire admiration or even emulation of their deeds in others. Some of Britain's most famous military heroes rose to prominence during the wars with France and it is a measure of their importance to this nation that new statues have been erected in honour of people who fought in the Napoleonic Wars over 200 years afterwards. There are many to be seen in town squares, churches and city halls around Great Britain and a few of the finest examples are described here with postcodes listed to assist visitors in finding them online or by satnav.

London – *Maps 1 & 2*

As the United Kingdom's capital city, London possesses a wealth of monuments and statues and is the most accessible travel destination for enthusiasts living outside the British Isles. There is a great deal to see in this extraordinary city and repeated visits are necessary to gain a true insight into the historical delights it has to offer. Dr Johnson effectively summarized the city's appeal when he wrote 'When a man is tired of London, he is tired of life; for there is in London all that life can afford'.

Marble Arch. W1H 7EJ

John Nash designed this monument as a triumphal arch commemorating the Napoleonic Wars in 1827 on King George IV's instructions. It was also intended to be a gateway for Buckingham Palace and Nash desired a more militaristic look than it now presents but his project was disrupted by the king's death and he was sacked for overspending by the Duke of Wellington. Architect Edward Blore took over his role and decided Nash's friezes of Trafalgar and Waterloo were better placed in the central courtyard of Buckingham Palace and the National Gallery. He also dispensed with the statue of George IV originally intended to top the arch, which now stands in Trafalgar Square.

Blore disliked military symbolism, adapting some decorative figures to represent Asia and Europe and adding allegorical female statues of England, Scotland and Ireland. This gave the arch a less elaborate appearance than Nash envisioned but it is an impressive structure clad in ravaccione (white marble from Italy) with its eight Corinthian columns cut from a single piece of marble nonetheless. Ceremonial processions regularly rode underneath Marble Arch while it was used as a state entrance for the palace's *Cour d'Honneur* but only members of the Royal Family and the King's Troop Royal Horse Artillery were permitted to ride beneath it. The arch was moved to its current site in 1851 by Decimus Burton (a former pupil of Nash) and has become a famous London landmark.

Statue of Achilles. W1J 7NT

This statue was gifted to Wellington as a war memorial commemorating his victories during the Napoleonic Wars and was paid for by donations from British women's societies totalling £10,000. Placed in Hyde Park on the seventh anniversary of Waterloo (18 June 1822) Richard Westmacott sculpted this 18ft/5.5m-tall statue of the legendary Achilles, greatest warrior of the Trojan War. The mound it stands upon elevates this monument to 36ft/10.9m and it was originally controversial as the first male nude to be displayed in public since Roman times. Even though the sculptor covered his subject's modesty with a fig leaf, there were protests led by George Cruickshank among others who claimed Achilles's bare backside was an affront to public decency.

Posed dramatically with raised shield and short sword at the ready, Achilles has a cloak draped over his shield arm, armour placed behind him and boasts a suitably muscular physique. While the statue is in marvellous condition, the inscription on the granite base is faded and reads: 'To Arthur Duke of Wellington and his brave companions in arms this statue of Achilles cast from cannon taken in the victories of Salamanca, Vittoria, Toulouse, and Waterloo is inscribed by their countrywomen. Placed on this spot on the XVIII day of June MDCCCXXII by command of His Majesty George IIII.'[1]

Wellington Arch. W1J 7J2

The Wellington Arch is also known as Constitutional Arch or Green Park Arch. It originally stood directly opposite the Hyde Park Screen but has been relocated a short distance to its current position upon an island surrounded by major roads before Apsley House with many other war memorials located in its immediate vicinity. Designed by Sir Decimus Burton, this monumental arch was intended to proclaim Britain's triumph over Napoleon but this martial purpose was mellowed to celebrate the Duke of Wellington's achievements along with acting as a grand entranceway to Green Park and Buckingham Palace Gardens. George IV commissioned the archway and construction took place from 1826 to 1830 with the project greatly overrunning its budget.

The link with Wellington was enhanced by placing a statue of him on the arch's summit in 1836. The Duke sat for its sculptor and is depicted in cocked hat and cape directing troops with his telescope at Waterloo. He sits astride his favourite horse, Copenhagen, and this colossal statue was designed and constructed by Mr Matthew Cotes Wyatt and his son James. It was made from bronze recast from cannon captured during the Napoleonic Wars, standing 30ft/9.1m high and weighing over 40 tons. Copenhagen's legs were cast in solid metal to bear this weight while most equestrian statues' legs are hollow to save on costs. Wyatt used a huge wooden cart 20ft/6m wide to carry the statue in six pieces that needed twenty-nine horses to drag it through London streets to this site. Raising the statue to the summit was a difficult operation and huge crowds gathered to see it unveiled in 1846 as one of the largest statues ever built at that time.

The statue's gigantic size made it appear out of proportion with the arch, even though the structure itself was three storeys high. Burton also raised doubts over whether his arch could withstand the statue's weight over a long period of time, adding that he never intended it to bear such a burden. Although people liked the statue's design, many considered its combination with the arch to be an eyesore and articles and letters appeared in London newspapers suggesting alterations but Queen Victoria would not hear of it as its removal might offend the Duke. After Wellington's death, Prince Edward (later King Edward VII) suggested relocating it to Aldershot 'where it will be highly regarded by the Army'. Parliament agreed and the statue was removed

---

1. Vitoria is usually spelt with a single letter t and four usually rendered IV in Roman numerals but this quotation is exact.

in 1883 while the arch was repositioned to lessen traffic congestion. The British Army took responsibility for dismantling and conveying the statue to Aldershot in 1885 where it now stands and a smaller statue of Wellington was eventually placed directly opposite Apsley House. A Triumphal Quadriga was set upon the archway's summit in 1912, which takes the form of the Angel of Peace driving a chariot.

The arch itself is hollow with rooms on three floors and was once a subdivision of Cannon Row Police Station and the smallest police station in London until the late 1950s. It is a popular tourist attraction today with rooms presenting historical displays and visitors can climb to a point just below the Quadriga where magnificent views of the city can be seen from its balconies towards Buckingham Palace and nearby parks. For details see – www.english-heritage.org.uk/visit/places/wellington-arch/

Hyde Park Screen. W2 2UH

Designed by Decimus Burton and completed in 1828, Hyde Park Screen is not a Napoleonic monument but was designed as part of an architectural composition with the Wellington Arch but the archway's relocation destroyed the impression of these monuments being linked. The 107ft/30m wide screen acts as a gateway to Hyde Park but its classic design is subtle with ionic columns and three archways containing ornamental wrought-iron gates and the frieze over the central arch's entablature blends well into the pale stonework. It shows Greek soldiers on foot or borne in chariots marching towards the Athenian Acropolis for a festival at the Temple of Athena. They are modelled upon figures from the famous Elgin Marbles, currently exhibited at the British Museum, and this work was carried out by John Henning and John Henning junior.

Duke of York's Column. SW1Y 5AJ

Prince Frederick, Duke of York and Albany, was Commander-in-Chief of the British Army during most of this period and the eldest son of King George III. He was mocked for poor leadership in Flanders in 1799 in the famous nursery rhyme 'The Grand Old Duke of York', which is perhaps unfair as the campaign was beset by overwhelming difficulties. He won far more respect as an able military administrator and reformer and the entire British Army sacrificed a day's wages when he died in 1827 to fund this monument that cost £21,000 (£1,858,690 in today's money).

Designed by Benjamin Dean Wyatt, it stands where Regent Street meets The Mall close to the Waterloo Gardens and the famous Athenaeum gentlemen's club. Three wide sets of steps lead down from the column to the

Mall, which are known as the Duke of York Steps. Constructed between 1831 and 1834 this Tuscan column is of grey granite with a lighter, bluer version used for its base and height of the entire monument is 137.9ft/41.99m. The statue at its summit is bronze, showing the Duke clad in the robes of a Knight of the Garter and was sculpted by Sir Richard Westmacott. When he died the Duke was £2,000,000 in debt and some joked that the column had been built this high so that he could escape his creditors. The column is hollow and a spiral staircase of 168 steps leads to a viewing platform below the statue but it has been closed for decades as it is small and thought to be weak. In 1850 the musician Henri Joseph Stephan hurled himself from this platform to his death and this incident also discouraged the authorities from allowing public access.

Case Study: Nelson's Column. WC2N 5DU – *Map 1*

Trafalgar Square and Nelson's Column are famous reminders of the Napoleonic Wars.

This memorial to Admiral Lord Nelson and his victory at the Battle of Trafalgar in 1805 is one of the most famous monuments in the world and is seen by thousands of visitors to London every day. There are very few monuments built on this scale in Britain with comparable works usually dedicated to Royalty and the fact that Nelson's statue gazes out over London from an incredible height speaks volumes about how he was regarded by the establishment and people of Britain in the nineteenth century and today. Members of both Houses of Parliament were among those who petitioned for a monument celebrating Nelson's achievements in 1838 to be paid for by public subscription. It would be placed in the newly renamed Trafalgar Square (renamed 1835) before the new National Gallery and a competition was held to select an architect. William Railton's proposals were eventually chosen by the project's sub-committee presided over by the Duke of Wellington.

Construction took place from 1840 to 1843 and the column was made in the Corinthian style from Dartmoor granite but Nelson's statue, sculpted by Edward Hodges Baily, was made from Craigleith sandstone and stands 18ft/5.5m tall. This statue is particularly impressive, showing Nelson in the cocked hat and uniform he wore at Trafalgar, holding a sword in his left hand with his right sleeve pinned to his breast. His decorations are prominently displayed over his heart and a cable (thick rope) adds a suitably nautical feature behind him. The statue faces south-south-east towards the Old Admiralty Building and the Corinthian capital beneath it is made from bronze cannon salvaged from the wreck of HMS *Royal George* that foundered at Spithead in 1782 and recast at Woolwich Arsenal foundry. The four bronze lions around the monument's base were added in 1867 and designed by Sir Edwin Landseer with flights of steps between them leading up to the column's base where observers can approach the bronze friezes adorning it.

When the column was measured in 2006, during a £420,000 renovation project, it was found to be 14.6ft/4.4m shorter than previously believed. The actual height of Nelson's Column, from the bottom of the pedestal to the top of Nelson's hat, is 169.3ft/51.6m but Railton had intended for it to be even higher at 203ft/62m but relented when concerns were raised about potential instability and ruinous costs. Four bronze friezes adorn the pedestal that are cast from captured French cannon and depict the Battle of Cape St Vincent, the Battle of the Nile, the Battle of Copenhagen and the Death of Nelson. They were set in position in 1854 and are each 18ft/5.5m square and sculpted by Musgrave Watson, William F. Woodington, John Ternouth and John Edward Carew.

The Death of Nelson is generally considered the best of the friezes and shows the mortally-wounded Admiral being carried below decks for treatment. Three seamen stand on the left of this composition with one sailor pointing at French sharpshooters in *Redoubtable*'s fighting tops while the others return fire with muskets. One of these represents George Ryan, who was 23 years old and one of the black sailors who served in the

Georgian Royal Navy. As he is shown holding a musket and trying to avenge the stricken admiral, it seems unlikely the artist would have given him this prominent position if Nelson was considered pro-slavery at that time.

The eventual cost of the monument more than doubled its original estimate of £47,000 (over £4,500,000 in today's money) and the Nelson Memorial Committee only raised £12,000 from public donations. Eventually, Tsar Nicolas I donated a further £12,000 in acknowledgement of the help Britain gave to Russia during the Napoleonic Wars and the British Government agreed to pay the remainder. Although the column and statue were swiftly constructed, the lions and friezes were added much later and the monument received a mixed welcome at first. Some malicious tongues even suggested that its statue looked like Napoleon, which was an easy mistake to make with their similar headgear, but Londoners eventually took Nelson's Column to their hearts.

The monument became so famous that it was soon recognizable around the world as a symbol of British pride and cultural identity. One unfortunate outcome of this was Adolf Hitler's intention to transfer the column to Berlin if London fell during the Second World War but luckily he was never able to carry his threat out. Trafalgar Square is a regular focal point of political demonstrations and Nelson's Column has been climbed with official endorsement by John Noakes for BBC's *Blue Peter* in 1977 and Gary Wilmott for LWT's *Six o'clock News Show* in 1989. Unofficial attempts have been made during demonstrations such as the Anti-Apartheid Movement's demonstration 1978, Greenpeace's campaign against acid rain in 1988 and stuntman Gary Connery parachuted from its summit during a demonstration against China's Tibetan policies in 2003. Filmmakers also paid £24,000 for permission to light the monument so that it resembled a lightsabre publicizing *Star Wars: The Force Awakens* in 2015.

The column faces south towards Whitehall, the Palace of Westminster (Houses of Parliament) and Westminster Abbey and the former headquarters of the Royal Navy (the Old Admiralty Building) is 7 minutes' walk away on Whitehall where Nelson attended meetings and lay in state on 8–9 January 1806. The famous Admiralty Arch was completed in 1912 and intentionally built in close proximity, providing an elaborate entrance to The Mall that connects Buckingham Palace and Trafalgar Square. Some memorials preceded its construction including the obelisk on Glasgow Green 1806, the statue of Horatio Nelson in Birmingham in 1809 and the Norfolk Column of 1819 in Great Yarmouth and many others have been dedicated to him afterwards in Liverpool, Portsmouth, Hereford, Edinburgh, Forres and Dublin but Nelson's Column is the most famous of them all.

Nelson Memorial. EC4M 8AD – Map 3

The statue of Nelson on this memorial in the south transept of St Paul's Cathedral is such a fine sculpture that some consider it superior to the statue on Nelson's Column. He is depicted bare-headed in full dress uniform with the cloak of a peer of the realm draped over his right shoulder that conceals his missing limb. Nelson stands upon a ship's quarterdeck with his left hand resting upon a rope coiled around an anchor and his determined expression gives no hint that he had lost the sight of one eye. Below the cylindrical plinth he stands upon are statues of Britannia, clad in Greek style, with two young boys on his right and a dedication to Nelson is inscribed on the monument's base – 'The pedestal allegories of the North Sea, German Ocean, Nile and Mediterranean express the geographical stretch of Nelson's career,' with his victories at Copenhagen, the Nile and Trafalgar listed and illustrated by images of pagan sea gods. A realistically-rendered lion with its teeth bared crouches at the foot of the pedestal on Nelson's left and symbolizes the fact he died in battle.

John Flaxman was once introduced to Nelson as the 'sculptor who ought to make your monument' and was chosen for the role after a government-run competition to select an artist for this work after Nelson's death. Flaxman laboured from 1808 to 1818 to complete this masterpiece, which was paid for by public subscription. His intention was to commemorate Nelson's bravery, patriotism and the nation's enormous pride in their hero. Its height illustrates the outstanding nature of his achievements and Britannia is shown commending him as an excellent role model to two young boys, who look up at Nelson in adoration. The facial expressions of these three figures clearly reveal that a fundamental purpose of this monument is to inspire British youth to follow in Nelson's footsteps and he is entombed in the crypt below (see Chapter 6).

Wellington Memorial. EC4M 8AD – Map 3

Following Wellington's funeral in 1852, designs for a monument commemorating his achievements were invited. It was destined for the nave of St Paul's Cathedral and Alfred Stevens, one of Britain's great nineteenth-century sculptors, was commissioned but asked for only £20,000 for expenses due to his respect for the Duke. He worked upon it from 1858 to 1875 but felt harassed by government interference and lack of funds, which probably contributed to his premature death. It was finished by his pupil, Hugh Stannus, who also died before the statue was set upon its summit and the monument was unveiled in 1912. It was moved to the small side chapel of St Michael and St George in 1892 during construction and languished there until transferred to its current position under the central arch of the north aisle in 1906. It is the largest monument in a cathedral containing over 300 monuments and a magnificent tribute to the Duke of Wellington.

The 40ft/12m monument is designed in the form of a sarcophagus with a pillared marble canopy and angular plinth above. There are two images of Wellington with the first being a recumbent bronze effigy lying in state upon the sarcophagus, resting upon a heap of martial spoils including cannon, shields and standards. The second is a bronze statue of the Duke by John Tweed at the summit high above the cathedral floor, showing him riding Copenhagen at Waterloo. Wellington wears uniform, cape and riding boots but is bare-headed and making a gesture of command with a field marshal's baton. Two groups of sculptures adorn the plinth, which are allegorical figures portraying 'Truth tearing the tongue out of the mouth of Falsehood' on the west face and 'Valour trampling Cowardice underfoot' on the east face. The virtuous figures are female while those representing vices are male and the sculptor was clearly influenced by Michelangelo. The nave's ceiling towers 91ft/27.7m above the cathedral floor and this incredible monument dominates the area with its dark bronze sculptures and adornments complimenting the pale stone of its main construction perfectly. Wellington is entombed in the crypt below (see Chapter 6).

Wellington Statue. EC3V 3ND

This is one of the few statues of Wellington built during his lifetime. The Court of Common Council of the City of London contributed money for it as a gesture of their appreciation for the Duke's contribution to the London Bridge Approaches Act of 1827, with other funds from public subscription. It is a bronze equestrian statue showing the Duke bare-headed and astride Copenhagen and cast from cannon captured at Waterloo. Sir Francis Chantrey began this work but died in 1838 and it was completed by Henry Weekes (his assistant). Lord Mayor William Magnay unveiled the statue in the presence of the King of Saxony and the Duke himself on the anniversary of Waterloo on 18 June 1844. A piece of granite from London Bridge is set into the pavement behind the statue and this memorial stands on the forecourt of the Royal Exchange (London's centre of commerce).

Waterloo Memorial. SE1 8SW

Modern memorials were erected for the bicentenary of the Battle of Waterloo and include this monument unveiled by the 9th Duke of Wellington at Waterloo Railway Station on 10 June 2015. It is the first monument to be dedicated to Waterloo participants alone in the United Kingdom but others can be found in

Belgium where the battle took place. It honours an estimated 24,000 soldiers thought to have been casualties from both the Anglo-Allied (British, Dutch-Belgian and Hanoverian) and Prussian armies that fought there against the French. At the unveiling, the 9th Duke commented 'It is an honour to unveil the Waterloo Memorial in tribute to the thousands of men from many nations who fought and died in just a few hours two hundred years ago.'

The monument was created by artist Jason Brooks in partnership with We are Waterloo, Waterloo 200 and the London Mint Office (who funded the project). Set upon an external wall, it takes the form of four white, oblong stone slabs with dedications above and below them. A circular bronze depiction of the reverse face of the Waterloo Medal is set in the centre, which was the first decoration awarded to men of all ranks in the British Army. Wellington influenced the creation of this medal that displays an image of Nike (Greek Goddess of Victory) and the lowest slab bears his famous words – 'My heart is broken by the terrible loss I have sustained in my old friends and companions and my poor soldiers. Believe me, nothing except a battle lost can be half so melancholy as a battle won.' Chief Executive Tim Shoveller of South-west Trains – Network Rail Alliance commented that the monument's prominent location means that 'it will be seen by the millions who frequent the UK's busiest railway station for years to come'.

Rifle Brigade Memorial. SW1X 7EQ – **Map 1**
Primarily dedicated to the First and Second World Wars, this monument displays three bronze statues of an officer of the Experimental Corps of Riflemen (1800), a Napoleonic Rifleman (1806) and a First World War Rifleman that were all designed by John Tweed. During the Peninsular War (1809–14) riflemen became famous, with the 60th and 95th Regiments of Foot wearing green rather than red uniforms and using Baker rifles. Ideal for skirmishing, rifles outranged the common musket and their use transformed the British Army's tactical use of small arms with the 95th Foot's exploits celebrated in Bernard Cornwell's famous series of novels about the fictional Richard Sharpe. The memorial stands at the junction of Grosvenor Gardens and Hobart Place near Victoria Station and is made of Portland stone with a curved screen placed behind its statues. Its inscription commemorates the loss of 11,575 men of the Rifle Brigade who fell during the First World War and the design was partly inspired by Colonel Willoughby Verner and paid for by the Riflemen's Aid Society with the monument unveiled on 25 July 1925 by Field Marshal Prince Arthur, Duke of Connaught (Colonel-in-Chief of the Rifle Brigade).

English Counties

Wellington Monument. TA21 9PA

When the Duke was elevated to his peerage in 1809, it was his brother William who suggested the name Wellington after the small town in Somerset that the Wellesley family originally came from. Wellington was derived from the Anglo-Saxon 'Weolingtun' (wealthy town or estate) and locals were proud of their association with the Duke, deciding to erect a monument to him in 1815. It stands on Wellington Hill 3.4 miles/5.4km south of Wellington where it dominates the Blackdown Hills. Construction began in 1817 using the plans of Thomas Lee (architect) but ran into difficulties that included damage sustained from a lightning strike, with Henry Goodridge finally completing the work in 1854.

It would have been higher with twenty-four French cannon placed at its foot along with a statue of the Duke at the summit but these elaborate plans were abandoned due to cost and design difficulties. It is built from local sandstone being 80ft/24m wide at its base and 175ft/53m high, making it the tallest three-sided obelisk in the world. Although the memorial has an Egyptian appearance, many liken it to the triangular-shaped bayonets used on Georgian muskets. An internal staircase ascends to a viewing platform, which has three circular windows cut into each face and the base has an Egyptian winged panel over its stairwell entrance. An internal counterweight hangs near the summit to assist the monument's balance in high winds and it has been restored several times. For opening times see – www.nationaltrust.org.uk/wellington-monument

Prisoner of War Memorial. ME4 4UH

Thousands of prisoners of war from France, Spain, America, Holland and other nations were held captive in Britain. Some were billeted in civilian residences if they gave their parole (promise not to escape) but many were housed in prison camps and fortresses or onboard prison hulks moored in rivers. Many perished from disease or deprivation during incarceration and monuments have been raised to commemorate their suffering.

The Admiralty ordered the expansion of Chatham Dockyard in 1861 and had the remains of hundreds of prisoners buried at Gillingham Reach cemetery reinterred at St Georges (Church) Centre where this monument now stands. It is constructed out of a mixture of granite, marble, limestone and sandstone in the form of a gothic spire with a statue of a Napoleonic sailor standing beneath an arch contained within it and set upon a square plinth bearing memorial plaques. Originally placed on St Mary's Island in 1869, it was moved here in 1904 along with the remains of prisoners disinterred from that site. An inscription on the front reads:

> Here are gathered together the remains of many brave soldiers and sailors who having been the foes, afterwards, the captives of England now find rest in her soil remembering no more the animosities of war and the sorrows of imprisonment they were deprived of the consolation of closing their eyes amongst the countrymen they loved but they have been laid in an honourable grave by a nation which knows how to respect valour and sympathise with misfortune.

This is probably the finest monument erected to commemorate prisoners of war but others include a plaque in Liverpool (L1 1HL) and a small cenotaph in Lothian, Scotland (EH26 8NU). Another fine monument is the Norman Cross Memorial for French Prisoners of War erected near the site of a purpose built military depot/prisoner of war camp. It is in the form of a stone pillar surmounted by a French Eagle and bearing a bronze plaque and can be found at Norman Cross, Huntingdon, Cambridgeshire, PE7 3TE.

Aldershot Wellington Statue. GU11 1QB

This is the statue that originally stood atop Wellington Arch described earlier in this chapter. The Duke of Rutland raised money for its construction from 1837 and engaged Matthew Cotes Wyatt to design and build a colossal bronze statue with Wellington sitting for the sculptor in person. Copenhagen had died by this time so another horse was used as a model for him whom some considered a poor likeness. The Duke is shown wearing a cocked hat and cape while gesturing commandingly with a telescope in his right hand. This imposing statue is doubly effective because of its vast size and was cast in a specially built foundry with two furnaces capable of melting 12 tons of bronze simultaneously but even this was insufficient so a third furnace was employed. Eventually it as cast in six pieces and the thickness of the bronze varied from 1–3in/25–76mm with the fully assembled statue being 40 tonnes in weight.

In the autumn of 1846 the statue was carried to its initial position on Wellington's Arch at Hyde Park Corner on a specially designed wooden carriage with huge wheels 10ft/3m in diameter, pulled by twenty-nine horses and assisted at various stages by a hundred soldiers. Crowds cheered enthusiastically as it approached the arch but it took many hours to haul it up to the summit and it was only in position the following day. The statue is 30ft/9.1m high and 26ft/7.9m from the horse's nose to tail being 22.8.ft/6.91m in girth. With these proportions, it was the largest equestrian statue ever constructed in Britain and probably in the world at that time.

It was removed from Wellington Arch after the Duke's death and Decimus Burton, who had disapproved of its placement upon his arch, left money in his will to contribute to its transferral. Edward Prince of Wales had suggested Aldershot as a new location and helped to choose Round Hill near the Royal Garrison Church as the new site for this great monument where it was placed in 1885. It now stands upon a gigantic, oblong red stone plinth that bears the single world 'WELLINGTON' with cannon barrels sunk into the area around it as fence posts and linked by a chain running through cannon balls protruding from their muzzles.

A smaller statue of Wellington that is similar but not identical to the original was designed by Edgar Boehm and placed opposite Apsley House (W1J 7NT). It is larger than life-size but far smaller than its monstrous predecessor but also stands upon a red stone plinth with 'Wellington' inscribed on one side and his dates of birth and death, 1769-1852, on the other. Four soldiers cast from the bronze of guns captured at Waterloo stand at each corner of its base. These are excellent studies and represent a Guardsman of the 1st Regiment of Foot Guards (Grenadiers), a Royal Highlander of the 42nd Regiment, a Royal Welsh Fusilier of the 23rd Regiment and a cavalryman of the 6th Inniskilling Dragoons.

Nelson and Wellington (Norwich). NR1 4DH

Statues of Nelson and Wellington stand in Upper Close before Norwich Cathedral (Norfolk) and both have been relocated from other parts of the city. Nelson is depicted in full-dress uniform with epaulettes, three stars on the cuff and the decorations he wore at Trafalgar are displayed along with two medals hanging from his neck. He is bare-headed and stands with left leg forward, resting a large telescope upon a cannon with a rope hawser attached. His right sleeve is pinned to his chest but Nelson's sea cloak is actually hung from this sleeve, which is an unusual feature. The plinth bears the single word 'NELSON' and it was moved here on 16 April 1856 from Market Street. Thomas Milnes was the sculptor and, although locals raised £400 in contributions, Milnes had to use his own money to complete what is one of his best works with Nelson's pose displaying considerable movement. His choice of Portland stone was unfortunate as it has deteriorated (particularly the head) but it is a fine statue situated in the grounds of one of Nelson's former schools (see Chapter 1). It was daubed with black paint by protestors in 2020 but swiftly restored as most people in Norwich are still proud of Norfolk's greatest hero.

An unusual statue of Nelson in the grounds of his former school in Norwich.

At a meeting held on 27 October 1852 in Norwich Guildhall, it was decided to erect a statue to Wellington's memory, who had died earlier that year. George Adams had already struck commemorative medals for the Duke along with making one of his death masks so he was commissioned as the sculptor of a bronze statue that eventually cost around £1,000. It was unveiled by City Mayor Sir Samuel Bignold before 20,000 spectators and the *Norfolk Chronicle* reported 'The hero is represented in the identical boots, cloak, and some other portions of dress actually worn at Waterloo, which were placed at the service of Mr Adams, the sculptor, when he was modelling the figure'. The Duke is shown bare-headed and leaning upon a drawn sword whose tip rests upon the ground. It was moved from Gentleman's Walk to its current position on 13 January 1937 a few yards from Nelson's statue that faces in the opposite direction. This is a particularly fine depiction of the Duke with a plinth emblazoned with insignia of a Knight of the Garter, Knight of the Golden Fleece and of the Bath. Wellington's four crossed marshal's batons are framed by the colours of many regiments with the granite plinth bearing the single word 'WELLINGTON'.

Admiral Nelson and Admiral Murray. PO19 1LX

Recent bicentenaries aroused great interest in this period and a monument of Nelson and Admiral Sir George Murray was unveiled in Chichester on 3 April 2021. They were close friends and Murray is renowned for his service at the Battle of Copenhagen with the unveiling taking place the day after its 220th anniversary. Local sculptor Vincent Gray depicted the admirals uniformed, wearing swords and standing side by side. Nelson wears a cocked hat while Murray is bare-headed and the statues are life-sized with Murray pointing into the distance while Nelson looks where he is indicating. Although Nelson's statue does not hold a telescope, this probably depicts the famous incident at Copenhagen where he held a spyglass to his blind eye and remarked 'I really do not see the signal' (see Chapter 1). The names and dates of both admirals are inscribed on the rear of the plinth while the words 'Murray or none' are emblazoned on the front, referring to Nelson's adage 'None but Murray will do' when selecting officers for a new command.

Gray commented that 'It has been a privilege to create a sculpture of Horatio Nelson, one of Britain's greats, and Sir George Murray, a true Cicestrian' (Murray was born in Chichester). Although Murray is an important figure in the Georgian Navy, he was not present at Trafalgar and therefore not as well-known as those who were. The ceremony was attended by Richard Plowman Mayor of Chichester and other members of the local Murray Club formed to commemorate this local hero's achievements. Murray's marble tomb lies on the wall of Chichester Cathedral and records the peak of his career as a Vice Admiral of the Red and is situated less than a mile away on North Street (6-7 minutes' walk).

Scotland – Edinburgh – *Map 4*

The National Monument of Scotland. EH7 5AA
This huge monument was constructed to honour Scottish soldiers and sailors slain in the Napoleonic Wars and bears the inscription 'A Memorial of the Past and Incentive to the Future Heroism of the Men of Scotland'. It stands upon Calton Hill to the north of the city centre, which offers spectacular views of Edinburgh, Arthur's Seat, Leith and the Firth of Forth. An imposing structure around 40ft/12m tall, it is renowned even in a city filled by fine memorials but it was never completed, thereby gaining the nicknames Edinburgh's Folly, Edinburgh's Disgrace and the Pride and Poverty of Scotland.

The Highland Society of Scotland called for a monument to commemorate their nation's war dead in 1816 and it was designed between 1823 and 1826 by Charles Cockerell and William Playfair who over-ambitiously based it upon the Parthenon in Athens. Lord Elgin also played a role in its planning and is known for obtaining the 'Elgin Marbles' from the Parthenon for the British Museum, an act that remains controversial to this day. The foundation stone was laid on 27 August 1822 during King George IV's visit, although the King did not attend the ceremony. The Duke of Hamilton was the senior Scottish noble present along with a large delegation of Freemasons who were escorted to the summit by contingents of the Scots Greys and 3rd Dragoons with cannon salutes fired from Edinburgh Castle, Salisbury Crags, Leith Fort and the Royal Squadron anchored in Leith roads.

The monument's construction began in 1826 by William Wallace & Son (builders) and it was originally intended to incorporate burial chambers beneath for military heroes. However, the estimated cost of £42,000 was enormous and public appeals for donations failed to meet this figure with only £24,000 eventually raised, so the project ran out of funds in 1829. Only part of the Stylobate (base) crowned with twelve Greek Doric columns and an architrave linking them together were ever completed. Its designers had intended the monument to have double the number of columns, a roof and triangular pediment at the front displaying images from antiquity. Even though only half the memorial was built, it is incredibly impressive and it took 'twelve horses and 70 men to move some of the larger stones up the hill'. It is built from Craigleith stone and some of the lintels topping the columns are among the largest pieces of stone ever quarried in Scotland. This is a grand tribute to the Scots who fell during the Napoleonic Wars and the vast scale of its construction is very much in keeping with the nation's proud military heritage.

The Nelson Monument. EH7 5AA

Edinburgh also boasts an exceptionally fine monument dedicated to Lord Nelson, which is a tower on the south side and highest point of Calton Hill, 561ft/171m above sea level. It can be seen from many parts of the city below and was built on the site of a signal mast once used to communicate with ships in the Firth of Forth and Leith Harbour. It was built from 1807 to 1816 to commemorate Nelson's greatest victory and several architectural designs were considered with those of Robert Burn eventually chosen. As the spyglass is an object closely associated with Nelson, Burn built this tower to resemble a telescope placed upside down which gives the structure an intriguing appearance. Burn died in 1815 and his scheme ran into financial difficulties but it was completed by Thomas Bonnar, who added the crenelated pentagonal building at the base of the structure between 1814 and 1816. The tower is 105ft/32m high with 143 internal steps up to a public viewing gallery, which offers fine views of Edinburgh and the estuary.

On the lintel over the tower's entrance is a three-dimensional depiction of the *San Josef* captured by Nelson at Cape St Vincent 1797 and a plaque below reads:

> To the memory of Vice Admiral Horatio Lord Viscount Nelson, and of the great victory of Trafalgar, too dearly purchased with his blood, the grateful citizens of Edinburgh have erected this monument: not to express their unavailing sorrow for his death; nor yet to celebrate this matchless glories of his life; but, by his noble example, to teach their sons to emulate what they admire, and, like him, when duty requires it, to die for their country. AD MDCCCV.

There is little doubt that Nelson would have approved of the addition of a mechanized time ball to the tower in 1852 as it offered a practical maritime device to this monument's commemorative purpose. Originally triggered by a clock in the nearby City Observatory, it allowed ships in Leith Roads and the Firth of Forth to synchronize the time when the ball rose and fell at one o'clock. It was also designed to operate in conjunction with the One o'clock Gun fired from Edinburgh Castle, especially if weather conditions concealed its position from below. It was operational from 1854 but it is now raised manually and only occasionally deployed at the time of writing.

When the tower was used a signal mast, sailors were accommodated in the rooms at its base but this practice ceased in 1820 and the lower rooms

Tower T at the mouth of the Deben River.

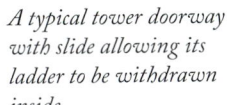

A typical tower doorway with slide allowing its ladder to be withdrawn inside.

Tower U overlooking the River Deben.

Most occupied towers have external stairways added to improve access.

The low, flat area behind the beaches north of the Deben meant a long line of towers was necessary.

Many towers had structures added during the Second World War.

*Tower W on
Bawdsey Cliffs.*

*The Wellington Arch
raised in honour of the
Duke's achievements.*

*Nelson's Column is
one of the most famous
monuments in the world.*

Colin Buttery (the author's brother) at the summit of Nelson's Column during the 2006 restoration project.

A detail from the 'Death of Nelson' frieze at the base of the column.

A detail from Nelson's Memorial of Britannia encouraging British youth to follow his example.

The Nelson Memorial in St Paul's Cathedral.

The statue at the summit of Wellington's Memorial in St Paul's Cathedral.

The memorial to the Rifle Brigade displaying statues of two Napoleonic riflemen.

The National Monument of Scotland dedicated to Scots who fell in the Napoleonic Wars.

Edinburgh's Nelson Monument designed in the shape of an upturned telescope.

The Duke of York's statue on the esplanade before Edinburgh Castle.

The Marquess of Anglesey's statue looks out over the Menai Straits.

The River Procession in Nelson's honour was a unique event in London's history.

Greenwich Dock, where Nelson's body was brought ashore and later loaded onto his funeral barge.

Nelson's spectacular tomb had been intended for King Henry VIII's use.

Wellington probably would have approved of the impressive but straightforward design of his tomb.

The memorial to Admiral Collingwood – the 'Forgotten Hero of Trafalgar'.

Generals Pakenham and Gibbs killed at the Battle of New Orleans in 1815.

A dramatic memorial commemorating the death of Captain Robert Faulknor.

Captain John Cooke's memorial, one of two Trafalgar captains commemorated near Nelson's Tomb.

ERECTED AT THE PUBLIC EXPENSE TO THE

The memorial commemorating over 20,000 officers and men buried in the grounds of the Old Royal Hospital, Greenwich.

Ensign Ewart's tomb on the esplanade before Edinburgh Castle.

The equestrian tomb of Colonel Edward Cheney.

Jemima Nicholas volunteered to fight the French and is buried in St Mary's Churchyard.

A monument over the grave of the first French soldier killed in the invasion of Ireland in 1798.

Irish exile Wolfe Tone presents his invasion plans to General Bonaparte.

Fishguard Fort.

The Royal Oak public house where negotiations took place.

A mural depicting General Humbert and his army.

Nelson's uniform jacket at the National Maritime Museum, Greenwich.

The remarkable ship in a bottle at Greenwich.

The captured Eagle of the 45th French Line Regiment in Edinburgh Castle.

A recreation of a Napoleonic POW dormitory at Edinburgh Castle.

The Royal Welch Fusiliers Museum has some particularly realistic Napoleonic mannequins.

are now used by staff who maintain the memorial. Although visiting this monument is worthwhile at any time of year, viewing the tower on Trafalgar Day (21 October) is particularly special as staff turn the entire structure into a signalling mast with the White Ensign flown from the summit and signal flags spelling out 'England expects that every man will do his duty' descending from spars on either side. A small fee is charged to ascend the tower, see – www.edinburghmuseums.org.uk/venue/nelson-monument

Wellington Statue. EH1 3YY

This statue was erected on 18 June 1852, the thirty-seventh anniversary of Waterloo and only a few months before the Great Duke's death in September that year. Placed before Edinburgh's General Register House, it is cast in bronze and is one of John Steell's finest works. It shows the Duke mounted on Copenhagen who is rearing upon two legs with his rider bare-headed, clad in a cloak and giving a gesture to advance.

Field Marshal Prince Frederick, Duke of York and Albany. EH1 2NH

This is one of a series of military statues and monuments placed on the north side of the esplanade before Edinburgh Castle, including Ensign Ewart's tomb (see Chapter 6), and all of them are provided with modern information panels. This large bronze statue stands upon a tall bronze pedestal with the Duke shown dressed in short breeches, tasselled cape and holding his field marshal's baton. It was cast by Thomas Campbell in 1836 and Princes Street (one of Edinburgh's important thoroughfares) is named after its subject, although the Duke never actually visited the city.

Scottish Counties

Nelson's Tower. IV36 3BT

Nelson's Tower stands upon Cluny Hill near the town of Forres, just under 30 miles/48km from Inverness (45 minutes' drive). This neo-gothic style octagonal tower is four storeys high (68.8ft/21m high) and was designed and built by architect Charles Stewart with a plaque placed on its exterior reading 'In Memory of Admiral Lord Nelson.' It is one of the earliest monuments dedicated to Nelson with the Forres Trafalgar Club and James Brodie laying its foundation stone on 26 August 1806. It was funded by public donations and completed in 1810 but was not opened to the public until Trafalgar Day, 21 October 1812. Cluny Hill is wooded in places and this fine white tower is located in an area of outstanding natural beauty with views of the town,

Findhorn Bay, Moray Firth and the Caithness Hills visible from its summit (96 steps to the top).

The Trafalgar Club held annual commemorations of the battle at this tower for many years and nautical items are kept here including two 4pdr cannon from the Bombardment of Alexandria in 1882, a large bust of Nelson, silver cup and bronze medal displaying Nelson's likeness (donated by the Duke of Gordon) and there is a war memorial dedicated to men from Forres who died in the Boer War located here. A near identical tower was built 20 years later to commemorate the birth of the Duke of York on a hill at Knock of Alves just under nine miles to the east. See – www.visitforres.scot/nelsons-tower/

Wellington Statue. G1 3AG

This bronze equestrian statue was created by Italian sculptor Carlo Marochetti and placed on Royal Exchange Square outside the Gallery of Modern Art in Glasgow in 1844. It stands on a rectangular stone base with bronze freezes inlaid upon it showing some of the Duke's battles and the statue is a classic representation of the Great Duke. In the 1980s, observing that Wellington's statue was bare-headed, drinkers scaled the monument and placed a traffic cone upon the Duke's head. This became a regular practice for drunken revellers in Glasgow city centre and is now a tradition as it appeals to the Glaswegian sense of humour. The Lonely Planet Guide's writers were so intrigued by this custom that they listed the statue in their 'top 10 most bizarre monuments on earth' in June 2010. While the council and police discourage this practice, fearing for the safety of those climbing the statue, this curious back-handed compliment to the Duke should not be taken too seriously. Images of the statue wearing a traffic cone are now sold on postcards, posters and even a 1/32nd scale model is sold in tourist shops.

Wales

Picton Monument. SA31 3BS

Lieutenant General Sir Thomas Picton has been celebrated as a hero in Wales for generations after his extensive military service and valiant death leading a charge at Waterloo. Many roads, public houses and buildings were named after him and this monument actually replaces a former memorial designed by John Nash in 1824 that was demolished in 1846. The current memorial stands on Picton Terrace, Carmarthen and was built by F. E. H. Fowler and takes the form of an obelisk 82ft/25m high of grey limestone upon a panelled pedestal. It is inscribed 'Picton born August 24 1758. Fell at Waterloo June 18 1815' and the names of other important battles, Busaco, Badajoz, Vittoria, Orthes and Toulouse that he fought at are also recorded. Wellington once called him a 'rough foul-mouthed devil as ever lived' but conceded that he was a fine commander and relied upon Picton in battle.

Following protests about who and what nineteenth-century statues represent, Carmarthenshire County Council received a petition with over 20,000 signatures requesting the renaming of this structure. Concerns were raised about Picton's investments in slave-supported industries, his profits from the same and brutal practices as a military governor that earned him the soubriquet 'Tyrant of Trinidad'. Some claimed he was unworthy of the respect he was formerly held in and believed Picton should not be celebrated in this fashion, so the council held a ballot to determine local opinion. Although two to one were in favour of keeping Picton's monument unaltered, information panels were erected exploring positive and negative aspects of his career by its side. They include QR codes and other internet links so observers can find out more about Picton and Town Mayor Gareth John hopes they will provide a fair summary of the General's life.

Marquess of Anglesey's Column. LL61 5NJ

This tall monument to Wellington's second-in-command at Waterloo rises 347.7ft/106m over the Menai Straits that separate the Isle of Anglesey from the mainland. He held the title Lord Uxbridge in 1815, commanding the cavalry at Waterloo, and was hit by one of the last French cannon shots that day as he rode forward to direct the pursuit of the enemy. This shattered his knee and he turned to Wellington beside him and gasped 'By God, Sir, I've lost my leg!' and the Duke replied 'By God, Sir, so you have,' grabbing his arm to prevent him falling from his saddle and calling for assistance. He survived the amputation and was created Marquess of Anglesey for his service in 1815. Locals began to raise this monument in his honour in 1817 (during the Marquess's lifetime) but he did not live to see it completed in 1860.

It is located just under 2 miles/3.2km from the house of Plas Newydd, which was the Marquess's main residence. The monument's hill top location makes it visible from a considerable distance and the column is 89ft/27m high. It is a Doric column, containing a narrow spiral staircase (115 steps) leading to a fenced viewing platform with magnificent views of the Menai Straits, Snowdonia, Anglesey and the Llŷn Peninsula. A brass statue of the Marquess in the uniform of the 7th Hussars wearing shako, braided dolman, pelisse (a jacket worn cloak style) and resting his cavalry sabre on the ground stands at its summit, sculpted by Matthew Noble.

An inscription at the column's foot (in Welsh and Latin) reads:

The inhabitants of the counties of Anglesey and Caernarvon have erected this column in grateful commemoration of the distinguished military achievements of their countryman HENRY WILLIAM, MARQUESS OF ANGLESEY the leader of the British Cavalry in Spain throughout the arduous Campaign of 1807 and Second in Command of the Armies confederated against France at the memorable battle of Waterloo on the 18th of June 1815. Thomas Harrison Architect.

Currently this column can be seen and photographed but the public are denied entry as the staircase is unsafe. A restoration project is underway and for updates on its progress see – www.angleseycolumn.com

Lord Nelson's Statue. LL61 6AE

One of the most delightful monuments in this study is the statue of Lord Nelson at Llanfairpwll on the Isle of Anglesey, which is located almost within the ocean at high tide. It stands on a hexagonal plinth enclosed by a small iron fence on top of a further square plinth. Nelson is depicted in his Trafalgar uniform and cocked hat with his left hand placed on his hip and right sleeve pinned to his breast. His famous quotation 'England expects that every man will do his duty' is inscribed on a panel beneath him and the monument rests on rocks along the shore line so the statue juts out about 20ft/6m into the Menai Straits and is surrounded by seawater at high tide.

The fact that this statue was placed here in 1873 and not during the aftermath of Trafalgar is a surprise to many visitors and its creator was Admiral Lord Clarence Paget (1811–95). He was the youngest son of the First Marquess of Anglesey and, in addition to his naval career, was a politician and sculptor who eventually took up residence in Plas Llanfair on the heights behind the statue. He believed bronze or marble statues were prone to damage from inclement weather, so he created this statue from concrete, which was more durable, cheaper and pliable. Paget initially planned to erect a statue of Neptune but when he discussed it with Sir Llewelyn Turner he responded 'What has Neptune done for us? Nelson is the proper subject', so he changed his mind.

Paget unveiled the statue in September 1873 and, during the dedication ceremony, recalled that he received great assistance from 'a loyal and patient Welshman called John Jones' during his speech. His connections with the Admiralty ensured that the structure appeared upon charts even before this ceremony as it was intended to act as a navigational aid for sailing vessels negotiating the Menai Straits. The tidal currents of this channel are notoriously unpredictable so Nelson would probably have approved of this additional but practical life-saving purpose.

Ireland

Monuments associated with the Napoleonic Wars are rare in Ireland but there are three commemorating Wellington in Dublin, Country Trim and Kilcooley (County Tipperary).

Wellington Memorial. D08 DF72

This monument is in the form of a vast obelisk (203ft/62m tall) and stands at the south-east end of Phoenix Park in central Dublin overlooking the River Liffey. It is the largest obelisk in Europe and designed by architect Sir Robert Smirke with its foundation stone laid in 1817. A more elaborate design was originally envisioned with an equestrian statue and other adornments but the project ran out of funds and these additions were abandoned. It was not completed until the anniversary of Waterloo on 18 June 1861, nine years after the Duke's death.

Four bronze plaques cast from cannon captured at Waterloo adorn the monument and three display pictorial images of the Duke's military and political careers, which are named 'Indian Wars' by Joseph Robinson Kirk, 'Waterloo' by Thomas Farrell and 'Civil and Religious Liberty' by John Hogan. The fourth bears a poetical inscription in English and Latin adorned with a crown, leaves and regimental standards that reads:

> *Asia and Europe, saved by thee, proclaim*
> *Invincible in war thy deathless name,*
> *Now round thy brow the civic oak we twine*
> *That every earthly glory may be thine.*

As a Protestant and Anglo-Irishman, Wellington's reputation varies considerably in Ireland but the erection of this vast and incredible monument testifies to the fact that many felt and still feel proud of him. The Provisional IRA targeted memorials dedicated to British subjects during the Troubles (1960s–1998) with the Nelson Pillar on Sackville Street, Dublin damaged so badly by a bomb in 1966 that it had to be demolished. When a member of this terrorist organization was asked why Wellington's obelisk was not attacked he replied 'Because he was an Irishman'.

1798 Monument Frenchill. RP7R+RM (Plus Code location)

There are numerous monuments commemorating the Great Rebellion, Wolfe Tone and General Humbert's invasion of Ireland 1798 in Ireland with examples in Castlebar, Ballinakill, Aughrim Bridge, Ballinamuck and elsewhere but this simple monument located 3 miles/4.8km south of Castlebar in Country Mayo is rather special.

In the wake of the British defeat at the 'Races of Castlebar' (see Chapter 7) a skirmish took place on this site as French forces pursued the British army, which is why it was named French Hill. A small party led by Bartholomew Teeling negotiated with British forces here but talks broke down and five French cavalrymen were killed in violation of their flag of truce. James Daly (editor of the *Connaught Telegraph*) and Patrick Nally built a small monument on this spot in 1876 in the form of a pyramid surmounted by a Christian cross. It bears the inscription 'In grateful remembrance of the gallant French soldiers who died fighting for the freedom of Ireland on August 27, 1798. They shall be remembered for ever.' It is a simple but striking monument erected by amateur builders and funded by local people.

The monument sometimes becomes overgrown but efforts are being made by Mayo County Council to maintain it and visitors are permitted access if they act with sensitivity as this is private land but the monument is easily reached on foot from adjacent roads.

Recent Controversy

Nineteenth-century statues on public display have recently become controversial with some questioning why society should celebrate individuals whose actions or beliefs they disapprove of. Protests erupted in the United States in 2019–20 demanding removal of statues of Confederate generals on the grounds that their southern rebel government supported slavery during the American Civil War (1861–5) and over a hundred monuments were covered, removed or relocated by 2020. Anti-racism groups like Black Lives Matter (BLM) rose to prominence during similar protests in Britain, Canada and some Caribbean states. Prominent figures from the past linked to the African slave trade were reviled in the media, although many had never heard of them before and their monuments caused little distress prior to these protests.

A statue of the Empress Josephine was beheaded due to her upbringing on a plantation, supposedly racist views and her husband (Emperor Napoleon I) restoring the slave trade in 1802. A statue of Nelson was also taken from its plinth in Bridgetown (Barbados) where it had stood for 206 years without causing concern, due to his tenuous links with anti-abolitionist groups. Canadian statues of Queen Victoria and Queen Elizabeth II were damaged even though the British Empire was instrumental in ending the slave trade in the nineteenth century. French President Emmanuel Macron spoke out on the bicentenary of Napoleon's death, proclaiming that the Emperor achieved good things for France and historical witch-hunts are misguided attempts to rewrite history. For example, the Emperor's restoration of the slave trade in Martinique and other West Indian colonies in 1802 was dictated by the necessities of war and intended as a temporary measure. Furthermore, Napoleon supported abolition in France during the Revolutionary period and personally outlawed slavery in Malta and Egypt in 1798, which failed to receive much publicity.

Statues of Churchill, Nelson, Cecil Rhodes, Sir Francis Drake and others were attacked and daubed with paint or graffiti in Britain in 2019–20. The most notorious event was the toppling of Edward Colston's statue in Bristol when his statue was pulled down and hurled into the river by an angry mob. Colston made his fortune in the sugar trade that used thousands of slaves but this was an act of vandalism nevertheless. When rioters were charged with criminal damage, they were cleared after admitting their guilt and this decision was met with incredulity.

Targeting the monuments of individuals or organizations for what they represent is nothing new. In Ancient Rome statues of people who fell from official favour were dragged from the Forum or Colosseum (Coliseum) and broken up in the streets by rioters, which is why few images of the Emperor Gaius Caesar Augustus Germanicus (Caligula) survive. After the fall of the Berlin Wall in 1989, statues of Communist leaders were taken down to suppress their political ideology and a statue of Saddam Hussein was pulled down by American soldiers and abused by an angry crowd of Iraqis at the end of the Second Gulf War in 2003.

The study of history is a continually evolving process with new information regularly emerging about historic events or personalities that sometimes results in modern reinterpretation but historians frequently disagree as sources often contradict each other. This makes conclusions a matter of opinion rather than being accepted as proven fact and it is also unrealistic to expect historical figures from 200 years ago to conform to modern beliefs or approaches. As L. P. Hartley said 'The past is a foreign country, they do things differently there'. Furthermore, it is unwise to judge nineteenth-century people by modern standards of morality as our supposedly enlightened philosophies may fall out of favour and be found wanting by future generations.

The theory that Nelson supported slavery is inconclusive, with the only serious evidence being a letter he wrote while under great emotional strain before Trafalgar. It was a private communication never intended for publication and what he said was ambiguous but amounts to the suggestion that Britain could ill-afford abolition while fighting a major war. It has also been suggested that elements of this letter were forged by anti-abolitionists when it was published years after his death. Even so, Nelson was a man of his times and what he believed should be viewed in that context along with the fact that he served his country from the age of 12, suffered terrible wounds and ultimately gave his life during a battle that effectively spared Britain from invasion. His decisive victory also led to British naval supremacy for over a hundred years making it possible for the Royal Navy to stamp out the slave trade.

A better case was made regarding Picton's statue in the Gallery of Welsh Heroes of Cardiff's City Hall. As the most senior British officer slain at Waterloo, his white marble statue was unveiled by Prime Minister David Lloyd George in 1916 and sculpted by T. Mewburn Crook but Picton was a slave owner and allegations of cruelty levelled against him as Governor of Trinidad between 1797 and 1803 were upheld during his 1806 trial when he admitted ordering the torture of a slave woman to extract a confession. Calls were made for the statue's removal and councillors voted to do so in 2020 with Lord Mayor Daniel De'Ath (the first black Mayor of Cardiff) being 'very pleased with the way we've chosen do it, democratically'. He considered Picton a monster but wished to see Welsh history preserved adding 'It's far more appropriate for Sir Thomas to be in one of our excellent museums rather than here'.

An investigation into 'offensive' monuments was recently commissioned to be funded by £800,000 of taxpayers' money for an entirely negative purpose at a time when Britain is undergoing financial austerity. Picton heads the list of controversial figures and demands for his monument in St Paul's Cathedral (see Chapter 6) to be removed were made but the Dean made a brave stand and stated that its removal is unlikely.[2] During the author's last visit, a staff member commented that this monument would undoubtedly stay as most subjects of the cathedral's numerous memorials have questionable incidents in their past, 'so where do you start?' This is a fitting Christian stance for a religion that considers no mortal free from sin.

As a modern comparison, Mahatma Gandhi is admired by many for working towards Indian independence in the 1940s but despised by some for his allegedly racist views, which made the 2009 erection of his statue in Leicester controversial and calls were made to remove it in 2020 but it remains in place. Winston Churchill was a contemporary opponent of Gandhi but acknowledged that few people who achieve great things do so without offending anybody, saying 'You have enemies? Good. That means you've stood up for something, sometime in your life'.[3] The deeds of most important historical figures should be viewed in conjunction with his perceptive comment and for debate on this subject see – Save Our Statues (@SaveOurStatues)/Twitter

---

2. See *The Times*, 10 November 2020 or *Daily Mail*, 2 March 2022 along with other newspaper articles.
3. Churchill then said 'But, whatever you stand up for must further truth, goodness, and righteousness, otherwise you're making the wrong kind of enemies.'

Chapter 6

Tombs and Graves

There are military tombs and graves relating to the Napoleonic period scattered all over the British Isles, with most individuals laid to rest in the counties of their birth but many of the most famous figures are buried or commemorated in the capital of the United Kingdom. It is a measure of how important the Napoleonic Wars were for the British that an individual's participation in this titanic struggle was often recorded on their grave marker even if they died many years afterwards and occasionally to the detriment of other achievements made in their lifetimes.

Taphophiles study burial rituals and various ways of commemorating the dead and engage in making brass rubbings of plaques, photography of tombs and detailed analysis of the art, heraldry and inscriptions displayed on headstones or tombs. Although some consider spending time in cemeteries morbid, significant historical knowledge can be derived from how an individual's friends, relatives or government chose to commemorate them. It is also worth recalling that funerals and memorials are also intended for the living rather than the dead, who have passed beyond the cares of this world. Memorials often have a number of functions in addition to providing a focal point for relatives or comrades to remember their loved ones. They also display national gratitude for achievements, provide inspiration for future generations and are tributes from those they left behind.

This chapter focuses on the largest concentration of relevant tombs and monuments in Britain within St Paul's Cathedral because of their number, significance and the fact that most people find London the easiest city in Britain to visit, particularly those living outside the United Kingdom. Two tremendous monuments dedicated to Nelson and Wellington are located here and both men are entombed in the crypt inside magnificent tombs that can be seen by the public. Other influential figures are also commemorated in this famous place of worship, which testifies to the respect they were held in at the time of their deaths. The second half of this chapter covers a small selection of tombs and graves from other parts of Britain with examples chosen from the author's own travel experiences.

St Paul's Cathedral – *Map 3*

A place of worship dedicated to St Paul the Apostle has stood on Ludgate Hill (highest point in the City of London) for over 1,400 years, with the original church founded in 604 AD. The Old St Paul's Cathedral was destroyed in the Great Fire of 1666 and the current structure created in English Baroque style by Sir Christopher Wren between 1675 and 1710. Cathedrals usually take decades to build so most architects do not live to see their work finished but Wren was lucky enough to see St Paul's completed in his lifetime. This Anglican cathedral is the seat of the Bishop of London and one of the most recognizable religious buildings in the world due to its impressive dome,

St Paul's Cathedral, which contains the largest number of Napoleonic monuments in Britain.

which is one of the largest ever placed upon a religious structure. St Paul's has dominated the capital's skyline for 300 years and was the tallest building in London until 1963 at 365ft/111m high.

St Paul's is located in central London and easily reached by bus, taxi or the Underground network as it is well signposted as a major tourist attraction. The nearest Underground station is St Paul's on the Central Line. As the cathedral is an active place of worship, it is worth checking what events are being held on potential visiting days as the crypt is sometimes closed to the public during religious services. For opening hours and visitors information Tel: 020 7246 8350 or see – www.stpauls.co.uk

Case Study: Nelson's State Funeral

As he lay dying, Nelson murmured 'Don't let them throw me overboard, Hardy,' receiving the reply 'Oh no! Certainly not.' It is a truism that most seafarers wish to be buried at sea but this was not the case with Nelson who saw other officers' bodies cast into the ocean to clear ships' decks during action and he wanted a Christian burial. This happened to John Scott (his secretary) who was killed standing very close to Nelson at the start of the battle and even senior officers like Captain Cooke of HMS *Bellerophon* were thrown overboard shortly after being killed. Many officers and men received formal committal to the deep the following day but Captain Hardy was true to his word and ensured that Nelson received the unique privilege of having his body carried back to England after Trafalgar.

Dr Beatty conducted a perfunctory examination of Nelson to locate the bullet (the full autopsy occurred later) and had his body placed in a leaguer filled with brandy to preserve it, which was the largest barrel carried on warships at that time. Major Rotely RM recalled 'The body was brought up by two men … I received it and placed [it] head foremost in the cask. The head of the cask was then replaced and filled with brandy, and a marine sentinel placed over it by night or day.' HMS *Victory* sailed to Gibraltar and eventually returned to the Nore (Thames Estuary) where Nelson's remains were transferred to the *Chatham* (a yacht belonging Mr Grey, Commissioner of the Royal Dockyard) which conveyed it to Greenwich. The journey lasted over two months so the brandy was replenished each week and Beatty soon had to blend it with wine spirit due to the large amount required to fill a leaguer (130-150 gallons). Tales of sailors siphoning brandy from Nelson's barrel to drink it are probably apocryphal due to the presence of an armed guard.

When the *Chatham* docked at Greenwich, the body was placed in an inner coffin made of lead contained within a wooden casket and eventually placed within a third outer wooden coffin. He lay in state in Greenwich's Painted Hall (see Chapter 1) and his inner wooden coffin was fashioned from wood and metal salvaged after the Battle of the Nile by Captain Ben Hallowell of HMS *Swiftsure*, a Canadian officer prone to eccentricity. Hallowell gave Nelson this unusual present in 1799 (partly to admonish him for his behaviour after Aboukir Bay) writing 'Herewith I send you a coffin made of part of *l'Orient*'s mainmast, that when you are tired of this life you may be buried in one of your own trophies but may that period be far distant'. Nelson appreciated this macabre gift and kept it within his cabin for a time before stowing it in the hold. The outer casket was decorated by Mr France (an undertaker on Pall Mall) with 'emblematic devices ... executed from designs, by Ackerman, of the Strand. The covering is of fine black velvet, with treble rows of double gilt nails, the whole finely enriched with gold matt, enclosed and chased', and its lid was inscribed with Nelson's titles and honours.

After a series of French victories on land, the British were delighted by the decisive naval victory at Trafalgar but celebrations were tempered by news that it had cost the life of their greatest hero. Therefore, guns were fired in celebration but followed almost immediately by the lowering of flags to half-mast signifying national grief. The establishment decided to honour Nelson with a grand funeral, knowing that the scale and sombre splendour of the occasion would have appealed to him, and the service would be preceded by a river-borne funeral procession, which had never been attempted before.

At 10:00am on 8 January 1806 Nelson was borne by pallbearers in a slow march from the Painted Hall to the landing stage before an honour guard of Deptford Volunteers who presented arms. His coffin was loaded aboard a funeral barge and placed upon a catafalque designed to be visible from the shore. The river procession then began and was an incredible spectacle with thousands of Londoners lining the banks of the Thames despite a cold south-west wind. There were seventeen large funeral barges and the first four were draped in black cloth and adorned with black ostrich feathers. Nelson's coffin lay on the third in line and his standards and banners were carried on other barges along with flags flown at half-mast. His personal barge flew a solitary Union Flag but also displayed four shields bearing his arms and three banner rolls were carried by officers who had fought aboard HMS *Victory*. The vessel carrying Nelson was originally King Charles II's state barge and he was accompanied by Admiral Lord Hood, Admiral of the Fleet Sir Peter Parker (Chief Mourner) and the Prince of Wales.

The other processional barges carried representatives of the Royal Family, the Admiralty, the Corporation of London, the Thames Navigational Committee and seven of the twelve Livery Companies of London along with the Apothecaries Company. A large flotilla of small vessels followed in their wake along with gunboats manned by Royal Marines and seamen, with the Tower of London's guns saluting the procession as it passed and signal guns from the gunboats firing in reply. A strong wind and choppy waves helped the rowers to maintain a deliberately slow course with the procession lasting three hours and ending at the Whitehall Steps, where the coffin was brought ashore and carried to rest overnight in the Admiralty Building.

The funeral had been organized by the College of Arms and its heralds, so numerous coats of arms were displayed on both days. Although Nelson's family (on his mother's side) possessed their own blazon, he had commissioned a personal coat of arms after the Battle of Copenhagen in 1801. This broke with heraldic convention by using a uniformed seaman as a supporter rather than a heraldic beast and the lion on the opposing side is rending the flags and staffs of France and Spain to pieces with its jaws. This unorthodox design was controversial but Nelson insisted upon it and the heralds permitted its inclusion due to his status.

After lying in state, Nelson's second funeral procession began on 9 January. A full state funeral was a privilege usually reserved for Royalty and reveals that Nelson was highly regarded by the government and loved by the people of Britain. The funeral car (hearse) was modelled upon HMS *Victory* with representations of her black and yellow prow and stern to fore and aft. An imitation of the ship's figurehead adorned the prow and the coffin lay under a black canopy supported by four pillars decorated as palm trees. A viscount's coronet was placed at the canopy's summit with Nelson's motto emblazoned underneath, reading '*Palmam Qui Meruit Ferat*' (let him who has deserved it wear the palm). A white ensign flown at half-mast protruded from the stern and traditional black drapes were dispensed with, allowing mourners a clearer view of Nelson's coffin.

The cortege route was only 1.4 miles/2.2km from the Admiralty Building but it took two hours for Nelson's funeral car to reach the cathedral steps due to the huge number of accompanying contingents and the procession's deliberately slow pace. Wartime requirements meant that most of the Royal Navy was on active service so there was a greater army than navy presence at the funeral with far more red than blue uniforms in evidence as 4,000 soldiers were provided for the event. A small contingent of forty-eight Royal Marines and seamen from HMS *Victory* stole the show, nonetheless. An estimated 20,000–30,000 people lined the cortege route who maintained a dignified silence and quietly doffed their hats as Nelson passed, while this contingent marching behind him regularly paused to open out a huge shot-torn colour they carried to its full extent. This clearly revealed the many holes that had been shot through it by enemy fire during the battle to the crowd, who applauded softly each time they did so.

Nelson's hearse arrived at St Paul's at 2:00pm and the vast cathedral was packed for the occasion with some spectators sustaining injuries in the crush as people had waited up to six hours for his arrival. The Prince of Wales was present (unofficially) along with other members of the Royal Family, thirty-six admirals, one hundred RN captains and numerous officers from both services attended in private or official capacities. Hundreds of civic dignitaries and Britons from all over the country were present along with most of Nelson's family but his wife, mistress and daughter did not attend as it was not customary for female family members to do so.

The magnificent four-hour service lasted until 6:00pm although many stayed till 9:00pm that evening. Six Rear Admirals acted as pallbearers and Nelson's coffin was carried to a point directly beneath the centre of the cathedral's dome. At the end of the service, the coffin was lowered into the crypt through a special aperture made in the cathedral floor that was later sealed. The ceremonial staves of office carried by the Comptroller, Treasurer and Steward during the funeral were ritually broken and cast into the tomb. Then flags and ensigns from HMS *Victory* were carefully furled and placed within but the large colour borne during the funeral procession had had so many mementos torn from it by its bearers or bystanders that only a small portion was eventually committed. Choirboy Henry Milman later wrote 'I remember the solemn effect of the sinking of the coffin. I heard or fancied that I heard, the low wail of the sailors who bore and encircled the remains of their admiral.'

Nelson's Tomb – Map 3

The heart of St Paul's is a fitting resting place for Britain's greatest naval hero and people come from all over the world to see his tomb, which is outstanding even in a cathedral containing so many impressive memorials. It is surrounded by eight white pillars and traces of the trapdoor that Nelson's coffin was lowered through can still be discerned above it. Its placement at the centre of the crypt directly beneath the dome was an extraordinary honour to bestow upon a commoner and its main rival is the tomb of the Emperor Napoleon I under the dome of Les Invalides in Paris. Some say Nelson would have preferred burial alongside kings having shouted 'Westminster Abbey or glorious victory!' as a battle cry at Cape St Vincent but it is hard to believe that he would not have been flattered by this incredible stone tribute. While Westminster is a traditional resting place of British monarchs, St Paul's rapidly became a pantheon for military heroes after Nelson's interment, making his place here even more appropriate and few boast a sepulchre as magnificent as this tomb intended for a king.

The tomb is made from Italian black marble and is 10ft/3.048m high. It was designed by the famous Florentine sculptor Bendetto da Rovezzano for Cardinal Wolsey in the sixteenth century but confiscated by King Henry VIII when his famous adviser fell from favour. Henry intended to use it as his own tomb but it lay unused in Windsor for over 300 years until the Prince of Wales (on behalf of King George III) presented it for Nelson's entombment. Wolsey had planned for three bronze angelic sculptures to surround his tomb but they had been lost by 1806 and have only recently been rediscovered. They now reside in the collection of the Victoria & Albert Museum.

A grey stone plinth was constructed for it to rest upon but 'A Viscount's Coronet, the Admiral's name and dates were the only additions made to the tomb [for Nelson]'. The coronet and cushion it lies upon are painted in red, silver and gold adding a touch of colour to this sombre but magnificent work. The words HORATIO VISC NELSON are picked out in gold beneath the sarcophagus and Nelson's remains lie within three coffins inside. The floor around the tomb is decorated in Romanesque mosaic style, its pattern showing nautical paraphernalia like anchors. This is sometimes referred to as the *opus criminale* ('criminal work') as it was carefully laid by female prisoners from Woking Prison in the 1860s and extends into the chamber holding Wellington's tomb. An encased copy of Nelson's Call to National Prayer written shortly before Trafalgar is also displayed here.

Wellington's State Funeral

Some criticized the Duke of Wellington's grand funeral, arguing that he would have disapproved of this ostentatious display and preferred a simpler affair, but Queen Victoria was determined to give her old friend and adviser a magnificent tribute in return for the services he performed for the country. Wellington was 83 when he died but the establishment were so accustomed to his presence that his death surprised them nevertheless. Therefore, preparations for his funeral were made swiftly with Prince Albert (the Prince Consort) taking a major role in its organization along with members from both Houses of Parliament. Even so, the Duke's body lay in state at Walmer Castle for eight weeks (see Chapter 2) while his entombment was planned and generals stood guard over his coffin for six more days as he lay in state at Chelsea Hospital. An estimated 200,000 people came to pay their respects at Chelsea and the crush of the crowds was so great that two women were killed and others injured with the army bringing in extra soldiers to control proceedings.

Wellington's funeral took place on 18 November 1852, a cold but sunny day, with a single cannon shot fired to mark its beginning at 8:00am. Representatives from every unit in the British Army attended and each regiment contributed a small contingent to march in the procession or act as guards along its route with at least 10,000 servicemen taking part. As Wellington's colossal funeral car (see Chapter 2) slowly set out from Horse Guard's Parade it proceeded past Buckingham Palace and went under Wellington's Arch. It then continued

Thousands of Londoners attended the Duke of Wellington's funeral.

along Piccadilly passing Apsley House and along Pall Mall. Passing Trafalgar Square it proceeded onto the Strand before eventual arrival at St Paul's Cathedral. A pair of his famous boots were inverted and placed within the stirrups of the riderless horse following his hearse. An estimated 1.5 million people lined the route of Wellington's funeral cortege and the gigantic hearse encountered difficulties negotiating the streets with dozens of sailors required to free it when it became stuck on at least two occasions. It set out at 9:30am and arrived at St Paul's at 12:15pm where the mechanism designed to unload the coffin malfunctioned, delaying the service by an hour.

Great wooden tribunes had been constructed inside the cathedral to increase the number of seats and provide mourners with better views of proceedings. Some 13,000 guests packed St Paul's, although many uninvited people quietly slipped in, concealing themselves beneath the tribunes or within the crowd sitting or standing in the cathedral. The sittings of both Houses of Parliament were suspended and nearly all their members attended along with a massive army and navy presence, dignitaries from home and abroad along with private subjects from all over the United Kingdom.

Eight generals acted as pallbearers bearing Wellington's coffin inside and it was placed under the dome at Dean Henry Milman's suggestion. He had been a choirboy at Nelson's funeral and had the privilege of witnessing both events at first hand. At the end of the service, Wellington's coffin was lowered into the crypt to rest near and to the east of Nelson's tomb with the strains of the Dead March by Handel playing as it descended. To the amazement of some foreign observers, ceremonial staves were broken and cast into the tomb according to tradition. As the Dean recorded 'the gradual disappearance of the coffin as it slowly sank into the vault below, was a sight which will hardly pass from the memory of those who witnessed it'. Sir Charles George Young (Garter Principal King of Arms) then read out an extensive list of Wellington's titles and tributes (military, foreign and domestic) and the hymn 'Sleepers Awake' by Mendelssohn was sung as the guns of the Tower of London were fired and trumpets were sounded at the cathedral's western entrance.

The elaborate funeral cost an incredible £80,000 (about £6.5 million in today's money), with Parliament paying for most of it. Wellington was not loved as Nelson had been but was held in enormous respect with his loss felt across the country. Lady Shelley wrote with pardonable exaggeration 'On this day, Arthur, Duke of Wellington, perhaps the greatest man that ever drew breath, departed'. Queen Victoria, who had been so upset that she collapsed in tears and was unable to view him lying in state, was consoled by the magnificent funeral and evident national grief, writing 'He was the greatest man this country ever produced, and the most devoted and loyal subject, and the staunchest supporter the Crown ever had'.

Wellington's Tomb – Map 3

The process of building Wellington's tomb began before the funeral but was only finished six years later in 1858. It was designed by architect Francis Penrose who also carried out significant internal work in St Paul's including the relocation of Wellington's Monument. The Duke lies inside a massive classically-designed brown stone sarcophagus made from Cornish porphyry (Luxullianite granite) with the words 'Arthur Duke of Wellington' in gold lettering inscribed on one side. The tomb is highly polished with simple Maltese crosses adorning each end and is exactly the kind of straightforward design the Duke would have approved of. It is 10ft/3.048m high, weighs 17 tons and presents an unmovable and imposing appearance.

The sarcophagus rests upon a block of unpolished Peterhead granite adorned with the heads of four sleeping lions, symbolising the tomb's guardians. Penrose also designed four large candlesticks (made from Cornish granite) which are movable and usually stand against the walls but are occasionally placed at each corner of the tomb. He also designed the mosaic floor that extends into Nelson's chamber (see Nelson's Tomb). Five ageing banners hang from the walls around the tomb, which were made for Wellington's funeral procession and were presented by European states. The Great Banner is among them and was carried by General Sir James Chatterton of the 4th Dragoon Guards who bore it on Queen Victoria's direct order. Originally there were six banners but the one presented by Prussia was removed during the First World War for political reasons and never restored to its position.

Other Memorials in St Paul's Cathedral – Map 3

There are over 300 tombs and monuments in St Paul's, commemorating many important national figures connected with politics, literature, religion, architecture, journalism and art as well as the army and navy. Most of these date from the late eighteenth century onwards although there are a few examples from earlier centuries. A significant number are of those who took part in the Revolutionary and Napoleonic Wars, with their largest concentration in the south transept on the cathedral floor. All of these monuments are of interest with many beautifully rendered, demonstrating how revered they were by their government, comrades in arms and families who paid significant sums of money to honour them in such fashion.

Most visitors will enter via the main entrance and walking into the nave will see the Wellington Monument on their left, which is difficult to miss because of its great height. This is an excellent monument to look at first during a tour of St Paul's (see Chapter 5) but then walk to the right through the nave and into the south aisle where visitors will find the first of many of monuments dedicated to military heroes from this era. Photographers will find that, depending upon the time of day and weather, sunlight often pours through the windows above, saturating many of these monuments with light that presents a challenge for taking good photographs.

The first monument commemorates Captain Richard Burges who was killed fighting the Dutch commanding HMS *Ardent* at the Battle of Camperdown in 1797. It was sculpted by Thomas Banks in a classical style that emerged in the 1770s using figures from ancient Greece or Rome, which occasionally presents an intriguing combination of pagan and Christian figures. Visitors will find this is a common theme used in monuments at St Paul's. Made from white marble, this shows Burges clad in a Roman cloak opposite an angel with the pair standing on either side of a naval cannon's breech. The angel is presenting Burges with a classical scroll and nautical items such as cordage and cannonballs lie in the background with classical figures represented on the plinth below and frieze behind them. A seated classical figure on the plinth divides the view of a ship in the background with the rear of this vessel appearing to be an ancient galley while the prow emerging on the other side is from a Georgian warship, implying that Burges's achievements mirror those of antiquity.

The next niche contains a monument to Thomas Middleton, first Protestant Bishop of India, but walk past this to the adjacent niche that contains a memorial dedicated to the memory of Captain George Westcott who was killed while commanding HMS *Majestic* at the Battle of the Nile after 30 years of service. His statue depicts him attired in Roman garb but collapsing into the arms of Victory mortally wounded, with this angelic figure supporting him and holding a victor's wreath over his head.

Walking past the stairs leading to the Whispering Gallery, visitors should turn right into the south transept, where they will see numerous statues. On the left, high up on the wall above, is a small tablet-style memorial, which is easy to miss due to its height. This is the first of a series of tabular/plaque-style monuments erected at public expense (as inscribed at the top of this memorial) which honours the fall of General Sir Isaac Brock, slain during the Battle of Queenstown Heights in Canada. Brock was assigned to Canada in 1802, fought against the United States during the War of 1812 and contributed to victories at Fort Mackinac and Detroit along with training militias at a time when many thought war could be avoided. An interesting feature of this memorial by Richard Westmacott is the Native American warrior on the left

A tablet memorial to General Isaac Brock, killed at the Battle of Queenstown Heights during the War of 1812.

holding a large axe (numerous tribes fought for the British) and Brock briefly co-operated with the famous Chief Tecumseh during that war and became known as 'The Hero of Upper Canada'.

Walking into the south transept, the first large monument on the right is dedicated to General Ralph Abercromby and was also sculpted by Westmacott. He was killed at the Battle of Alexandria in 1801 as the British invaded Egypt to liberate that country from French occupation. This equestrian statue shows him slipping from his horse's saddle after being shot, with a fellow officer arresting his fall. Two large and very impressive Egyptian sphinxes sit on either side of the monument's pedestal, which is inscribed with details of Abercromby's military service.

A statue commemorating Sir Astley Paston (1768–1842), who was Sergeant-Surgeon to two monarchs, stands next to Abercromby's memorial but most visitors will find the monument adjacent to his of even greater interest. This is dedicated to Lieutenant General Sir John Moore and was sculpted by John Bacon. Moore saw extensive service, being renowned for his pioneering role in training light infantry, and was wounded many times. His command skills rivalled Wellington's but his superiors found him difficult to deal with. After leading an army into Spain, he was forced to withdraw before Napoleon's superior forces and faced Marshal Soult at the Battle of Corunna in 1809,

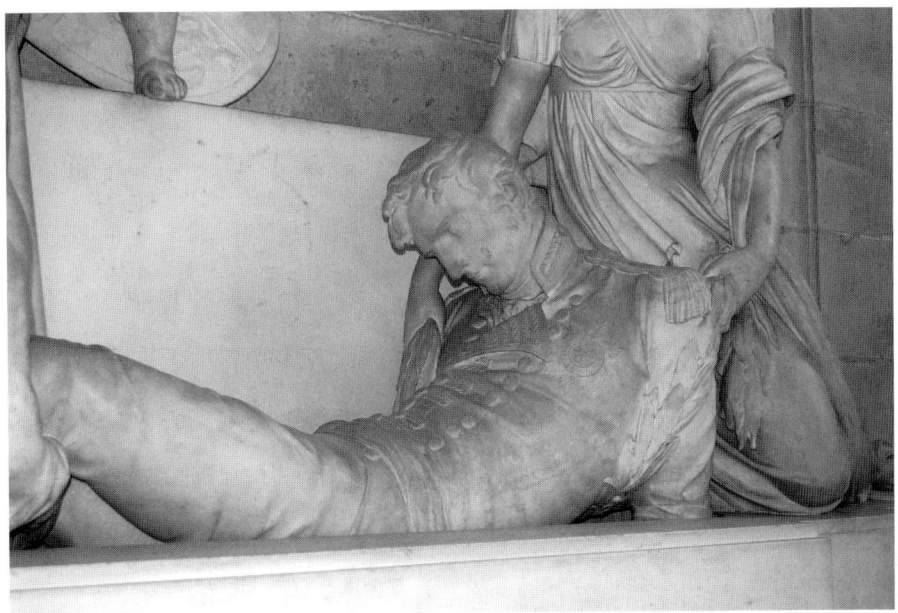

A detail of the monument to General Sir John Moore, who was killed in Spain 1809.

where he was killed by a cannonball. Moore's successful defence delayed the pursuing French army long enough for the British to embark and sail back to England. He was wrapped in a cloak and buried hurriedly as his army prepared to evacuate and this monument provides an excellent representation of the tragic scene with Moore's distressingly realistic corpse being lowered into his grave by two figures. One is a semi-nude allegory of Victory and the cherub-like genius of Spain (representative of the divine nature of an individual or place) stands over the scene holding a standard to display Spanish gratitude for Moore's sacrifice.

The next monument is dedicated to General Robert Gillespie and stands on the left of the cathedral's south door but is often obscured by piled chairs and tables. Gillespie's tall statue is shown in full uniform with a hooded cape, grasping a map in his left hand with his right placed on a sheathed and grounded sword. He was killed on 31 October 1814 leading an assault on the Fortress of Kalunga in the Kingdom of Nepal, which was the campaign that ultimately led to Nepalese soldiers joining the British Army and the creation of the renowned Ghurkha regiments.

A beautiful statue rendered in white marble by Thomas Campbell stands roughly opposite Gillespie's monument and depicts the heroic Captain Sir William Hoste. The placement of his statue so near the Nelson Monument is appropriate as he was one of his protégés, who was renowned as an outstanding

The monument to Sir William Hoste, one of the greatest frigate captains of the era.

frigate commander, took part in six major actions (including Cape St Vincent, Santa Cruz de Tenerife and the Nile) and became an acting captain aged only 18. The inscription records that this monument was erected by 'his brother officers and the admirers of his services', and Nelson once remarked that 'His worth as a man and an officer exceeds all which the most sincere friend can say of him'. Dismayed that he could not fight alongside Nelson at his final battle (due to the demands of the service) Hoste recalled the great admiral as 'Him I look upon as almost a second father, a sheet anchor whom I shall always have to trust to'.

Hoste came from the Norfolk village of Ingoldisthorpe, 16 miles from Nelson's birthplace, and his statue shows him in uniform and draped in a long peer's robe holding a large telescope and wearing tasselled Hessian boots. He is bareheaded and stands upon a rectangular pedestal displaying an elaborate insignia with oak leaf surround, emphasizing the word 'Cattaro' upon a flag held over a naval crown and 'Lissa'[1] on a medal below it. Hoste flew the signal 'Remember Nelson' to inspire the sailors as they went into action at Lissa and Hoste Island (one of the southernmost isles in Chile) was named after him. His naval career was so dramatic that Patrick O'Brian and C. S. Forrester modelled the fictional characters of Jack Aubrey and Hornblower upon his exploits, although Captain Edward Pellew was also influential.

General Eliott's memorial stands to the left of Hoste's statue. He is best known for his valiant defence of Gibraltar during the Great Siege of 1779–83 when Spain tried to seize the Rock while the British were distracted by the war in America. Although Eliott served before the period this book concentrates upon, it is a particularly fine memorial displaying details of the general's army uniform magnificently with his cloak draped over one shoulder, sword held in the crook of his arm and a large cannonball at his feet. Furthermore, his stubborn resistance prevented this vital naval base from falling into Franco-Spanish hands, which gave the Royal Navy an immense strategic advantage between 1792 and 1815 by allowing secure access to the Mediterranean.

The Nelson Monument stands behind and to the left of Hoste's statue (see Chapter 5) and above it is another national memorial to Captain George Hardinge by Charles Manning. He was killed by grapeshot during a running ship-to-ship engagement near Ceylon in which his ship, HMS *San Fiorenzo* (36 guns), was outmatched by *La Piédmontaise* (50 guns) but prevailed nonetheless. *La Piédmontaise* was taken as a prize with an eyewitness recalling:

---

1. The Battle of Lissa on 13 March 1811. O'Brian even borrowed Hoste's actions at Cattaro and Ragusa for plot lines in the Aubrey-Maturin series

She came in under jury masts and was towed in by the boats of the men-of-war from the mouth of the harbour to her mooring ground. The flags of all the vessels in the harbour were hoisted half-mast high, and minute guns corresponding to the age [28] of the excellent, brave, and lamented Captain Hardinge, were fired from the flag-ship …– *Bombay Courier*, 23 April 1808.

His memorial shows a sarcophagus emblazoned with a lion with a standard draped over it. A Lascar (Indian sailor) sits with his back to the tomb, bare-chested and bald except for hair tied in a topknot while an angelic figure lies sprawled in grief before the sarcophagus, weeping and holding a victor's wreath.

Opposite the Nelson Monument is a tribute to General Charles Cornwallis (1st Marquess Cornwallis) who is best remembered as one of the most able British commanders of the American War of Independence but his surrender at Yorktown in 1781 lead directly to the end of hostilities and Britain's only loss of a major war in the last 300 years. Cornwallis was appointed Lord Lieutenant of Ireland from 1798 to 1801 and opposed the French invasion attempts (see Chapter 7). He also helped bring about the Act of Union of 1800 with Ireland and was reappointed Governor-General of India in 1805 to curb the ambitions of Richard Wellesley. This monument shows his statue standing upon a fluted column, cloaked and dressed in the garter robes of a peer of the realm while holding a scroll. It was sculpted by John Rossi and the statues of three allegorical figures stand below the column representing Britannia, a native woman and a muscular, bearded Indian man with his hair coiled up who all display signs of grief.

Above Cornwallis's statue is a tabular monument to Captain Ralph Miller, sculpted by John Flaxman. American-born and one of Nelson's 'Band of Brothers' at the Battle of the Nile, he was an officer of great experience having fought at the battles of Chesapeake and Cape St Vincent, the sieges of Toulon and Acre and many other engagements. This memorial shows angelic depictions of Britannia and Victory in the act of hanging a medallion upon a palm tree emblazoned with his name and portrait. To the right is the stern of HMS *Theseus* that Miller commanded at the Nile and a crouching lion is shown on the left. Miller was one of twenty men killed in an accidental explosion as he prepared to sail from Alexandria to Jaffa. Forty-five men were wounded in the tragedy and the ship was only narrowly saved from fire in the conflagration that followed. Nelson knew Miller well and commented 'he is not only a most excellent and gallant officer, but the only truly virtuous man that I ever saw', upon learning of his death.

The next monument stands on the eastern side of the south door and is easy to miss as chairs and tables are often stacked in front and obscure it. This is a joint memorial to Generals Sir Edward Pakenham and Samuel Gibbs who were killed in the Battle of New Orleans on 8 January 1815. This presents a more modern impression than nearby classical style memorials, showing them realistically without religious embellishment in the high-collared uniforms of the day and standing side by side. Westmacott sculpted it between 1870 and 1879 and depicted Pakenham in a long cloak with both hands resting on the pommel of a sheathed sword held before him. Gibbs's cloak is draped over his shoulder and he holds his sword in his left hand with his right placed upon Pakenham's shoulder in a gesture of brotherly affection. It is rendered in white marble and the simple rectangular pedestal records how both generals were killed leading attacks against fortified American positions.

The adjacent sculpture is one of the finest Royal Navy memorials in the cathedral and dedicated to Vice Admiral Cuthbert Collingwood. Some consider him as 'the forgotten hero of Trafalgar' because he is overshadowed by Nelson's actions. He enjoyed a long career in the Royal Navy 'but most conspicuously in the decisive victory of Cape Trafalgar, obtained over the combined Fleets of France and Spain to which he eminently contributed, as Vice Admiral of the Blue, commanding the Larboard[2] Division', while commanding his flagship HMS *Royal Sovereign* and Collingwood assumed command after Nelson's death. He was a vocal opponent of press gangs and flogging, which made him so popular that many seamen thought of him as a father figure. He died in service aboard HMS *Ville de Paris* in 1810.

Sculpted by Westmacott, this white marble memorial was funded at public expense and shows Collingwood lying upon a classically-inspired funeral barge and naked but for a light covering. He clasps his sword hilt upon his chest with the blade lying down the centre of his body pointing towards his feet in the style of a medieval knight. The barge is sailing upon the mythical River Styx, so the reclining figure watching its progress is a river god rather than Neptune (although there is a marked resemblance). Naked infants clamber around this deity while a protective winged angel crouches over Collingwood, resting her right hand against his cheek and indicating the way to the afterlife with her left. There is a large monument dedicated to his memory at Tynemouth (he was born in Newcastle-upon-Tyne) and Collingwood is buried near Nelson in the Crypt below.

Admiral Richard Howe's stark white monument stands in the eastern corner of the south transept beneath one of the great windows, which often

---

2. The old term for port.

saturates it in light making it appear even more magnificent. Howe served in the War of the Austrian Succession, Seven Years War and War of American Independence, and his successful relief of the Great Siege of Gibraltar in 1782 towards the end of the latter is given a place of prominence revealing that the presence of Eliott's memorial nearby is intentional. During the Revolutionary Wars, Howe commanded the Channel Fleet, participated in the Battle of the Glorious First of June in 1794, became Admiral of the Fleet in 1796 and is renowned for the role he played during successful negotiations with the Spithead mutineers in 1797 shortly before he retired. This sculpture was rendered by John Flaxman who depicted Howe in uniform and a boat cloak holding a large spyglass and reclining slightly with a remarkably solemn look upon his face. A lion lies on his right while two female figures read the inscription on the podium beside him and a figure representing Britannia, dressed in Graeco-Roman attire and holding a trident, sits behind him. A depiction of a Georgian warship appears at the rear of the monument.

Two tabular monuments are located to the north of Howe's memorial and before one of the entrances to the Crypt below. One of these is dedicated to Colonel Henry Cadogan who fell while commanding a brigade at the Battle of Vitoria 1813 aged 34. It shows him wounded and bare-headed, holding a broken sword while staff officers and men try to catch him and prevent his fall. The mortally-wounded Cadogan watches as his men advance in the background. Wellington mentioned his bravery in his Vitoria despatch and Foreign Secretary Lord Castlereagh proposed that a monument be placed here in a motion that was passed by the House of Commons later that year.

The second tablet commemorates Major General Robert Ross who captured the American capital of Washington during the War of 1812. He served during the Peninsular War at Vitoria, Sorauren and Orthez and was appointed commander of all British forces on the East Coast in North America. He defeated an American force at the Battle of Bladensburg and subsequently entered Washington on 24 August 1814, setting government buildings alight in revenge for American troops sacking York and burning Government House (the Canadian Parliament), and the White House was set on fire and badly damaged. Ross was killed at the North Point during the early stages of the Battle of Baltimore on 12–15 September 1814 and this tablet shows an allegorical figure of Britannia weeping over his tomb while a figure representing Valour drapes an American flag over it. A bust of Ross is set upon the tomb and an angelic figure representing Fame holds a wreath of laurels over his head.

The last monument on this side of the cathedral lies just beyond the Crypt entrance on the corner of the south transept and south quire aisle. It is dedicated to John Howard (1726–90) who was a reformer of prisons and hospitals, which depicts its subject dressed in Roman garb with manacles at his feet, holding a key and a scroll. Walk from this statue under the great dome to the second entrance to the Crypt below located in the eastern aisle of the north transept. Opposite this stairwell are two more tabular monuments and the first was sculpted by Francis Chantrey and dedicated to Major General Bernard Bowes who fought at the battles of Roliça and Vimeiro along with the siege of Badajoz in the Peninsula. It shows his fall at the Battle of Salamanca on 22 July 1812 with the mortally-wounded Bowes falling backward as a soldier tries to support him. His scabbard is empty and he holds a broken sword with his soldiers depicted marching onward in the background.

The second tablet honours the memory of Major General John Le Marchant, who was also killed at Salamanca. A cavalry general who served in Flanders as well as the Peninsular War, he helped found the academy that eventually became the Royal Military College at Sandhurst. He was killed by a musket ball at the head of his brigade in the latter stages of a highly successful cavalry charge against French infantry. James Smith began this monument in 1816 but died before he completed it with his assistants finishing the tablet. It displays an image of a tomb with a portrait of the general on its side and a female allegorical figure leaning weeping over it. Several military standards are placed upon the tomb and on the right is a seated female figure wearing a Minervan helmet with her hand upon the shoulder of a boy whom she is comforting.

There are four monuments in the centre of the north transept. The first is a large memorial dedicated to Major General Thomas Dundas, sculpted by John Bacon. Dundas saw extensive service in the American War of Independence, served as Lieutenant Governor of Jersey and took part in a military expedition to the West Indies in 1794 where he died of yellow fever. The monument shows a bust of the general upon a pillar displaying a battle scene. A helmeted allegorical figure holds a wreath over his head and dominates this montage in the centre with a seated lion between her and the pillar with a second female figure and cherub behind her.

A tablet is set on the wall above Dundas's monument is in memory of Major General Jeremy Mackenzie and Brigadier General Ernst Langwerth, who both fell at the Battle of Talavera in 1809. This was Wellington's first major victory in Spain and it displays a tomb in the centre with a kneeling angel pressing her face against it on one side while a cherub bearing a military colour stands opposite. A figure representing Britannia sits behind the cherub with her shield emblazoned with the union flag resting against the tomb and this monument was sculpted by Charles Manning.

These monuments are mirrored by two military memorials directly opposite. The first is a highly dramatic example of one of Rossi's works. It shows Neptune God of the Sea grasping his trident in his right hand while turning quickly to catch the naked figure of a sailor in his left. This is Captain Robert Faulknor who holds a shield in one hand and a broken sword in the other as he plummets down into the depths. On the left side is a figure depicting Victory who is about to crown him with a laurel wreath and the inscription explains how Parliament funded this memorial. It also records how Faulknor fell on 5 January 1795 commanding an action between HMS *Blanche* (his command) and *La Pique* when 'having lost most of his mast and rigging, snatched an opportunity of the bowsprit of *La Pique* coming athwart the *Blanche* and with his own hands lashed it to her capstan: and thus converted the whole stern of the *Blanche* into one battery: but unfortunately soon after this bold and daring manoeuvre, he was shot through the Heart'. He died almost at the moment of victory aged 32.

A tablet commemorating Major Generals Robert Craufurd and Henry MacKinnon is placed on the wall above Faulknor's memorial. Both men were killed storming the Spanish fortress of Ciudad Rodrigo in 1812, which was an important stronghold on the Spanish-Portuguese border. Although considered a stern disciplinarian, Craufurd was highly respected and considered a rising star within Wellington's army and was mortally wounded leading an attack into a breach blasted through the town walls. Their monument shows a ragged soldier and an angelic allegory holding a standard upon a tomb with a lion and military paraphernalia in the background.

Walk behind these monuments into the western aisle of the north transept where there are two more tabular memorials. The first is dedicated to Lieutenant Colonel Sir William Myers who fell at the Battle of Albuera on 16 May 1811 where the British suffered terrible losses in an action where both sides claimed victory. Although Marshal Beresford led the army at Albuera, Wellington wrote to Lady Myers and an extract from his letter is inscribed:

It will be some consolation to you to know that your son fell in an action in which, if possible, the British troops surpassed all their former deeds, and at the head of the Fusilier Brigade, to which a great part of the final success was to be attributed. As an officer he had already been highly distinguished and, if providence had prolonged his life, he promised to become one of the brightest ornaments to his profession, and an honour to his country.

The memorial shows a central bust of Myers flanked by sculptures of Britannia in Greek dress and a muscular Heracles (Hercules) clad in lion skins.

On the wall opposite is a memorial to Major General Daniel Houghton who also fell at Albuera. His brigade withstood numerous attacks with three quarters of them falling dead or wounded and Houghton was killed by a musket ball just as he gave the command to advance. Wellington commented 'I understand that it was impossible for anybody to behave better than he did … he actually fell waving his hat and cheering his brigade on to the charge.' The tablet depicts this moment with Houghton in uniform and reclining into the arms of an angelic figure in the foreground, delivering his last command as he dies. The angel holds a banner that she is pointing in the enemy's direction while British soldiers advance in the background with levelled muskets and fixed bayonets.

Walk north from here and the last memorial for this era on the cathedral floor is located on the western side of the north transept. It is also one of the most controversial, being dedicated to Lieutenant General Sir Thomas Picton whose reputation has been attacked recently. Picton is the only Welshman with a monument dedicated to his memory in St Paul's and it is undeniable that he died a hero's death at Waterloo, even if other aspects of his personality and career are less creditable. During the final campaign against Napoleon, he was struck in the hip at the Battle of Quatre Bras but concealed this wound so he could continue to fight. He was killed two days later at the decisive battle of the Napoleonic Wars leading a bayonet charge that helped repulse the first major French infantry attack on the British ridge.

He is buried in his family's vault at St George's Church in Hanover Square and this classically-inspired monument was dedicated to his memory by order of Parliament. It displays a bust of Picton in Roman garb set upon a pedestal with three life-sized classical figures standing before it. The two angelic figures represent Fame and Victory with the latter presenting a symbolic wreath to a Roman general with a lion watching as she does so. The lion's presence signifies Picton's death in battle and this monument was sculpted by Sebastien Gahagan between 1816 and 1820.

The Crypt – Map 3

Two staircases descend into the crypt from the cathedral floor located in the eastern aisles of the north and south transepts. Plaques set above both entrances display three human skulls with bones behind them, providing a macabre but necessary reminder that human remains are entombed here so visitors should explore the crypt in a respectful manner. Entering is always a sobering experience as most of this area is deliberately lit in soft light, which creates difficulties for photographers even though flashguns are permitted. Nelson and Wellington have the largest, most impressive tombs but there are many plaques and memorials dedicated to famous architects, poets, writers, artists, philosophers and journalists here.

The following route is for visitors entering the crypt via the staircase on the east side of the south transept. Upon reaching the floor of the crypt, turn left and there are a group of monuments and plaques on the right. One of these is a plain white plaque with lettering inscribed in black and no illustrative adornments. This is dedicated to the Reverend William Nelson who bore the titles Baron Nelson of the Nile, Viscount Merton, 1st Earl Nelson and 2nd Duke of Bronte who is buried in this area near his brother Horatio along with his wife Sarah Countess Nelson. He served briefly with his brother as a naval chaplain aboard HMS *Boreas* but obtained a discharge in 1786 and continued his career in the church, dying without issue in 1835.

Take the south aisle corridor to the left of Reverend Nelson's plaque, which is lined with statues and monuments. One of these is dedicated to General Sir William Napier (1785–1860) who served in the Peninsular War but also became a military historian and was present at some of the events he described. Defending the reputation of Sir John Moore was his primary motive for writing and he produced a six-volume history of the Peninsula, which is still widely read, along with other works. A statue of General James Napier (1782–1853) is located further down this corridor and he also fought in the Napoleonic Wars with both brothers serving into the Victorian period. William's statue depicts him standing with his hands placed on the hilt of a sheathed sword, bare-headed, bearded and cloaked in Victorian British Army uniform. James's memorial is similar, showing him in the uniform of the same period with hand on sword, bearded and bare-headed.

Between the two Napier statues but on the opposite side of the corridor is a large monument in memory of Admiral Lord George Rodney (1718–92), sculpted by Rossi out of white marble in 1811. While Rodney's career pre-dates the Revolutionary Wars, visitors can catch a glimpse of Nelson's tomb through the railings behind his monument.

Further along the south aisle is a statue dedicated to Vice Admiral Sir Pultney Malcolm (1768–1838) rendered by Edward Hodges Baily. Malcolm was a captain by 1805 and participated in Nelson's celebrated pursuit of Villeneuve's fleet to the West Indies but did not fight at Trafalgar. He fought at the Battle of San Domingo in 1806 and carried out naval operations in support of the British Army in the Peninsula and during the Hundred Days Campaign in 1815. He briefly commanded naval forces guarding Napoleon on St Helena in 1816–17 and was an Admiral of the Blue at the end of his career. This statue is an imposing depiction of Malcolm wearing a long collared cloak and a uniform postdating the Napoleonic period with a large telescope tucked under his left arm and clasped in both hands before him. Malcolm's receding hairline and proud demeanour give an impression of a man who had earned and received great respect.

At the end of this aisle, turn right, then right again and head towards Nelson's tomb. Immediately before his tomb are memorials on either side of the corridor dedicated to captains killed at Trafalgar. Both were buried at sea and the first is for Captain John Cooke. It was created by Westmacott and shows Britannia kneeling and holding her chin in her palm while two cherubs in the background carry her trident and helmet. The prow of a two-decked battleship is shown in the background and the inscription reveals that Cooke was 44 when he was killed after serving 30 years in the Royal Navy. He died in a savage melee as French seamen and marines of the *Aigle* boarded HMS *Bellerophon* but they were repulsed and the *Aigle* surrendered towards the end of the battle.

Captain George Duff's plaque is located opposite Cooke's memorial and shows his visage emblazoned in profile upon a tomb adorned with oak leaves. A kneeling, bare-chested seaman leans against the side of his tomb weeping and holding a standard over his shoulder. Britannia stands opposite with her left arm draped over the tomb as she lays a garland upon it with a lion in the background symbolizing Duff's death in battle commanding HMS *Mars*. The monument was sculpted by John Bacon (junior) and records that he died in his 42nd year after 29 years of service.

Beyond these memorials is Nelson's tomb in the heart of the cathedral – see Chapter 5. After viewing this, turn right to see Admiral Collingwood's simple rectangular stone tombstone to the south of Nelson's tomb and directly behind Rodney's monument. It is plain and unadorned but carries the inscription 'Cuthbert Lord Collingwood. Died 7th March 1810 Aged 61'. Its position so close to the resting place of Britain's greatest naval hero tells visitors all they need to know about the high regard Collingwood was held in.

Near Collingwood's tomb is a tablet dedicated to Admiral Codrington, showing him in profile with naval crown, flag and his coat of arms adorning this composition and the word 'Navarin' prominently displayed. It was sculpted by Albert Bruce Joy and the inscription describes Codrington's extensive career including ships he served in and major actions he fought at. The Glorious First of June and Trafalgar stand out but his more obscure service in the Scheldt, on the east coast of Spain and during the War of 1812 are also listed along with the Battle of Navarin on 20 October 1827, which was a notable victory. There are also monuments dedicated to Royal Navy officers of the Victorian period and from both world wars in the area around Nelson's tomb.

Wellington's tomb lies directly east of Nelson's sepulchre and there is a small plaque on the right of the archway leading into this area for Colonel John Gurwood. It shows Gurwood in profile with an inscription describing that he 'served with distinction in the Peninsular, France and Waterloo'. It also records how he led a 'forlorn hope' at Ciudad Rodrigo, a term given to the first unit entering a well-defended breach blasted into the walls of a fortification. Defending enemy garrisons concentrated their fire into breaches, inflicting great casualties in the unit spearheading the first assault but their participants' courage was rewarded by promotion if they survived. This memorial records how Gurwood received the task of compiling Wellington's despatches and died on 27 December 1845 aged 57.

Walk directly east from Gurwood's plaque to see Wellington's incredible tomb, surrounded by tabular monuments dedicated to army officers from later wars – see Chapter 5. After viewing the tomb, turn right to find a small white marble tablet placed at the corner of the right hand passage and southern aisle. This recalls the service of Captain Alexander MacNab of the 30th Regiment who served as an aide de camp for General Picton at Waterloo. He was killed during the battle but his body was never identified and cremated or buried in a mass grave after the battle. This memorial was placed here by his nephews in 1876.

Continuing east along the south aisle, visitors may wish to see monuments dedicated to the early war correspondents and pay their respects to the memorial of Sir Christopher Wren, architect of St Paul's Cathedral. Turn left at Wren's monument and walk to the north aisle running along the northern side of the crypt and along this corridor is a monument dedicated to Sir William Q. Orchardson (1835–1910). His memorial is rendered in black and white marble and shows an artist's palette on a tomb flanked by an angel with a statuette of Napoleon I on the other side This is based upon Orchardson's famous painting 'Napoleon on board the *Bellerophon*' that depicted the Emperor's journey into final exile and shows him standing on deck looking grimly towards the horizon while a group of officers regard him in the background. Sculpted by Sir William Reynolds-Stephens, it is one of the very few nineteenth-century monuments displaying Napoleon's image in Britain.

Retrace your steps, passing Nelson's tomb and head towards the exit at the western end of the crypt to find the last three monuments for the period near the cathedral cafe and gift shop. On the left is a statue of Admiral John Jervis (Earl St Vincent) (1735–1823). He served during the Revolutionary and Napoleonic Wars and earned the title Earl St Vincent for his victory at the Battle of Cape St Vincent in 1797. A fierce disciplinarian, he was nicknamed 'Old Jarvie' by his sailors but they respected his courage and seamanship. As they approached the enemy fleet at Cape St Vincent, Captain Calder counted their ships by telescope and gave a running commentary as they came into view. Beginning at eight, the number rose rapidly to twenty and finally twenty seven before Jervis stopped him and growled 'Enough, Sir, no more of that, the die is cast and if there are 50 sail I will go through them!' This monument was created by Edward Hodges Baily and shows Jervis uniformed and wearing a boat cloak with his hands clasped upon a large collapsed telescope. His stern countenance makes it easy to imagine him as a martinet and the statue's plinth is inscribed with a summary of his career.

Walk west and turn to the left to see the next monument, which is in memory of Major General Sir William Ponsonby who served in the Peninsula but is renowned for his valiant death at the Battle of Waterloo. There he commanded the Union Brigade comprised of English, Scottish and Irish cavalry regiments drawn from the nations of the United Kingdom. The brigade charged, repulsed and pursued the first major French infantry attack but elements of the brigade overextended their advance by going on to attack French artillery batteries. They were badly mauled when French cavalry counter-attacked and Ponsonby was cut down as he tried to rally his men. This monument portrays a dramatic composition as the fallen General is raised to his feet by an Angel bearing a victor's wreath while simultaneously lifting him to heaven. Ponsonby is almost naked but for a classical robe and is dropping his sword as he rises with a wounded horse foundering on its knees in the background. This memorial was rendered in white marble by Edward Hodges Baily in 1815.

To the right of Ponsonby's memorial and near the exit is the final monument, which is dedicated to Captains' James Mosse and Edward Riou on the north side of the crypt. Created by John Rossi in 1806, it is flanked by two winged angelic sculptures, holding a medallion showing portraits of the officers in the centre. The medallion bears an inscription and a tomb is depicted above it. The inscription reveals how they were killed during the Battle of Copenhagen 1801 fighting under the combined command of Admirals Hyde Parker and Nelson. Mosse commanded HMS *Monarch* and Riou HMS *Amazon* and details of their careers are described here.

*   *   *

The following are a few good examples of monuments chosen by the author during his travels around Britain.

Greenwich

Adjacent to the National Maritime Museum at Greenwich (see Chapter 8) are monuments and graves of officers and men in the grounds of Devonport House Hotel (formerly the Old Royal Navy Hospital burial ground). Near the gateway into this area by the museum's entrance is a memorial to Vice Admiral Thomas Thompson. He served at Copenhagen and Aboukir Bay and was one of Nelson's 'Band of Brothers' at Trafalgar. He lost a leg at Copenhagen and from 1816 until his death in 1828 (aged 62) was Treasurer for Greenwich RN Hospital. The memorial is a freestanding obelisk, surrounded by iron railings, inscribed with the names HMS *Leander* and HMS *Bellona* (two of his ships) and features a stylised flag flying at half-mast near its summit. Thompson is buried in the Officers' Vault 100ft/30.48m behind his monument.

Tom Allen, who was Nelson's personal servant, is buried nearby and commemorated with a square, pillar-style gravestone surrounded by an iron railing. It was unusual for a man of his social status to receive such an expensive grave marker and a sure sign of the regard the Royal Navy had for him as they paid for its creation. Allen was a Greenwich Pensioner and the inscription on this grave reads 'To the memory of Thomas Allen, the faithful servant of Admiral Lord Nelson born at Burnham Thorpe in the County of Norfolk 1764, and died at The Royal Hospital Greenwich on the 23rd of November 1838.'

A tall monument surmounted by a statue of Britannia dedicated to officers and men of the Royal Navy and Marines also stands within this grassed area. It records that an estimated 20,000 former inmates of the hospital were buried here between 1749 and 1869 and was erected by the Lord Commissioners of the Admiralty in 1892. Its inscriptions extol the virtues of Valour, Honour, Loyalty and Duty along with commemorating the battles of Trafalgar, St Vincent, Camperdown and the Nile and the monument bears nautical images including an anchor on its north side and a shrouded gun on its south face.

Behind this area is the Old Mausoleum Pavilion, placed over the vaults where many officers were laid to rest. It is fenced and private but visitors can photograph this structure, which is constructed from dark brown brick with white stone facings and has three archways blocked by iron gates. A manual lift within this building once lowered coffins into the subterranean vaults after funeral services. The public are usually allowed limited access to this area that contains monuments and headstones during the annual London Open House weekend in September.

Vice Admiral Sir Thomas Hardy died at the age of 70 and is the most famous occupant of this mausoleum. After the notable role he played at

Trafalgar, many thought Hardy deserved an elaborate funeral ceremony but he left instructions in his will forbidding an ostentatious show at his interment. Nevertheless, many Greenwich Pensioners and members of the public lined the route as his small cortege marched here and saw him buried in a simple ceremony. A miniature that Nelson gave him was placed around his neck as he lay in the coffin, which sculptor William Behnes earlier made a cast of so that he could represent it on Hardy's bust. This can still be seen in the Old Royal Naval College Chapel nearby.

A memorial tree has been planted before the pavilion and its plaque records:

The Hardy Oak – This English oak (*quercus robur*), grown from 2002, was planted here on 8 April 2014 by the Nelson Society, to mark the 180th anniversary of the appointment of Vice Admiral Sir Thomas Masterman Hardy as Governor of Greenwich Hospital, on 8 April 1834. Born in Dorset on 5 April 1769, he died at Greenwich on 20 September 1839 and is buried here in the Hospital officers' vault, under the Mausoleum pavilion.

For further details of this fascinating area see – www.nelson.greenwich.co.uk/things-to-see/

Deal

Captain Edward Parker participated in Nelson's abortive attack on Boulogne on 15–16 August 1801 and was severely wounded with his thigh being shattered by a roundshot. He was brought back to Deal where he died following the amputation of his leg and was buried in the graveyard of St Georges Church. He was a close personal friend of Admiral Nelson, who treated him like a son and helped him to rise within the service. The attack on Boulogne was one of Nelson's few defeats with Admiral Latouche-Tréville predicting that he would assail his defensive line of ships anchored across the harbour mouth using a similar strategy to that he used at Aboukir Bay. The French took care not to be outmanoeuvred and repulsed two British attacks with concentrated cannon fire, inflicting heavy losses.

Nelson paid for Parker's funeral and his large gravestone is the only monument he is known to have bought for a fellow officer. Nelson wept openly during the funeral over the loss of his friend, who was only 23, and often leant against a tree near the graveside during the burial ceremony. This tomb's inscriptions are indistinct but local historians have interpreted them with its dedication recording 'Captain Edward Thornborough Parker. Died Sept. 27th 1801' and a poem on its north side reading:

> *This stone records a gallant hero's name,*
> *Whose youthful bosom glow'd with virtue's flame:*
> *A nation heard with tears his mournful doom;*
> *The flow'r of Valour, wither'd in its bloom.*

Leicestershire

Two riflemen of the 95th Regiment of Foot are buried in Welford Road Cemetery, central Leicester. The first is John Winterton in Plot CE13 beneath a simple headstone adorned with an oak leaf. He was born in 1796 and his inscription records that he fought at Waterloo where he suffered life-changing wounds. It reads 'In Remembrance of John Winterton who departed this life February 16th 1870 in the 74th year of his age. He was severely wounded at the Battle of Waterloo and after lying three days and two nights on the field had his left leg amputated at Brussels. May he rest in peace.' Sadly Winterton's slow treatment in the aftermath of a Napoleonic battle was not unusual.

Private William Green (1769–1881) of the same regiment is known for his book *Where Duty Calls Me*, an account of his nine years' service in the British Army. He was present at Corunna, Busaco, Ciudad Rodrigo and Badajoz but also wrote rare accounts of the Battle of Kiöge and Siege of Copenhagen 1807. Learning that his grave was unmarked, historian Mel Siddons and the Friends of Welford Road Cemetery took action and on 6 April 2002 (the anniversary of Badajoz's fall in 1812) they dedicated a permanent gravestone in the presence of his great-great-great nephew Gerald Green with 95th re-enactors sounding the last post and firing a volley over the grave. It lies in Plot L23 and the regimental badge is inscribed at the top of Green's headstone along with a quotation from his book 'I shall go where my duty calls me' at its base. Few working class people could afford headstones before the late nineteenth century and most graveyards contain thousands of unmarked graves. Some of Green's relatives are buried nearby who also lacked markers so the names of six of them were recorded under Green's personal inscription. This cemetery has a visitor's centre, see – www.fowrcl.org.uk/contact-us/

The most famous Waterloo veteran from Leicestershire was Colonel Edward Cheney (brevet Major during the battle) who is buried in St Luke's Church in Gaddesby Village (11 miles/17.7km north-east of Leicester) in a tomb with an equestrian statue of Cheney dismounting from a wounded horse above it. He is depicted bare-headed with his bearskin lying at his feet

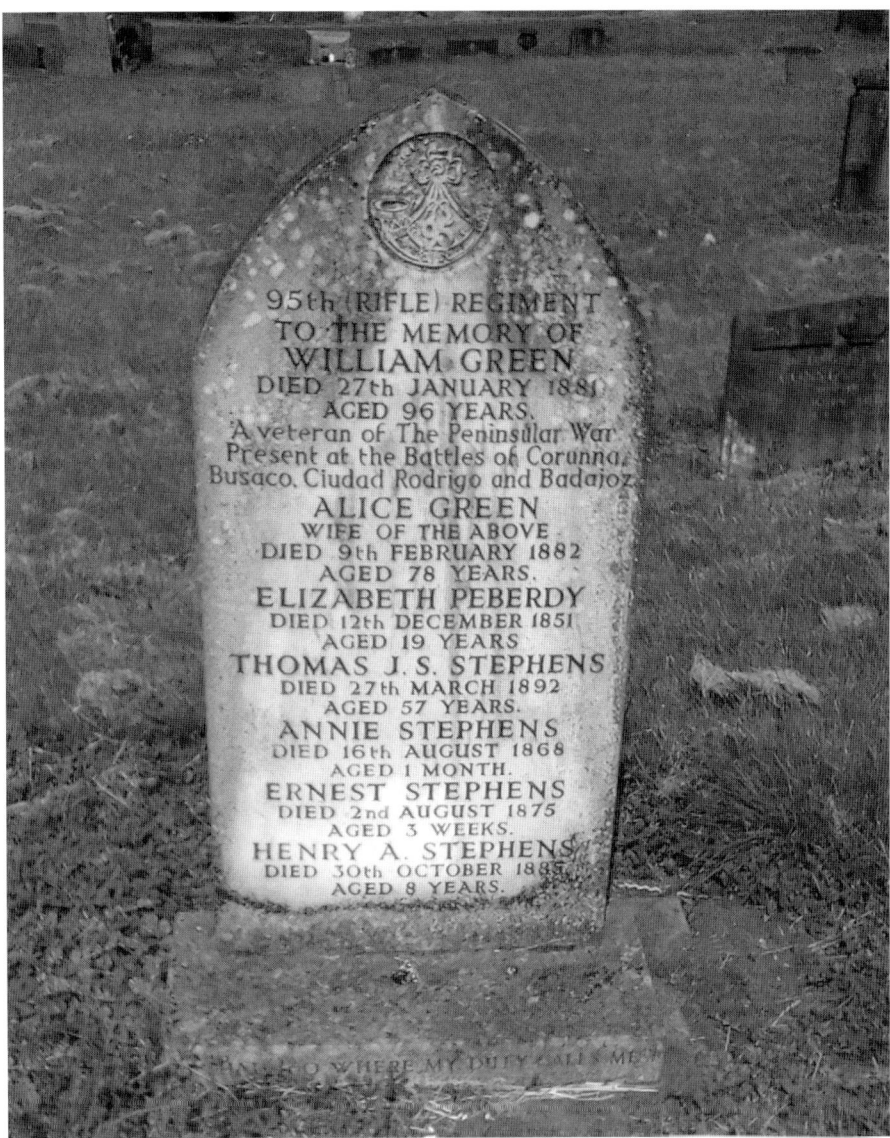

The gravestone of Private William Green of the 95th Foot and his relatives.

and dressed in the uniform of the 2nd Royal North British Dragoons (Scots Greys). His horse's jaws are bared in agony as he dismounts and an apple is sometimes placed between them during the church's harvest festival. The monument's base is elaborately decorated with friezes including a depiction of Sergeant Ewart seizing the Eagle of the French 45th Line Regiment along with representations of both standards captured by the brigade. It was sculpted by Joseph Scott shortly after Cheney died in 1845. Cheney took part in the charge and went on to assail French artillery batteries as his brigade overextended its attack. As French cavalry threatened to cut off their withdrawal, a fellow officer shouted 'How many minutes have we yet to live, Cheney?' Seeing the odds heavily stacked against them, he responded 'Two or three at the very utmost, most probably not one.' Cheney survived unwounded but had four horses shot from under him and assumed command of the regiment following the death of his colonel.

Edinburgh – *Map 4*

Ensign Ewart's tomb is easy to find in the Scottish capital as it is located at the top of the Royal Mile on the esplanade before Edinburgh Castle, which is a major tourist attraction and well signposted. Ewart became famous after capturing a French Eagle at Waterloo in a particularly bloody melee and this is exhibited along with his sword and other related items in the regimental museum inside the castle (see Chapter 8). A painting entitled 'The Fight for the Standard' by Richard Ansdell illustrates Ewart's courageous exploit in the Great Hall and he is said to have cut down the standard bearer, at least one infantryman and a lancer (cavalryman) to seize and bear his trophy away.

He died in 1846 and was originally buried in the churchyard of New Jerusalem Chapel in Salford but his grave was eventually paved over and forgotten. It was rediscovered in the 1930s by members of his regiment who applied for permission to disinter his remains and transfer them here. The new tomb is made from a large block of grey granite and the top of his former gravestone is set into the pavement behind, reading 'In memory of Ensign Charles Ewart who died March 23rd 1846, aged 77 years.' The modern tomb is inscribed on its south side with the words 'Here lies Ensign Ewart, Royal North British Dragoons. He captured the standard of the French 45th Regiment from which the Eagle Badge now worn by the Royal Scots Greys is derived. Erected to his memory in April 1938 by the officers, warrant officers, non-commissioned officers and men past and present of the Royal Scots Greys.' The date 1815 is incised on the memorial's western side with a graphical rendition of an eagle on its east face.

The Ensign Ewart public house, which Ewart ran after retiring from the army, is a few minutes' walk from his tomb on the Royal Mile at 521–523 Lawnmarket, Edinburgh, EH1 2PE. This marvellous old pub has a low, wooden-beamed ceiling and dates back to 1680 according to some accounts. It contains paintings, prints and other items relating to this Scottish hero and the French Eagle he captured. See – www.ensignewartpub.co.uk/

Fishguard (Wales)

An unusual headstone is displayed at St Mary's Church dedicated to a woman involved in repelling the French invasion. Its inscription reads;

> In Memory of Jemima Nicholas of this town The Welsh Heroine who boldly marched to meet the French Invaders who landed on our shores in February 1797. She died in Main Street July 1832 aged 82 years. At the date of the invasion she was 47 years old and lived 35 years after the event. Erected by subscription collected at the Centenary Banquet July 6 1897.

Nicholas is buried in the churchyard but the precise location of her grave is unknown so this fine headstone stands in a prominent place in the knowledge that her remains rest nearby. Accounts of Nicholas's actions during the last invasion of Britain (see Chapter 7) vary but local tales agree that she and other women armed with pitchforks and improvised weapons captured French soldiers they caught looting and possibly drunk. Her participation goes unrecorded by reliable sources but Nicholas represents local civilians who volunteered to help militia and regular army soldiers resist the French.

Ireland

On an isolated road near Killala in County Mayo stands an unusual monument recording the death of the first French soldier to die in Ireland during General Humbert's invasion in 1798, which is an obscure event even in Ireland (see Chapter 7). French forces landed near Kilcummin Village and the soldier was a cavalryman who died reconnoitring the route of their advance as they marched on Castlebar but shot himself accidentally rather than being killed by the enemy. This was easy to do with a short weapon, especially if a pistol was thrust hurriedly into a belt or sash and the soldier died before his comrades could staunch the blood flow.

The grave is covered by a large stone base and topped with two sculptures, rendered in fibreglass or resin rather than stone, although their green colour makes them appear to be bronze from a distance. One is dressed in rural clothing and sprawls at the other's feet while the standing figure bends down in the act of helping him to his feet. The stricken figure represents an oppressed Irishman while his rescuer is a French soldier dressed in Revolutionary-period uniform and cocked hat. It symbolizes the fact that the French came to support Irish patriots resist British rule and is a remarkably poignant monument, especially as it is backed by woods and overlooks an isolated rural landscape. It is difficult to locate and the author would not have found it without the assistance of locals as many roads and lanes in the vicinity are unnamed. It lies between Kilcummin Harbour and the town of Killala with nearest the village being Castlelacken. The monument is located on the road to the Old Lacken Graveyard at Grid Reference (N 54°16'19" - W 9°16'4").

There is a plaque with inscriptions written in French, English and Irish (Gaeilge) that reads 'Here in Garrai Franncach lies the body of a French soldier who died in August 1798. He arrived at Kilcummin with General Humbert and his forces. He was the first soldier of that expedition to die on Irish soil.' Although the soldier's name is long forgotten, *Garrai Franncach* means French Garden or Frenchman's Garden in Irish and Killala is now twinned with the town of Chauvé where the soldier is believed to have come from.

Summary

It would be easy to write an entire book on the large number of Georgian military graves and tombs scattered around Great Britain in graveyards, churches and cathedrals but this chapter attempts to provide a strong introduction of what can be seen along with details about the most important concentration of memorials and tombs in St Paul's Cathedral. Enthusiasts will find it worthwhile to seek these monuments out and reflect upon what their inscriptions, symbolism and expense signify about their subjects and how the British regarded these wars.

Chapter 7

Facing Invasion

Many British people are unaware of the French invasions in Ireland and Wales during the Revolutionary Wars. The reasons for their obscurity are that these landings were small scale, militarily unsuccessful and overshadowed during two large conflicts that witnessed far more significant events. Nevertheless, enthusiasts can learn a great deal from visiting the sites of these invasions as studying them provides an insight into how people thought during this period when real-life adventures were attempted and political radicals believed that anything was possible. Although often treated as separate incidents, these invasions were part of a larger plan to invade Ireland in support of the Society of United Irishmen who planned to rebel against British rule.

General Lazare Hoche intended to land his main force in Bantry Bay in Southern Ireland where he hoped to receive support from Irish people who wanted independence and might ally themselves with Revolutionary France in its attempt to spread reform throughout Europe. He also dispatched secondary forces to Newcastle in northern England and Fishguard in Wales, with these smaller contingents acting as diversions to draw British reinforcements away from repelling the main invasion. It was a bold plan but in common with all seaborne invasions it relied heavily upon close coordination between army and navy units, minimal naval interference from the enemy, reasonable weather and good luck.

Bantry Bay – *Map 7*

Towards the end of the eighteenth century, Ireland was poorly governed and the British Government knew it. Ireland had been split along religious lines for centuries with Catholics denied the vote and the right to hold most offices and most influential figures were Protestants. The Dublin Government was dominated by an elite group whose policies were based on self-interest thereby ensuring that land rents remained high, which provoked great resentment in the rural-based economy of the south. The north was more prosperous but landowners were predominantly Protestant descendants of English and

Scottish settlers and many Catholics felt oppressed or ignored by the state. The land in the south was sparsely populated as many had emigrated to escape poverty and the political situation was widely considered unjust.

Although serious political changes were proposed, the British Government felt obliged to postpone reform in the wake of the French Revolution, fearing a potential spread of republicanism to Ireland. The United Irishmen, whose membership included Catholics and Protestants, was a nationalist organization that sought an independent Ireland and its leader fled to Paris to solicit French support. This was Wolfe Tone who so impressed Lazare Carnot (French Minister for War) with his petitions that he ordered the formation of a military expedition on Tone's assurance of attracting widespread support from the people. Although the French Directory would be delighted by the emergence of a republican Ireland, what it really wanted was a secure base to support an invasion of England.

Admiral Justin Morard de Galles left the Port of Brest on 15 December 1796 commanding a sizable fleet of seventeen ships-of-the-line, twenty-six smaller warships and troop transports that carried an army of 15,000 French soldiers under General Hoche. However, the fleet soon encountered difficulties trying evade the Royal Navy blockade and it dispersed during foul weather. Three ships were wrecked in storms and a brief fight ensued when elements of the fleet encountered the frigate HMS *Indefatigable* under the command of Captain Pellew. The fleet had been split into three formations but a sizable number managed to rendezvous off the south-west coast of Ireland and enter Bantry Bay on 22 December 1796.

Tone accompanied the fleet in an advisory capacity and was greatly frustrated when the French declined to go ashore as the ocean was calm enough for landings and opposition would be minimal with the element of surprise. This was largely because Hoche's frigate became separated from the fleet and the army felt obliged to delay until he rejoined them. Over the next few days, gales blew up making it almost impossible to land and Admiral Bouvet (acting commander) cancelled the invasion on Christmas Day. The French sailed back to France in squadrons with the last ships leaving on 3 January 1797. Although the *Droits de l'Homme* was intercepted by HMS *Indefatigable*, the British failure to prevent the French fleet's departure was considered a poor performance by the Royal Navy.

Tone wrote that the English had not experienced such a narrow escape since the defeat of the Spanish Armada and the invasion was foiled by a combination of bad luck, lack of initiative on the part of subordinate officers and stormy weather. The main result of this failed attempt was to forewarn the British of French intentions so they increased the size of garrisons in Ireland and began fortifying its coastline.

The Invasion of Wales

The mission against northern England was beset by poor discipline in the French army regiments involved and naval mutinies over arrears of pay but it was actually thwarted by atrocious weather in the North Sea with the squadron turning back well before it reached its destination. Bad weather also delayed the small squadron headed for Wales and the expedition only arrived after the Bantry Bay invasion had been abandoned. They set out from Brest on 16 February 1797 under Commodore Jean-Joseph Castagnier with the frigates *La Résistance* and *Vengeance* accompanied by a corvette and a lugger. Castagnier was ordered to land his invasion force in Pembrokeshire on the south-west coast of Wales before joining the main fleet off Southern Ireland.

The small army carried by the squadron was led by 44-year-old Colonel William Tate who was an Irish-American veteran of the American War of Independence. His force comprised about 1,400 men with the bulk of regular soldiers (600 men) drawn from La Légion Noire, who were so called because they were issued with former red British Army jackets dyed dark brown or black. Tate's other troops were a mixture of republican volunteers, former convicts, pardoned deserters and former Royalists and deemed highly unreliable but this force was well armed and commanded by French and Irish officers.

On 22 February, the French squadron arrived off the Welsh coast having successfully evaded Royal Navy patrols by adopting the ruse of sailing under Russian colours. Castagnier began landing troops under cover of night and by 2:00am seventeen boatloads of soldiers had been rowed ashore along with 2,000 muskets, 50 tons of cartridges and 47 barrels of gunpowder with only one boat overturning in the surf during this swift and efficient operation.

The Fishguard and Newport Volunteers were a Yeomanry regiment raised in 1794 for the war effort under local landowner Colonel William Knox. His son, Lieutenant Colonel Thomas Knox, received warning of the invasion when a messenger arrived at a social gathering he attended at Tregwynt Mansion on the evening of the 22 February. Initially disbelieving the report, Knox's reaction was slow but he returned to Fishguard Fort and ordered the regiment's Newport contingent to join him. News of the invasion spread swiftly and Captain John Campbell (Lord Cawdor), commanding the Castlemartin Troop of the Pembrokeshire Yeomanry, rapidly assembled troops when he heard, including men from the Cardiganshire militia. Captain Longford and other officers also brought sailors ashore at Milford Haven along with nine cannon to swell the forces massing to repel the invasion.

Upon landing, Colonel Tate marched his men inland to secure farm buildings to shelter them from the elements as the February weather was extremely cold.

Almost immediately he had trouble with discipline breaking down among his irregulars and some of those sent to find supplies failed to return. One group broke into Llanwnda Church, burning its pews to keep warm and using bible pages as kindling. Lieutenant St Leger occupied Trehowel Farm, roughly a mile from the landing site, where Tate established his headquarters. Here he held a council of war and revealed his orders were to march on the English port of Bristol.

On the morning of 23 February, Knox arrived with just under 200 soldiers and was alarmed to see the French had taken up strong defensive positions on the heights between the craggy outcrops of Garnwnda and Carngelli. He believed the enemy outnumbered his force by at least six to one and considered withdrawal as the French could observe his manoeuvres from the heights. Knox reconnoitred their positions but fell back towards Fishguard where he ordered the small unit of Royal Artillery at Fort Fishguard to spike their guns and retreat, which they refused to do. Shortly afterwards he encountered Lord Cawdor bringing up reinforcements, including at least six cannon, at about 1:30pm. After a short argument about seniority, Lord Cawdor assumed command.

However, Colonel Tate's apparently strong position was deceptive as he was suffering increasing problems with his irregular troops. There had already been violent clashes with civilians and militia and at least six deaths but the discovery that local people possessed large amounts of Portuguese wine (seized from a recent shipwreck) resulted in many irregulars dispersing to search for it. Others mutinied and refused to obey orders and there were many desertions, with only Tate's hard core of 600 regulars staying true to their colours.

Lord Cawdor decided to attack late that afternoon and advanced up the narrow Trefwrgi Lane towards the French position. However, progress was slow dragging artillery and, with the light fading fast, the attempt was abandoned. This was fortunate for the British as Lieutenant St Leger had prepared an ambush along this route with his grenadiers that could have inflicted serious losses. British headquarters were established at the Royal Oak public house in Fishguard Square and two French officers arrived here that evening under flag of truce. They requested terms from Lord Cawdor but he insisted that they must surrender unconditionally, trying to bluff them into thinking that his forces were far stronger than they actually were. Following these negotiations, he gave them till 10:00am the following morning to march down and surrender on Goodwick Sands or he would attack.

Back in the French camp, Tate's French and Irish officers counselled immediate surrender with half their force absconded, drunk, mutinous or unreliable. They faced an enemy that was rapidly increasing in strength and the locals, far from joining them as hoped, were arming themselves to support the British. Their ships had left that morning and there was nowhere to retreat to.

British forces assembled in battle order on 24 February on Goodwick Sands and prepared to assault the heights. Many locals had gathered on the cliffs to watch the battle and it is thought the traditional Welsh garb of some women (tall black hats and red shawls) deceived the French into thinking that regular British Army regiments had arrived when viewed from a distance. Tate negotiated and the French tried to prolong talks but agreed to surrender unconditionally by 2:00pm. By 4:00pm they had piled arms and marched down from the heights in a column towards captivity with 1,360 men eventually imprisoned in Haverfordwest. Casualties were slight during the invasion with just over thirty people wounded or killed and after a brief period as prisoners of war Tate and most of his forces were repatriated in 1798. What is often called 'the last invasion of mainland Britain' was over.

Half of Castagnier's squadron made it back to France but the frigates HMS *San Fiorenzo* and HMS *Nymphe* intercepted half his squadron in the Irish Sea as it headed towards Southern Ireland. The frigate *La Résistance* and the corvette *La Constance* were damaged and slowed by storms during their return journey but resisted for over half an hour in a brief fight, suffering a combined eighteen killed and fifteen wounded with both ships taken as prizes.

Visiting Fishguard

Fishguard is in an isolated part of Pembrokeshire and is a long distance from most major British cities. It is just under 270 miles/434.5km from London and driving from the capital via the M4–A48–A40 takes around five and a half hours. Alternatively, Fishguard can be reached by train from Paddington Station with changes at Newport and Haverfordwest, with the last leg of the journey along the A40 requiring bus or taxi services. Travelling from the Welsh capital of Cardiff, which has its own airport, is another option via the M4 for drivers (two hours and fifteen minutes). Travellers taking the train from Cardiff can reach Haverfordwest before having to switch to bus or taxi for the remainder of their journey. Drivers should keep in mind that the immediate area is hilly and mountainous (the town lies at the foot of the Preseli Mountains) with steep and winding roads making the last stage of the drive into Fishguard challenging, especially in inclement weather.

The name Fishguard is derived from the Norse word 'fiskigarðr' (fishtrap) as the bay was an excellent place to catch shellfish in traps placed on the mud flats and retrieved at low tide. There are three main locations to visit in the town itself, the first being the Royal Oak public house in the Market Square on the corner of the High Street (A487) and West Street. It was here that Cawdor and his staff negotiated with French officers and presented an ultimatum. This charming pub is one storey high, stone faced and slate roofed. Inscribed into the door frame above the entrance are the words 'Last Invasion of Britain Peace Treaty was signed here in 1797' in gold lettering. Inside are various items including a musket and powder flask above the bar, prints, carved wooden panels, images of the Invasion Tapestry (see below) and the table negotiators sat around and signed a preliminary agreement on. The pub serves good food and is an excellent place to rest and recuperate after a long journey here.

The Town Hall is located across the road from the Royal Oak and has a cannon placed outside. The barrel is from a large-calibre gun and lacks any obvious identifying markings but it is almost certainly British and probably unrelated to the invasion. Its wooden carriage is a modern reconstruction intended only as a representation of a naval gun carriage as it is far too small with inoperable wheels. In 1997 a tapestry in the style of the famous Bayeux Tapestry was sewn by seventy-eight local volunteers. At 100ft/30.48m long it is longer than its Norman inspiration and depicts events and personalities involved in the French invasion to great effect. It is colourful and benefits from the elaborate style of French and British uniforms of the late eighteenth century. Landings, French looting and Welsh volunteers are all represented along with a colourful group of officers in blue and red uniforms discussing surrender terms. This remarkable representation is definitely worth seeing and is kept in Fishguard Library within the Town Hall. For details of opening times see – www.fishguardgoodwick-tc.gov.wales

The third location in the town is Saint Mary's Church, which is located nearby on the High Street. The churchyard contains a headstone dedicated to Welsh heroine Jemima Nicholas who was one of the locals who volunteered to help resist the invasion and is said to have participated in the capture of French soldiers caught looting nearby (see Chapter 6).

For sites outside Fishguard, visitors may find it convenient to visit Fishguard Fort before entering the town as the A487 following the coast runs past it before it reaching Fishguard itself. The fort has its own car park and a postcode for satnav location, which is SA65 9NB. It can be easy to miss with the turning near a sharp bend just before Fishguard and drivers may find they have to turn around in town and return. The road to the fort is steep and a difficult walk down to if visitors choose to walk here from town and it is always worthwhile to take hats, coats and sturdy boots for walking in this area as the Welsh coast is often wet and windy. A footpath leads to the fort from the west end of the car park and is roughly 328ft/100m away. Halfway along this is a small area of level ground where visitors can see down into the fort, which is useful for photographers, and it stands on a rocky promontory jutting out over the ocean.

The remains of a gate stand at the bottom of this slope and the first building (on the left) is the old powder magazine, which is almost complete. From here, visitors can walk out on to the gun platforms where four cannon are placed. Their gun barrels are eighteenth or nineteenth century but the naval carriages are modern reconstructions. Some walls remain but most have crumbled due to age and the elements and they would have been higher in 1797. The gunners' officer considered this position so strong that he refused an order to disable his cannon and retreat and it is easy to see why the fort was sited here as it dominates the approaches to the harbour (the old fishing harbour is obscured by the headland) and also possesses good views northward out to sea. The fact that this fort was manned is probably why the French decided to land further along the coast rather than make an attempt to seize the harbour and town.

To reach Goodwick, drive back through Fishguard and drive north-west along the A40 where the beach where the British formed up is easily found. Here visitors can walk the stretch of beach where the final confrontation between the invaders and British forces took place. Walking along this beach is pleasant but most of the area where the French took up positions is built over and it is difficult to be precise about their exact location.

The French invasion monument on the Carrag Wastad headland.

Driving further along the A40, Llanwnda (SA64 0HX) is just under 4 miles/6.4km from Fishguard and is a small hamlet rather than a village but its church still exists. Accounts vary but the French soldiers who took shelter here either burned church property for warmth but did little real damage or came close to burning down the entire church in an act of wanton pillage, depending on which sources historians choose to believe. Saint Gwyndaf's is a small, five-celled church that dates back to the medieval period, which was partially restored in the 1880s and has good views out over the ocean.

The small stone memorial placed to commemorate the invasion on the Carrag Wastad headland can be seen in the distance from the churchyard. Its location marks the eastern flank of the French landing zone and it can be reached by walking along a footpath from the churchyard and is three-quarters of a mile/1.2km away. It presents a challenging walk at most times of year and some may think the distance is further than claimed with the route well marked with signposts or arrows but deeply rutted and muddy in places. Before reaching the monument, walkers are faced with a final gate with a sheer drop behind it and should proceed carefully as the route down the hillside is treacherous, especially in wet or windy conditions. At the bottom of the slope is a large stream running through a ravine spanned by a wooden plank bridge with no railings. After crossing this, the land rises and walkers will have to clamber up a gorse-covered slope before emerging onto the rocky headland.

The point and the views it presents are beautiful and worth the walk to reach it but beware of high winds on this headland. Observers can see along the entire area where the four French ships brought men, munitions and supplies ashore with the inlet where the stream from the ravine emerges into the sea on the right (east). Landings also took place to the left (west) all the way to Strumble Head, which was the western end of the landing zone. Visitors will observe that this rocky coastline has steep cliffs along most of its length and was a strange place to land an army. Bringing troops, munitions and especially artillery ashore would have been hazardous and it is a tribute to French seamanship that they managed it. Even so, the boat that turned over in the surf is said to have contained some or all of their artillery, which would have reduced their chances of success considerably. Most accounts of the invasion fail to mention any cannon that the French brought ashore.

One advantage to the site from the French point of view was its isolation and Fishguard cannot be seen from here, which gave them hopes of remaining undetected for a while. However, local observers swiftly alerted the authorities about the landing and the lack of communicating roads in the vicinity meant they could not move inland as quickly as hoped if they were to march on Bristol. The exposed nature of this coastline also reveals why the French squadron left the area as soon as their troops landed as the Royal Navy would have made them pay a heavy price had they come upon them during landing operations.

The memorial stone was set up here in 1897 to mark the centenary of the French invasion and is a simple stone marker set upon a circular group of small stones that anchor it in place upon this windswept headland. It is partly covered in lichen but its Welsh language/English inscription can still be made out and reads 'MEMORIAL STONE OF THE LANDING OF THE FRENCH FEBRUARY 22 1797.' It gives one pause to stand here and consider the brave optimism of men who landed at this isolated spot hoping to bring revolution to this land along with the determined stoicism of those who prevented them.

Tregwynt Mansion, where news of the French invasion spoilt Lieutenant Colonel Knox's entertainment on the evening of 22 February, still stands and is located nearby along with Trehowel Farm, where Colonel Tate established his headquarters. Unfortunately, both are private residences and not open to the public.

The Great Rebellion – *Map 7*

The United Irishmen were undismayed by the dismal failure at Bantry Bay and continued with their plans for an uprising in the belief that military support might still come from France. The Irish exiles redoubled their efforts to win support in Paris and Wolfe Tone arranged a meeting with General Bonaparte. Unfortunately, they failed to get along, with Tone recalling that the rising star of the French military looked and acted like a mathematician rather than a general while Bonaparte scorned the patriot's lack of military experience. He also considered tales of widespread discontent in Ireland exaggerated and was sceptical about recruiting forces other than ill-trained militia in the Irish countryside. While Bonaparte considered a successful invasion of England vital for the Republic to survive, he believed this proposed venture poorly planned and declined to get involved, especially as his Egyptian Expedition was about to set out.

Nevertheless, Carnot and other politicians were optimistic about French intervention in Ireland and General Cherin was appointed as Commander-in-Chief of the French 'Army of Ireland' assembled near Brest. Hearing news of a major uprising, a small force under General Joseph Humbert was dispatched to Ireland as a vanguard in four ships that sailed from Rochefort on 6 August carrying 1,150 men and 3,000 weapons for the Irish rebels. However, Cherin's main army soon encountered problems including major pay disputes with soldiers and sailors. As gales set in along the French coast, Cherin realized his departure would be delayed and his chances of evading the Royal Navy blockade were slim. He resigned in despair at this chaotic situation as Humbert sailed onwards blissfully unaware that he was now on his own.

Unfortunately for the French, the Great Rebellion of 1798 had already taken place and was crushed before Humbert embarked. Protestants in the north rebelled that March but were swiftly defeated and while small-scale revolts took place in many parts of Ireland, the insurgency in County Wexford was the only uprising to gain any real success. Rebels received the active support of the Catholic clergy but were disorganized and poorly armed, with most having pikes or improvised weapons rather than muskets. Atrocities occurred in the countryside against landowners or recent settlers and local militias reacted savagely with massacres committed by both sides.

Most rebel bands were swiftly isolated and defeated and the largest group brought to bay at the Battle of Vinegar Hill, where it was decisively beaten. An estimated 30,000 people were killed and over £1 million-worth of property destroyed during the Great Rebellion, with largely Protestant militias exacting a terrible revenge in some areas with reprisals changing Irish nationalism into a bitter sectarian conflict that continued into the twentieth century and beyond. Lord Cornwallis (Viceroy of Ireland) was appalled by these outrages and issued amnesties to those who agreed to lay down their arms but many militiamen had lost family or friends and even hanged rebels who were granted amnesty. General Moore wrote that 'I cannot but think that it was their harshness and ill treatment that in a great measure drove the peasants to revolt,' and despaired that the landowning gentry had 'learned nothing by the lesson'.

Case Study: Vinegar Hill – *Map 7*

The Battle of Vinegar Hill on 21 June 1798 was the largest engagement fought during the uprising and took place near Enniscorthy in County Wexford on the heights and within the town's streets. Most of the rebellions in Ireland had been put down by June so the British Army and militias were able to concentrate around 20,000 troops to pacify Wexford and fielded 15,000 men against 20,000 rebels at Vinegar Hill. With the countryside in a state of uproar, over a thousand women and children had taken refuge in the rebel camp and at least half the insurgents were armed with pikes rather than muskets. They concentrated their captured guns on the hill around a windmill near its summit and built barricades for their infantry using stone from farm walls and felled trees. The rebels knew

The Irish rebel camp on Vinegar Hill.

their best chance of victory against well-trained soldiers lay in fighting a defensive action.

General Gerard Lake planned a major assault on the hill dividing his army into three main columns to do so but also sent a quarter of his force to cut off the enemy's escape route to the west, hoping to end the rebellion with this action. The fighting began with a bombardment of rebel positions and British artillery used the new 'shrapnel' shells that caused more wounds than deaths as they landed behind the barricades, showering their defenders with musket balls and fragments of casing. Rebel gunners were unable to match the speed of professional artillerymen and British cannon soon dominated the battlefield, allowing their infantry to advance under cover of their fire up the hillside. Faced with massed musket fire, the rebels charged down the slopes twice but suffered heavy losses, failed to break the enemy lines and were forced back into a steadily-shrinking defensive area as the British advanced.

Meanwhile, General Johnson's column entered Enniscorthy and his light infantry skirmished with rebels in the streets or assailed fortified houses, encountering stiff resistance. They were driven back at first but a second assault backed by cavalry inflicted losses on the rebels and the

The Battle of Vinegar Hill.

town fell, although the insurgents continued to hold the bridge over the Slaney River. As British troops crested the hill and overran the barricades, the hill's defenders broke and ran. General Needham's troops had failed to completely surround Vinegar Hill as planned and the area that most rebels fled through became known as 'Needham's Gap'. Cavalry were brought up and pursued the insurgents, cutting down many in the rout.

British regulars and militia suffered at least a hundred casualties but sources disagree over the number of rebels killed or wounded at Vinegar Hill, with estimates varying between 400 and 1,200 men. Thirteen cannon were recaptured along with rebel supplies and there were accusations that many women in the insurgent's camp were beaten and raped. The fact that regular troops easily overcame ill-trained rebels was unsurprising so the British Army never celebrated Vinegar Hill as a victory. Many insurgents escaped over Slaney Bridge and fought a bitter guerrilla war in Wexford for years afterwards but this was the last significant action of the uprising.

Considering the brutal events that took place there, Vinegar Hill is a surprisingly attractive location with spectacular views of the Irish countryside from its summit. The original bridge over the Slaney (built in 1795) was demolished and rebuilt in 1866 but provides a good impression of what the original looked like and the tidal River Slaney would have presented a fearsome obstacle to the rebel retreat if this crossing point had fallen into British hands. There is a battlefield centre that holds regular historic re-enactments along with exhibitions, lectures and guided tours. Archaeological digs have recently been made on Vinegar Hill that may eventually tell historians more about how events transpired from the location of musket and cannon shot recovered.

Driving from Dublin to Enniscorthy takes roughly 2.5 hours via the M50–M11 and the Battlefield Centre is located at Vinegar Hill, Vinegar Hill Lane, Templeshannon, Enniscorthy, County Wexford, Ireland. See – www.vinegarhill.ie

Killala Bay – *Map 7*

On 23 August 1798, Dr Stock, who was the Protestant Bishop of Killala, heard that warships flying British colours had anchored in Kilcummin Harbour, having arrived late the previous day. He sent his sons to invite their officers to dine with him but they were taken prisoner and soldiers began to land. As weapons were brought ashore, the warships raised the French tricolour along with a new standard displaying a gold Irish harp on a green field with the legend '*Erin Go Bragh*' (Ireland Forever).

Killala's militia were swiftly overcome and the Bishop was forced to act as a translator when Humbert took over his house as French headquarters. He considered Humbert an ill-mannered adventurer and 'no gentleman' while the general was equally unimpressed by the clergyman. When locals refused to lend their fishing boats to unload munitions, he turned on Stock and 'poured forth a torrent of vulgar abuse, roared, stamped his foot, laid his hand frequently on a scimitar, levelled a pistol at the bishop's eldest son, and finally told the cleric he would punish his disobedience by sending him to France'. After witnessing this abuse of a clergyman, shocked local fishermen swiftly provided the French with the boats they demanded.

Humbert rapidly formed an Irish Legion but his officers were appalled by the poor quality of recruits they attracted, who shot at wildlife and nearly hit the general when a ball shattered a second-storey window he stood at while watching their training. Few were proficient with firelocks and one officer recalled that they had no idea of how to clear a blockage and 'When stuck in the passage (as they often did), the inverted barrel was set to work against the ground, till it was bent and useless.' After several unfortunate incidents, gunpowder was temporarily withheld. The French were horrified by the religious divide in Ireland and bemused by their volunteers' political naiveté, one officer remarking 'Take up arms for France and the Blessed Virgin? God help these simpletons. If they knew how little we care for the Pope or his religion, they would not be so hot in expecting help from us.' They desperately needed educated and experienced men to officer the Irish Legion but few volunteered.

General Cornwallis had seen how fast dissent could spread during the American War of Independence and decided to amass a vastly superior force to crush this incursion before Humbert attracted significant support. He began to raise forces in Dublin and when he marched against the French became the first Irish Viceroy to take to the field in a hundred years.

The Races of Castlebar

As the French squadron sailed for France, Humbert's forces skirmished with local militias and captured Ballina before turning inland and marching on the town of Castlebar. General John Hutchinson commanded a militia-based force of 3,500 men here and took up defensive positions on Sion Hill that lies between two loughs (small lakes) north of the town. He placed the 6th Foot, his only regular regiment, in the centre along with guns manned by the Royal Irish Artillery. The hillside presents a gentle slope on its north side but General Lake thoroughly approved of Hutchinson's positioning when he arrived and assumed command. Following a French reconnaissance, Humbert planned a frontal assault on the hill believing that he could rely on his 900 regulars who were veterans of German or Italian campaigns but could only bring one cannon up in time to support the attack

The French attacked at least three times in column formation but were driven back by artillery fire while attempting to assault the British centre and accounts vary over whether the Irish Legion formed their own column and participated. Colonel Sarrazin (Humbert's second-in-command) then led a determined outflanking attack around Rathbawn Lough where his grenadiers encountered the Fraser Fencibles and Galway Yeomanry (militia) and were stopped by musket fire. This coincided with a renewed attack on the centre where the Kilkenny and Longford militias opened fire prematurely, which encouraged the French to mount a bayonet charge. In the face of this fierce assault, the militias broke and ran and, although the 6th Foot stood their ground for a while, the British were soon in headlong retreat. This battle is one of the few instances where a French column formation overcame a line of British infantry whose greater firepower usually ensured victory in continental battles.

Humbert only had half a squadron of the 3rd Chasseurs and some hussars but he sent this small cavalry force in pursuit of the enemy who fled over

CASTLEBAR.

Castlebar witnessed a rare example of a French column overcoming a British line.

the single bridge leading into the town. Lake did his best to slow the British retreat and a running fight ensued in Castlebar's streets with a sizable force of militiamen making a stand in Christ Church as the churchyard possessed a high wall. French forces and Irish rebels pressed the retreat and Castlebar soon fell with the British failing to check their flight till they reached Tuam (30 miles/48km away). Some even reached Athlone, covering 63 miles/101km in 27 hours, leading locals to name the battle 'The Races of Castlebar'. Officially the British lost 53 dead, 36 wounded and 278 missing with the French suffering around 50 casualties.

After Castlebar, Humbert marched north-east towards Belfast and skirmished with a force under General Charles Vereker at Collooney, who slowly withdrew before the French advance. He tried to evade two approaching armies under Cornwallis and Lake but was outmanoeuvred and trapped at Ballinamuck where he surrendered on 8 September after offering token resistance. He later wrote 'After having obtained the greatest successes and made the arms of the French Republic triumph during my stay in Ireland, I have at length been obliged to surrender to a superior force of 30,000 men.' French prisoners were marched to Dublin and treated decently but the Irish Legion was less fortunate and treated as rebels. As their French allies surrendered, Captain Pakenham rode up to their line and shouted 'Run away, boys, otherwise you'll be cut down!' They were not permitted to surrender and many were sabred by militia cavalrymen who pursued them through the countryside. Many were hanged when captured and but for the restraining presence of the regular British Army and French officers, reprisals could have been worse.

The following week saw a French force accompanied by James Napper Tandy of the United Irishmen sail into Rutland Harbour in Northern Ireland. The ships of this expedition only carried 300 soldiers but their holds contained thousands of muskets and artillery pieces. Tandy came ashore on 18 September but swiftly returned to France after learning of Humbert's defeat.

A far larger French squadron under Commodore Bompart arrived off the north-west coast of Ireland on 11 October, intending to enter Lough Swilly. Bompart commanded the *Hoche*, a 74-gun ship of the line, and his squadron comprised eight frigates and some sloops that conveyed 3,000 troops and artillery. Had this force landed, it would have caused the British considerable difficulty but Commodore Warren intercepted it near Tory Island off County Donegal. Warren had three ships of the line, three frigates and two sloops and the French attempted to flee. In the running battle that followed, the *Hoche* resisted bravely for two hours but eventually struck her colours in the face of overwhelming firepower. Three French frigates were taken that day and, when the French scattered and headed for home, three more vessels were overtaken and captured.

The French suffered around 700 casualties at the Battle of Tory Island with the Royal Navy sustaining about 150 killed or wounded. Wolfe Tone accompanied this expedition and took part in the fighting but was captured along with at least 3,000 Frenchmen. He had been commissioned as a French officer and wore a general's uniform in combat but Tone was put on trial for treason in Dublin and sentenced to death. He won great respect by pleading guilty on the grounds of patriotism and requesting 'As ... I occupy a high grade in the French army, I would request that the court, if they can, grant me the favour that I may die the death of a soldier'. His appeal to be executed by firing squad was denied so Tone committed suicide in his cell and cheated the hangman.

The Battle of Tory Island marked the end of French attempts to invade the British Isles and dashed the hopes of the United Irishmen to secure foreign aid. These invasion attempts convinced the British of the need to fortify their coasts and they continued to spend vast sums on this strategy but the saddest result was that brutal suppression of the rebellion lingered in Irish memory and contributed to political unrest there for another 200 years.

Visiting Castlebar

There are numerous battlefields related to the Great Rebellion and French invasions in Ireland but Castlebar offers a particularly large concentration of relevant sites for events that occurred during 'The Year of the French' as it is referred to in the town. County Mayo is in Southern Ireland on its north-west coast so Castlebar is a long journey from most major cities. It is a three hour drive from Dublin via the M50–M4 and almost four hours from Belfast using the M1–N5. The best way to get there is to fly from London or either of these Irish cities to Knock Airport, which is a 35-minute drive from Castlebar with taxis available at this airport. For details see – www.irelandwestairport.com

Castlebar is the capital of County Mayo and rose to prominence when Norman invaders of the De Barrie family built a stronghold here from 1235–40 and has often been used as a garrison town since that time. Locals are proud of their connections with the invasion but some interesting items have disappeared since the author's first visit in 2005 such as a house mural of General Humbert on horseback leading his troops into Castlebar with the French line of march snaking back into the hills behind him rather effectively. Furthermore, the famous Humbert Inn on Main Street closed in 2006, which bore a sign reading 'On Aug. 27th 1798, General Humbert routed the British Garrison from this town and deemed this building Headquarters of his expeditionary forces. From within its walls he declared that John Moore of Moorehall be proclaimed President of Connaught. To celebrate the occasion a banquet was held here, followed by a victory ball in The Linen Hall… .'. This building still exists but has been divided into retail units although a new sign is likely to be placed upon it.

The 1798 memorial is a tall monolith commemorating the Great Rebellion and French Invasion near The Mall, which is a grassed area in the centre of town. It bears the date 1798 emblazoned in bronze near its summit along with images of an Irish Harp and the Fleur-de-Lys, symbolising its connection with the French. It was designed by local art teacher Frank Hourigan and a bronze frieze on one side shows St Brigit of Kildare and an Irish inscription above '*A Muire na nGael guid orainn*' ('Mary of the Gael pray for us' – St Brigit is known by both names). On the other side is a depiction of a kneeling Irish pikeman receiving a blessing from a priest below the words '*i gCuimhne 1798*' ('In memory of 1798'). It is a dark and imposing monument and was erected on Sunday 30 August 1953 by President Sean T. O'Ceallaigh and the Archbishop of Tuam, Dr J. Walsh.

On The Mall nearby is a stone tombstone surrounded by a short iron railing. This is the grave of John Moore (1767–99) who was proclaimed First President of Connaught by Franco-Irish forces but later captured and imprisoned by the British. He died in captivity at Waterford Gaol awaiting deportation in 1799 but his remains were reinterred here in 1961 in a ceremony attended by President Eamon de Valera, where he received the full honours of church and state. Another ceremony was held in 2015 when the US Ambassador planted a commemorative tree near these memorials and an information panel and a flagpole now stand nearby.

Christ Church stands on the edge of The Mall across the road from the 1798 Monument. It is one of the few remaining Protestant churches in Castlebar being founded in 1739 and restored between 1800 and 1828 due to damage sustained during the battle. The church is encircled by a tall stone wall and was defended by elements of Lake's army as they tried to cover their withdrawal. The churchyard contains a gravestone dedicated to soldiers killed in the battle and bears the inscription 'erected to the memory of … the FRASER HIGHLANDERS who were killed in action at CASTLEBAR with the FRENCH invaders on the 27th August 1798'. Another memorial remembers Major George O'Malley from Ballinvilla who served in the British Army in North America and Egypt among other campaigns. He was wounded twice at Waterloo but survived the wars to die in 1847. He is buried in his family plot at Murrisk Abbey, 16.7 miles/27km west of Castlebar. The gate in the church wall is sometimes locked so it is wise to contact www.tuam.anglican.org/aughaval-westport/castlebar-christ-church/ in advance if visitors wish to gain entry.

There are many modern plastic plaques on walls and buildings around the town including one near the centre recording the 1998 bicentenary bearing the French Revolutionary slogan *Liberté–Égalité–Fraternité* along with pictures of Irish and French flags unfurled by Humbert when he came ashore. It reads 'To celebrate the spirit of solidarity with the Irish struggle for liberty by General Humbert and his French Army on these streets', along with Irish script recording its unveiling by Bertie Ahern (Deputy Leader of Fianna Fáil) on 3 July 1998. A modern sculpture recalling the Great Rebellion also stands in Market Square, displaying a forest of Irish pikes with bronze tips and curved secondary blades designed for hooking horsemen out of the saddle. They are inclined at an angle on a concrete base with a flock of birds flying around the pike heads, which may be doves of peace.

The battlefield is located across the Castlebar River 2 miles/3.3km north of the town on Pontoon Road (R310). Most fighting took place between the two small lakes (Rathbawn and Tuckers Loughs) at the foot of Sion Hill, which make this area easier to locate as there are no signs or monuments. A modern road dissects the battlefield and visitors will arrive at the British position on

Sion Hill first when walking or driving from the town. This battlefield is largely unspoilt with most of the land uncultivated due to marshland around the lakes. It is easy to see that the gentle northern slope of Sion Hill would not have slowed a determined infantry assault for long or deterred pursuing cavalry. The skeletal remains of at least thirty men were discovered when Pontoon Road was widened who were probably French soldiers killed during the battle. The location of this mass grave is unmarked but there is a monument to the French killed at Castlebar on the outskirts of town (see Chapter 6).

Chapter 8

Museums and Heritage Centres

The British are privileged to possess an incredible range of museums and heritage centres, covering a wide range of subject matter and most are easily accessible to the public. Some of these institutions have long histories, amassing their collections over hundreds of years, with the Ashmolean Museum in Oxford being one of the oldest surviving museums in the world having been founded in 1683. Their collections contain exhibits from across the globe obtained by a variety of means including purchase, persuasion and occasionally military compulsion, with the British Museum in London boasting items from antiquity that cannot be seen anywhere else in the world.

This chapter contains details on military museums from around the country devoted to the British Army or Royal Navy along with some heritage centres that have relevant items on display. Their circumstances vary enormously and some national museums do not charge an entry fee while others are forced to do so or request charitable donations. Apsley House (see Chapter 2) and other institutions have already been described and this list is not definitive as there are too many regimental museums with relevant collections to be described in a single chapter but it provides Napoleonic highlights of various collections and details of research facilities for some of the most remarkable museums in Britain.

England – *Map 8*

Portsmouth Historic Dockyard

National Museum of the Royal Navy, Visitor Centre, Victory Gate, HM Naval Base, Portsmouth, PO1 3LJ.
Website: www.historicdockyard.co.uk/

Overview: This large dockside area offers an impressive range of maritime centres, including authentic ships moored on the dockside or within dry dock that can be boarded and viewed. Attractions include the National Museum of the Royal Navy, Mary Rose Museum (containing the wreck of Henry VIII's flagship), Submarine Museum, HMS *Victory* and the Victory Gallery, HMS *Warrior* 1860, HMS *M.33*, Action Stations and Explosion! The Museum of Naval Firepower. Tickets can be bought for museums as single attractions, for several or all the museums on site (see website above). Harbour tours are available and there is much see here relating to different periods of nautical history.

Napoleonic Highlights: The best attraction by far is Nelson's flagship HMS *Victory* (see Chapter 1) and it is a crucial asset of the National Museum of the Royal Navy (Portsmouth) located nearby. This is the most relevant museum for the 1793–1815 period here and contains galleries on HMS *Victory*, Nelson, Sailing Navy and HMS Hear My Story galleries. The museum possesses a vast array of objects including weaponry, busts, prints, charts, paintings, models, uniforms, telescopes, quadrants, sextants, letters, diaries, ships' logs and other exhibits donated by the Royal Navy with an enormous panorama of the Battle of Trafalgar being particularly impressive.

There are three exhibits of particular note, the first being a large section of HMS *Victory*'s original wooden foremast, which is scarred by shot marks along with a hole punched straight through it by a direct hit from a cannon ball. The other is this flagship's damaged foretopsail, which is thought to be the largest surviving relic of the battle other than the ship itself. It measures 80ft/24.3m at its foot, 54ft/16.4m at its head and 54ft/16.4m deep and is riddled with shot holes from cannon and muskets. Due to conservation issues, the sail is displayed for limited periods of time but seeing it makes a viewer pause in contemplation of the firepower levelled against HMS *Victory* and what her crew must have suffered. The third exhibit is a gold betrothal ring gifted to Emma Hamilton by Lord Nelson during a private ceremony at his house in Merton shortly before he left England. This intimate relic implies that Nelson intended to seek a divorce and marry his mistress had he returned from Trafalgar.

The Historic Dockyard Chatham
Chatham Historic Dockyard Trust, 1st Floor
North, Fitted Rigging House, Anchor Wharf,
The Historic Dockyard, Chatham, Kent, ME4 4TZ.
Website: www.thedockyard.co.uk

Overview: Chatham Dockyard lies on the River Medway in Kent and dates back to the mid-1500s. By the eighteenth century it was the Royal Navy's most important shipbuilding and repair facility and the wars against France required a huge expansion of this dockyard to cope with demand. Chatham retained its importance throughout the Victorian period and beyond and now presents exhibitions devoted to the Age of Sail but it is a multi-period heritage site incorporating the Victorian Master Rope Makers (whose factory still operates) and ships such as HMS *Gannet* (Victorian sloop), HMS *Cavalier* (Second World War destroyer) and HMS *Ocelot* (Cold War period submarine).

Napoleonic Highlights: Many ships that saw action during the Napoleonic Wars were built here including HMS *Victory* that was constructed between 1759 and 1765. There are four main galleries devoted to this period including the 'Hearts of Oak' cinematic experience. They explore concepts such as ship design, building and preservation (particularly against dry rot) along with explorations of what life was like working on the docks. Highlights include archaeological displays of items recovered from the wreck of HMS *Invincible* (1758) and a large-scale model of HMS *Victory* used in the film *That Hamilton Woman* (1941). Many historic buildings still exist on this site that strove to produce ships capable of increased speed, efficiency and endurance including ironworking facilities at No. 1 Smithery (1808), the Ropery (1809) and the first steam-powered sawmill (1814).

Case Study: The National Maritime Museum

Park Row, Greenwich, London, SE10 9NF.
Website: www.rmg.co.uk/national-martime-museum
Overview: This is the largest maritime museum in the world and is located behind the former Greenwich Royal Hospital (see Chapter 2). It is divided into three major display areas, which are Ship Stories (Level 0), Ocean Stories (Level 1) and Epic Stories (Level 2). Exhibitions cover a variety of time periods with galleries devoted to Voyages of Exploration, Maritime Trade, Tudor and Stuart Seafarers, Piracy and separate galleries for various wars fought at sea among other subjects. Highlights include 'The Great Map' of the world, which is so large that visitors can walk upon it to study it, ships' figureheads and small boats.

Napoleonic Highlights: 'Nelson's Ship in a Bottle' is an external exhibit before the museum Parkside Cafe and was originally intended to be placed on the fourth plinth in Trafalgar Square. It measures 16.4ft x 9.1ft/5m x 2.8m and contains a 1:30 scale replica of HMS *Victory*. Yinka Shonibare, a British/Nigerian artist, made the model's thirty-seven sails from a multitude of patterned textiles, symbolizing the multinational nature of British maritime history during the Imperial and Commonwealth periods. The ship is accurately represented and the bottle rests upon a wooden base pierced by representations of portholes. It has the kind of handle with a finger or thumb hole for a drinker and is corked, wrapped with cordage around its neck and adorned with a red seal. This is a highly original work of art and a fine tribute to the famous warship.

There is a display on Level 0 examining Turner's famous painting 'The Battle of Trafalgar' commissioned by King George IV in 1822. Painted on a gigantic scale (8.5ft x 12ft/2.61m x 3.68m) it presents a fascinating analysis of how historically accurate the artist's portrayal was with a film show. Located nearby are a stern and figurehead from a warship mounted on the wall that rises into the atrium above. These were from the *Duguay Trouin*, a 74-gun *Téméraire*-class ship of the line that fought at Trafalgar but was captured by the Royal Navy at the Battle of Cape Ortegal two weeks later. She was renamed HMS *Implacable* and was the second oldest vessel in the Royal Navy after HMS *Victory* before she was scuttled in 1949 and the navy donated these exhibits.

The 'Nelson, Navy, Nation' gallery is located on Level 2 and displays unique items that should delight the most demanding enthusiast including an incredible number of sea chests, charts, swords, telescopes, flags,

Part of the stern of HMS Implacable *at Greenwich.*

cutlasses, uniforms, muskets, a volley gun, ships' figureheads, paintings, busts, surgeon's implements and many other exhibits. Two items of special note are a French cannon ball recovered from HMS *Victory* after Trafalgar and the masthead/lightning conductor of *l'Orient* brought back from the Battle of the Nile and kept by Nelson as a souvenir. There are other items once owned by Nelson, including a bespoke combination knife-fork he had made to help him eat one-handed and a face mask made during his lifetime, rather than the more common death mask. The most interesting exhibits are items of clothing he wore at Trafalgar such as his blood stained breeches and stockings. Blood on the stockings largely came from John Scott who was killed standing next to him on the quarterdeck but bloodstains on the breeches are Nelson's own and this item displays cut marks made by Surgeon Beatty to remove them prior to medical treatment.

Pride of place is given to the uniform coat that Nelson wore at Trafalgar, which is a flag officer's undress coat. It is displayed in a case before a large Union flag from HMS *Minotaur* and, considering it is over 200 years old, the coat is in a remarkable state of preservation. The admiral's decorations are displayed in a cluster around his heart and some sources say that he was advised not to wear them in battle as they marked him out as a high-ranking officer and an inviting target. Part of the coat's left epaulette has been shot away and the hole in the left shoulder marks where the French sharpshooter's musket ball entered. This is an iconic exhibit and many observers will share the author's sense of awe when standing before it and wonder how such an important item has survived all this time.

A more elaborate full-dress uniform belonging to Nelson stands in a nearby case alongside uniforms worn by a captain and a midshipman. Comparing the sizes of these uniform coats says a lot about Nelson's physical stature, revealing that he was slight but broad-shouldered. Detailed descriptions are also provided here relating to the decorations on his Trafalgar uniform, which were the Order of the Bath (British), Order of the Crescent (Turkish), Order of St Joachim (German) and Order of St Ferdinand and of Merit presented by the King of Naples.

Research Facilities: The Museum's Research Library contains many original documents, rare books, charts and other resources with some items dating back as far as the 1400s. To use this facility, apply for a reader's ticket online (see website above) where a description of how to use the library is provided along with details about restrictions to ensure that ancient documents are well treated and preserved.

The National Army Museum
Royal Hospital Road, London, England, SW3 4HT
Website: www.nam.ac.uk/contact-nam

Overview: This museum is the best resource in the country for examining the role of the British Army from the British Civil Wars of the seventeenth century right up to the modern conflicts of today. It has galleries devoted to the Civil Wars, Napoleonic Wars, Crimean War, Boer War, Victorian and later period Colonial Wars, the First and Second World Wars, the Korean War, the Falklands War and more recent conflicts. The museum is particularly renowned for its archive that holds items that historians will find invaluable for research.

Napoleonic Highlights: Galleries contain a variety of Napoleonic uniforms, weaponry, musical instruments, paintings and prints. Exhibits of particular note include the skeleton of Marengo, who was one of Napoleon's favourite horses and captured at Waterloo. There are items of uniform belonging to soldiers who fought during the period including a sash worn by General Sir John Moore (killed in Spain in 1809) and a coat worn by Major Thomas Harris who fought at Waterloo. The right sleeve of this jacket has been cut by a surgeon in order to amputate Harris's arm after he was struck by case shot during the battle and recent studies on the garment revealed that he may also have been wounded in the side by a musket ball.

A huge model (21.4ft x 19.9ft/6.5m x 6m) of the battlefield of Waterloo made by Captain William Siborne is an interesting exhibit. In order to make his model as authentic as possible, he wrote to participants, using the accounts of over 700 officers in addition to spending eight months personally surveying the battlefield. It is made in 35 sections with over 75,000 model soldiers (each representing two men) showing approximate positions of formations at 19:45, which was a pivotal moment in the struggle. Wellington disapproved of Siborne's project and some experts dispute its accuracy as he failed to use French or Prussian sources along with other factors but it is a magnificent tribute to those who fought there and took eight years to construct from 1830 to 1838.

Research Facilities: This museum possesses some of the best primary source material available for this period along with references to documents held in other military archives. The website above provides lists of the NAM collection's contents and visitors can apply for a readers' card to use the Templer Study and Archive Centre for research.

Norwich Castle Museum and Art Gallery
Castle Hill, Norwich, Norfolk, NR31 3JU.
Website: www.museums.norfolk,gov.uk/norwich-castle

Overview: The Castle was built in the aftermath of the Norman Conquest in 1066 on the orders of King William I circa 1067 with its museum founded in 1894 and holding significant collections of artwork, archaeological finds and natural history specimens. There are special exhibitions on Queen Boudicca (Boadicea) and the Iceni tribe's revolt against Roman occupation, Anglo-Saxons, Vikings and Normans and the museum is renowned for collections of Norfolk paintings, glassware and porcelain.

Napoleonic Highlights: At the time of writing, the castle is undergoing internal restoration but the displays on the Norfolk Regiment (9th Foot) were only recently completed. These concentrate on modern conflicts but exhibits from the Napoleonic Wars include musket balls and shrapnel from the battlefield of Salamanca 1812 in Spain and displays of decorations like the Military General Service Medal and Army Gold Medal awarded for service during the Peninsular War. Portraits of some medal recipients are included such as Major Dallas and Lieutenant Colonel John Stewart (killed at Roliça in 1808 and commemorated in Canterbury Cathedral). One notable portrait is that of William Tapp of the North Norfolk Militia, who served at Norman Cross Prisoner of War Depot and died there in 1797.

Nelson is Norfolk's greatest son and this museum holds one of the Spanish officers' swords surrendered to him at Cape St Vincent along with original paintings including 'Horatio Nelson' by William Beechey RA (1801), 'The Return of the Hero (Lord Nelson)' by Fred Roe (1909) and 'View of Nelson's Monument, Great Yarmouth' by Joseph Stannard (circa 1815–30). These are currently in storage but the museum hopes to present an exhibition on Nelson and display them in the near future. However, the Art Gallery's porcelain section currently exhibits a commemorative range of jugs, goblets, pots, plates and cups (pottery, glass and chinaware) recording Nelson's achievements from 1797 to 1805. Most celebrate him as the Hero of the Nile or Victor of Trafalgar in a patriotic style that remained popular during the Victorian period and well into the twentieth century.

Scotland – *Maps 4 & 8*

Edinburgh Castle

Castlehill, Edinburgh, Scotland EH1 2NG.
Website: www.edinburghcastle.scot

Overview: As the foremost attraction in Edinburgh, the castle is placed on a high position of obvious strategic value and this site has been used for defence since the Iron Age. Its fortifications have been updated many times but the castle has also been used as a garrison, prison and royal residence. It has been besieged numerous times with the 'Lang Siege of 1571–73' being the most notable but its defences were so strong by 1745 that Bonnie Prince Charlie's army declined to attack it and marched away. Its collections contain relics such as the Royal Honours of Scotland (Crown Jewels), Stone of Scone, Mons Meg (Medieval cannon) and the Scottish National War Memorial. It is enormously popular so visitors are advised to use the website above to book advance tickets.

Napoleonic Highlights: The Esplanade before the castle is where Edinburgh's famous Military Tattoo is held along with other major events and war memorials and tombs are also located here with some relevant to the Napoleonic period (see Chapter 6). The National War Museum is located within the castle and explores the history of Scots at war from the seventeenth century to the present day and displays some Napoleonic exhibits but the regimental museums have major exhibits specific to this period. These are the Museum of the Royal Scots and the Royal Regiment of Scotland and the Regimental Museum of the Royal Scots Dragoon Guards. First raised in 1633, the Royal Scots are the oldest regiment of the British Army and have been awarded an incredible 146 battle honours for service in many conflicts. These include the Peninsular War and 1815 campaign and it displays a permanent Napoleonic section.

The second museum explores the history of Scotland's most famous cavalry regiment, which played a prominent role in the charge of the Union Brigade at Waterloo. This was the Royal North British Dragoons (Scots Greys) that were eventually amalgamated with the 3rd Carabiniers to form the Royal Scots Dragoon Guards. There are numerous Napoleonic exhibits in the collection but most famous by far is the standard of the 45th French Infantry Regiment that Sergeant Ewart captured during the battle. Capturing an Eagle was a rare event as they were guarded by men who had sworn to give their lives to protect them as Eagles symbolised a regiment's honour. An eyewitness recalled

I saw Ewart, with five or six infantry men about him, slashing right and left … [he] finished two of them, and was in the act of striking a third man down who held the eagle; next moment I saw Ewart cut him down … Almost single-handed, Ewart had captured the Imperial Eagle of the 45th 'Invincibles'.

Ewart received great acclamation for this act and the Eagle is exhibited in a large case along with Lady Butler's famous painting of the charge known as 'Scotland Forever!'

Prisoners of war were imprisoned in the castle within two great stone vaults beneath the Great Hall and the Queen Anne Building. Their dormitories have been faithfully re-created in a display examining the conditions they endured that includes original graffiti drawn by inmates, iron grille doors, items made by prisoners and details of escape attempts. POWs were brought here during the Seven Years War and American War of Independence but most famously during wars against France 1793-1815. Many were sailors and not all of them were French with Dutch, American, Spanish, Irish and other nationalities among them.

Dalmeny House and Estate

Dalmeny Estate Office, Dalmeny House, South Queensferry, EH30 9TQ. Website: www.roseberyestates.co.uk

Overview: Dalmeny House lies ten miles from Edinburgh, enjoying incredible views of the Firth of Forth and has been the home to the Earls of Rosebery since 1662 with the current structure built in 1817. A large bronze statue of a racehorse named King Tom stands outside its main entrance, which was owned by the 5th Earl and won the Derby, 1000 Guineas, Oaks and St. Leger in the same year (1871). The house is a magnificent gothic revival mansion with many rooms decorated in Regency style and holds numerous paintings, furniture, porcelain and other items from the Rosebery and Rothschild collections. The family still reside here so access to the house is by guided tour alone during the summer months and booking is essential.

Napoleonic Highlights: Archibald Primrose, 5th Earl of Rosebery (1847–1929) was a scholar and politician who eventually became Prime Minister in 1894–95. As a historian, he was fascinated by the lives of great men who changed history and foremost among them was the Emperor Napoleon I with his book *Napoleon: the Last Phase* (published 1900), considered a classic work on the subject. He amassed one of the largest collections of Napoleon related memorabilia outside France including busts, paintings, prints, books and furniture. There are many representations of Napoleon as First Consul or Emperor along with members of the Bonaparte family and their contemporaries with original works by artists like David, Appiani, Girolet and Wicar. The Earl acquired items owned by the Emperor including a shaving stand from the Palace of Compiègne but the most impressive is one of the thrones he used as First Consul. The collection also includes relics from Napoleon's exile on St Helena such as a desk, chair, shutters and a pillow from his deathbed. While most objects relate to Napoleon, there is also a folding campaign chair supposedly used by Wellington on display.

Wales – *Map 8*

Monmouth/Nelson Museum
Market Hall, Priory St, Monmouth NP25 3XA
Website: www.visitmonmouthshire/things-to-do/monmouth-nelson-museum.
com

Overview: Located in the old Market Hall in the centre of Monmouth, this museum is famous for its collection of Nelson memorabilia but also holds numerous items on Monmouth's local history and archaeology.

Napoleonic Highlights: The majority of this collection was donated by Lady Georgiana Llangattock in 1923, whose husband and son amassed a vast amount of Nelson memorabilia. It includes letters written by Nelson to his wife, Lady Hamilton and Royal Navy officers along with his fighting sword, enemy swords surrendered at Trafalgar and a stunning array of commemorative silverware, pottery and glassware. In addition to paintings, prints and models, local relevance is added by exhibits linked to Nelson's visit to South Wales and Monmouth in 1802 accompanied by the Hamiltons. There are also some interesting fake items created by those hoping to profit by selling 'Original Nelson memorabilia' including a glass eye (he never wore one) that was bought and used by a surgeon for lecturing his students for a time.

Waterloo Museum
Plas Newydd, Llanfairpwllgwyngyll, LL61 6DQ
Website: www.nationaltrust.org.uk/features/plas-newydd-anglesey

Overview: Plas Newydd is an aristocratic house that was owned by the Griffiths, Baylys and Paget families until bought by the National Trust in 1976.

It is located on the north bank of the Menai Straits in near Llanfairpwllgwyngyll on Anglesey and possesses stunning views with the house set in magnificent grounds.

Napoleonic Highlights: The house was once home to Henry Paget, 1st Marquess of Anglesey, who famously lost his leg to an enemy cannon shot towards the end of the Battle of Waterloo. Renowned as a great cavalry commander, he saw action in Flanders and the Peninsula (under Sir John Moore) and in 1815 under Wellington. He was Lord Paget from 1784 to 1812 before becoming Earl of Uxbridge from 1812 to 1815 and was created Marquess of Anglesey in honour of his military service and is among the most famous British officers of the wars. There is a small museum dedicated to the Battle of Waterloo at Plas Newyyd, containing unique items such as weapons, busts, silverware, prints, statuettes, paintings and uniforms. Notable among them are uniforms owned and worn by the Marquess along with one of his prosthetic legs and a spyglass that reputedly belonged to Napoleon. Statues of the Marquess and Nelson overlook the straits nearby (see Chapter 5).

Royal Welch Fusiliers Regimental Museum
The Castle, Caernarfon, Gwynedd, North Wales, United Kingdom, LL55 2AY
Website: www.rwfmuseum.org.uk/contact.html

Overview: This museum's collections include items such as weaponry, band instruments, paintings, standards, medals, silverware and statuettes typical of most regimental museums except that the Royal Welch Fusiliers (RWF) is among the most famous British regiments, having served in conflicts for over 300 years and boast an incredible fourteen Victoria Crosses (the highest British military award for valour). It presents exhibitions covering the campaigns of William III, the American War of Independence, Crimean War, Victorian Wars, First and Second World Wars and modern conflicts in Northern Ireland, Bosnia, Iraq and Afghanistan.

Napoleonic Highlights: There are a number of Napoleonic exhibitions and some use highly effective life-sized mannequins of red-coated infantrymen using scaling ladders on the walls of Badajoz during the siege of 1812 during the Peninsular War. A French Eagle of the 82nd French Line Regiment captured at Martinique 1809 by the RWF is displayed along with material relating to Colonel Sir Henry Ellis who was mortally wounded at Waterloo and died on 20 June 1815 along with original uniforms and medals awarded for service during the Napoleonic Wars.

Research Facilities: The RWF Museum acts in partnership with Wrexham County Borough Council to offer the public access to the RWF Archives to research service records of family members who may have served in the regiment. Contact RWF Enquiries Service at: localstudies@wrexham.gov.uk

Chapter 9

Exploring Great Britain

England is among the oldest nations in Europe and the United Kingdom provides a unique mixture of customs, accents and laws that can easily confuse visitors from other nations. An American guest on a battlefield tour once told the author that his state was larger than this entire country but he could travel around it and expect to encounter people whom he shared a similar upbringing, accent and even a common outlook on religion or politics but the opposite is true of this small nation. Here one can travel 20 miles and find people whose regional accents, beliefs, traditions and politics vary enormously. The Spanish philosopher George Santayana once wrote 'England is paradise of individuality, eccentricity, heresy, anomalies, hobbies and humours', and it is easy to see why he believed this. While this is true of England, the additional languages, accents, values and traditions of Scotland, Ireland and Wales make the British Isles an even more diverse and interesting place to be. The following chapter offers general hints and advice about what travellers are likely to encounter and how to get the best out of their visit.

Travelling to Britain

Flying to Britain is easy with almost every international airline operator running services to London, which handles 60 per cent of UK air travel. Many of the general travel directions in this guidebook are given on the assumption that most travellers will be able to reach London as the British capital has six major airports alone (Luton, Heathrow, Stansted and Gatwick being the most famous). It is also easy to reach the cities of Edinburgh, Cardiff, Belfast and Dublin by air and there are numerous smaller airports around the country.

Visitors from Continental countries can also travel to Britain by ferry and there are currently over 1,200 ferry routes sailing from sixty-four nations including France, Spain, Italy, Ireland, Holland, Germany, North Africa and the Baltic States. For details on the services available see – www.ferryto. co.uk/routes.html and the vast majority of these services allow travellers to bring a vehicle with them. A relatively new service is the rail link via the Eurotunnel (Channel Tunnel) with high-speed services available from

Brussels, Amsterdam, Berlin, Cologne and other major cities on the continent to London. The Eurostar service has earned an enviable reputation for speed, comfort and efficiency and some services allow vehicles to be carried.

While travellers from outside the UK should encounter few difficulties in reaching Britain, the country left the European Union (EU) in 2020 and negotiations are ongoing about borders and travel requirements now that the country is no longer a partner in the Schengen Agreement. Britain left the EU during 'Brexit' and the results of this move will not become clear for some years but will hopefully allow Britons greater autonomy over their economy, borders, national currency and laws but whether this will be an advantage or disadvantage to travellers visiting Britain remains to be seen.

Personal Identification

Unlike the EU and most nations outside Europe, the British do not enforce an identification card system, which can be a two-edged sword depending on the circumstances. Visitors will regularly be asked by quality hotels to give their credit or debit card details as a form of ID or simply to secure a booking. If travellers are stopped by the police for any reason, a national ID card or driving licence from another country is usually sufficient but a passport is universally acceptable by authorities.

Planning an Itinerary

Great Britain is exceptionally interesting to travel around with a host of things to see. This is particularly true of its capital cities and it is best to plan intended routes and make a rough calculation of how many sites travellers expect to see each day, how long they hope to spend viewing them and the time it takes to get there and back. In the case of cities like London or Edinburgh, it is advisable to make a list of priorities as these cities contain many distractions that can cause travellers to divert from their plans and steal time set aside for major attractions. For example, it is best to set aside at least three hours to look around Edinburgh Castle but most visitors will approach it along the Royal Mile that has a spectacular range of churches, museums, shops, pubs and graveyards along its route that may prove irresistible. This is worth factoring into an itinerary, along with researching the opening times of desired locations in advance as visitors will often be pressed for time.

Travelling around London presents a visitor with similar distractions and the author encountered two unexpected sites of interest on the way from the nearest Underground station to St Paul's Cathedral that could easily have taken hours to look around when he required at least half a day to devote to his destination that day. As Walter Besant perceptively remarked 'I've been walking about London for the last 30 years, and I find something fresh in it every day', which was true when he wrote it in 1922 but even more so in today's London with its greater size and additional attractions.

Essentially, visitors should be prepared to adapt their plans by allowing extra time for potential difficulties in reaching locations, such as traffic congestion, and be prepared to abandon secondary locations if a site proves so fascinating that they wish to spend more time there than expected. Every tour guide understands the concept of planning ahead to show their guests as much as possible in the time period allowed and those using organized tours will find all these considerations have been taken into account on their behalf. However, for those conducting their own personal visits it is well worth taking the time to draw up a short and practical itinerary.

Tour Companies

There are numerous historical tour companies offering in-depth visits for many of the locations described in this book. They excel when it comes to visiting locations that are difficult to reach or have limited opening times with Wellington's house of Stratfield Saye being a prime example. A wide range of tours and prices are available but visitors generally get what they pay for in this sector and quality tours are recommended such as www.theculturalexperience.com. The advantage of using a professional tour company is that almost everything is handled by tour guides and managers with minimal effort required on the traveller's part. Most use coaches as their main form of transport and guests do not need to concern themselves about driving, map reading, opening times, hotel bookings, historic site reservations, restaurant bookings or negotiating with hotel staff. Furthermore, they will benefit from the historic knowledge of an experienced tour guide in the company of fellow enthusiasts. Disadvantages are that travellers cannot divert from the tour company's itinerary, which may not be specialized enough and tours are often expensive.

Do-It-Yourself (DIY) Tours

Travellers with an amateur or even professional interest in studying Napoleonic sites, writing books or magazine articles for example, will do well to make their own travel arrangements as this allows total freedom of choice for destinations, itinerary and the ability to visit obscure sites that tour companies may not cover. The drawback is the responsibility for handling tasks such as driving, map reading, booking hotels, buying site entry tickets, researching opening times, buying rail or bus tickets and other requirements. One advantage is that DIY tours are invariably cheaper. Fortunately, there have never been better maps or guidebooks available than at the present time and the internet enables travellers to consult maps or weather sites online that make organization easier. See – www.google.co.uk/maps for maps and www.bbc.co.uk/weather for checking weather conditions and the beauty of the internet is that it can be accessed by transportable devices such as mobile phones (cell phones), tablets, or laptops in transit.

Money and Cash Cards

British currency is the Pound Sterling, which is based on the decimal system with 100 pennies to the pound and coins for 1 pence, 2p, 5p, 10p, 20p, 50p, £1 and £2 in general circulation. Pound notes include £5, £10, £20 and £50 and England, Scotland and Northern Ireland produce their own national designs that can be used throughout the United Kingdom. Southern Ireland uses the Euro currency of the European Union and visitors will find it necessary to exchange Euros at a bank or *bureaux de change* to convert to or from British currency when applicable. While payment by cheque is gradually being phased out in Britain, a range of credit and debit cards can be used and cashpoints are commonplace in towns and cities, although less frequent in isolated rural areas. Visitors from the EU but especially from countries outside Europe should check if their credit/debit cards can be used before travelling.

The cost of living in Britain is high compared to many countries and prices in the capital cities of London, Edinburgh, Belfast and Cardiff are often more expensive than the rest of the country. As a general rule, those staying in Britain spend more on accommodation and eating out than anything else, so if travellers have a budget trip in mind it is better to use self-catering accommodation, which is usually located outside the more expensive areas.

Language

Although English is by the most common language used in the United Kingdom, the population is becoming increasingly diverse and other languages are spoken in cities where there are large ethnic minority communities. Welsh, Scottish Gaelic and Irish Gaelic (also known as Old Irish or Gaeilge) are also used but mostly in the rural areas of those nations. Visitors who speak English should have little difficulty in communicating with the vast majority of British subjects but be aware that there is also a bewildering array of national and regional accents that occasionally cause confusion.

Where to Stay

The reputation of British hotels varied enormously in the past but has drastically improved over the last 15 years. The international hotel star rating system is used here and travellers able to afford 4 to 7 Star hotels can expect an extremely high standard of service with even those of 2 or 3 Stars being acceptable to most travellers. Many public houses and Inns offer accommodation and the service offered in capital cities such as London and Edinburgh can be exceptional, with everything from grand old establishments to modern hotel chains being available. Visitors can expect to find reasonable parking, internet facilities, attached restaurants, travel advice and clean rooms along with all the usual services at most hotels but their main disadvantage is that quality comes at a price so visitors should budget for large bills, particularly in London or other capital cities.

A brief internet search reveals that Britain offers numerous alternative forms of accommodation such as bed and breakfast establishments, which are commonplace and often use a star rating system similar to hotels but are more economical. Travellers receive a far less formal service and should be aware that fewer facilities are available and that entry times may be restricted. They can also make use of the Youth Hostel network that offers basic accommodation in a communal style with facilities such as shared kitchens and bathrooms, see – www.yha.org.uk

A recent innovation is Airbnb for travellers operating who wish to save money. This offers a range of accommodation varying from renting a simple room in a private individual's house to self-contained flats or houses. While a high standard of cleanliness is demanded by this service, facilities vary and many are self-catering (a significant way to reduce costs). This service has allowed the author to carry out economic research by staying on the periphery of expensive cities like London or Paris. Although many locations lack the convenient central position of hotels, Britain enjoys extensive communication networks and travelling to various historic sites is usually easy. See – www.airbnb.co.uk/

There are many campsites in Britain for caravan or tented accommodation. Campsites of both kinds can be extremely economical and self-catering in caravans or tents, rather than using campsite restaurants, is an excellent way of reducing costs. Quality and prices vary enormously but they are popular ways of staying in an isolated area for a few days and the author used a static caravan to explore Martello towers in the Felixstowe area to great effect. See –www.ukcampsite.co.uk for details.

Travel by Car or Taxi

Britain enjoys an extensive network of motorways and trunk roads that make travelling around the country straightforward but although modern facilities like satnavs are available, it is wise to plan travel routes in conjunction with old fashioned maps or internet navigation facilities. The best of these is www.google.co.uk/maps/ that allows travellers to insert their locations and destinations with the site providing accurate estimations of journey times by motor vehicle, public transport, cycling or walking.

Drivers will need a valid and up to date driving licence or international driving permit and visitors from abroad should check with their embassies if unsure what documentation is required. It is also wise to have proof of ownership, rental agreements and insurance documents to hand just in case. Visitors from outside the United Kingdom may find hiring a car a viable option but it is worth researching this well in advance of a trip. Car rental services are available at most major airports or coastal ports and there are many hire companies to choose from including Hertz, Europcar, National Hire and Avis. Be aware that most companies will need to see some form of ID with an address in addition to a current driving licence.

Visitors from outside the UK may find it useful to acquire a Highway Code from the Department of Transport website – www.gov.uk/government/organizations/department-for-transport – that provides up to date information on traffic regulations in detail. Electronic signs on motorways also advise drivers about speed restrictions, weather conditions and what to do if an accident occurs. British vehicles drive on the left-hand side of the road and most distances on signs are only given in miles. Traffic lights use the Red (Stop) Amber (also Stop until Green) and Green (Go) system and most railway crossings employ an automatic safety barrier but a flashing red light means a train is approaching and motorists should stop. Directional signs are colour coded with blue representing Motorways (M-roads), green for major roads (A-roads) and white for minor roads (B-roads). Advisory and warning signs are usually white, triangular and outlined in red with simple pictorial symbols. Signs indicating areas of historical interest are in brown.

The obvious benefits of using a car for a historical tour are the ability to carry overnight luggage, extra clothing and equipment such as cameras, tripods, food, water and other useful items. Using a car also allows travellers to follow their own itinerary and enables them to be more adaptable if circumstances force them to change their plans. Disadvantages include possible diversions, traffic congestion, refuelling and finding safe parking areas.

Taxis are a great form of travel, especially in big cities, and travellers using them will not have the stress of driving, refuelling or finding parking spaces along with the benefit of the driver's local knowledge. Their disadvantage is price as taxis can be expensive, especially for long journeys, but booking in advance may gain some discount. Country taxis are available in rural Britain but fares are higher than in urban areas and drivers may charge a fee for driving to an isolated pick-up point in addition to that charged for conveying passengers to their destination.

Rail Travel

Travel from city to city is usually swift and efficient but it is generally easier to travel along lines between the north and south than those running between the east and west of Britain. This is due to line closures during the 1950s but this form of travel is an efficient, comfortable and quick way of travelling around the country. Rail staff are usually helpful and will find the most economical train route for passengers with a minimum number of changes when buying tickets at a station, although booking in advance online often confers considerable discounts, see – www.nationalrail.co.uk. The main disadvantage for train travel is high ticket prices and travellers on tight budgets may wish to consider other forms of travel. The opening of the Channel Tunnel was a major step forward for international travel and passengers from the Continent can board Eurostar trains in Berlin, Amsterdam, Paris, Brussels, Rotterdam or Lille and arrive very quickly in London with HS1 (High Speed 1) being the fastest line between London and the Channel Tunnel. The future looks even more promising with talk of re-opening old train lines and plans to construct HS2, which should enable high-speed travel between London and Edinburgh by the 2030s.

London Underground

This is the easiest form of public transport to use in London and its key advantages are that visitors can travel around this vast city swiftly and precisely as numerous Tube stations are built near famous attractions. Although tickets can be purchased with cash, users increasingly rely upon Oyster Cards that can be bought and topped up with further credit at machines provided at stations. Large wall maps are regularly displayed around the network and small paper or card versions can be bought to enable travellers to navigate around London with confidence. The Underground allows travellers to avoid traffic congestion and, even though some lines become busy at commuting times, regular trains make it a swift form of transportation. It is the oldest underground network in the world with the Metropolitan Line built in 1863 and therefore some stations are more suited to use by disabled passengers than others. Tube maps employ a disabled friendly symbol for stations that have wheelchair access so disabled travellers or carers should consult these when planning journeys. The Underground currently operates 272 stations in or around London and for further information see – www.tfl.gov.uk.

Coach or Bus Travel

Coach travel is the cheapest form of transport in the UK and more economical than rail or car travel. All major cities possess coach and bus stations along with most towns and large operators such as National Express, FlixBus and Megabus offer a diverse range of services. Coaches generally suffer from fewer delays or industrial action than rail services and drivers can swiftly change to alternative routes if they need to avoid diversions, accidents or congestion. While they are more economical than train travel, coaches are generally less comfortable for passengers on long journeys and it takes more time to reach destinations due to the need to pick up passengers at stations along their routes but they are a great choice for those travelling on a budget nonetheless. For more details see – www.omio.co.uk/coaches.

Buses operate on local routes and are used for shorter journeys than coaches and travellers using public transport often find that they can get nearer to an isolated destination by train or coach but will require a bus for the last leg of their journey. With cars being the predominant form of travel in Britain, many bus routes have been closed down in rural areas so it is wise to check online in advance that buses are still available. For example, the bus service to Nelson's birthplace (Burnham Thorpe) closed down years ago and travellers can only get as close as the neighbouring village by bus and will have to walk or use a taxi to complete their journey. Passengers should also be aware that contactless payment is increasingly used on buses and that many minor stations are now closed or unmanned so it may be wise to print out bus timetables in advance of a journey.

Walking and Cycling

Walking or cycling are often the best or only methods of reaching isolated areas or approaching a specific site such as Martello towers or monuments. Even in busy cities, limited walking is usually required with the monuments high on Edinburgh's Calton Hill being a prime example. For longer walks it is advisable to carry useful items in handbags or small rucksacks such as money, debit cards, mobile phone, binoculars, cameras, bottled water, a compass and some kind of timepiece. Britain is a temperate country and weather is unpredictable so taking sun cream, hat, decent footwear and a light raincoat is always worthwhile, recalling the adage 'There's no such thing as bad weather, only unsuitable clothing' – Alfred Wainwright ((British guidebook author, fellwalker and illustrator). Carrying something to drink is wise as dehydration is the walker's worst enemy and can strike swiftly either in the wilds or an urban area.

There are some instances where a bicycle is extremely useful, such as visiting the line of Martello towers beyond the River Deben in Suffolk or cycling along the coastal path from Deal to Walmer Castle. While visitors often see more at a leisurely walking speed, cycling saves considerable time and bikes are widely available for hire in Britain. However, cyclists are vulnerable to collisions with other vehicles and travellers should consider using helmets and high visibility clothing. It is also worth carrying a lock, repair kit and panniers if further equipment is required.

Safety and Security

Britain is a fairly safe country to visit but it is wise to take care of valuables and carry a mobile phone in case of emergencies. Tourists and travellers are at greatest risk from pickpockets and scam artists, who rarely cause physical harm but are capable of spoiling a trip if a significant sum of money is lost. Travellers should be especially careful walking around urban areas after dark and be aware that over drinking is commonplace in Britain and drinkers' behaviour in establishments selling alcohol can be unpredictable. Britain has a fine police force along with good ambulance and fire services. Dial 999 to call these emergency services by phone if there is a serious problem and, the event of an injury, the NHS treats foreign nationals in an emergency but travellers from outside Britain are advised to take out health insurance prior to visiting. For general advice see – www.holidaysafe.co.uk/general-travel-advice/

Photography and Drones

Most sites described in this book permit photography but there are a few exceptions, usually relating to areas where a family's privacy must be respected or copyright rules are imposed. Such rules are usually clarified by staff upon entry or outlined on a location's website. A typical example is Walmer Castle, where photography is permitted in its grounds and gardens but prohibited inside. Sometimes museums and cathedrals allow cameras but forbid the use of flash photography, usually because it may damage old exhibits such as

Regency period uniforms, paintings or room decoration. It is always best to ask staff about restrictions if in doubt.

Drone photography is another matter as they are recent inventions and laws governing their usage are still under consideration in Britain. Visitors are advised to check with owners of private sites before using drones as their wide field of vision enables users to see into areas beyond the range of conventional cameras. As a general rule, the use of drones in open public areas where there are few private residences is unlikely to cause serious issues, such as recording images of isolated Martello towers along a coastline. However, authorities are increasingly suspicious of drones in areas with security concerns or where images of individuals in their homes could be taken without their knowledge and publicised. Drones flying over secure areas like military bases can be legally shot down and their owners detained so it is best to avoid using them in built up areas and particularly large cities at risk of terrorism where an operator's motives may be misinterpreted.

Summary

Great Britain is an exciting country to visit with a wide range of accommodation services available and enjoys reliable communication routes by road, rail or air. This guidebook provides visitors with details about some excellent historic sites and travellers should look forward to a comfortable stay with stunning locations to see.

Annotated Bibliography

Books

Anonymous, *Stratfield Saye House*, Blacker Design, Hampshire, 2015.

Brown, Paul, *Maritime Portsmouth*, The History Press, 2009.

Bryant, Julian, *Apsley House: the Wellington Collection*, English Heritage, 2005.

Coad, Jonathan and Willard-Wright, Rowena, *Walmer Castle and Gardens*, English Heritage, 2015.

Corke, Jim, *War Memorials in Britain*, Shire Publications Ltd, Buckinghamshire, 2005.

Clements, Bill, *Martello Towers Worldwide*, Pen & Sword, Barnsley, 2011.

——, *Towers of Strength*, Pen & Sword Books, Barnsley, 1998.

Edwards, Jason, Harris, Amy and Sullivan, Greg, *Monuments of St Paul's Cathedral 1796-1916*, Scala Arts & Heritage Publishing Ltd, 2021,

Eastland, Jonathan and Ballantyne, Iain, *HMS Victory First Rate 1765*, Seaforth Publishing, Barnsley, 2011.

Eley, Jamieson and Limbert, Matthew, *Redoubt Fortress*, Jarrold Publishing, Eastbourne, 2017.

Glover, Gareth, *The Duke of Wellington in 100 Objects*, Frontline Books, Barnsley, 2020.

Harwich Society, *The Harwich Redoubt*, Harwich Society, Harwich, 2018.

Higgins, David, *Springboard to Victory*, Phoenix Publications, King's Lynn, 2020

Holmes, Richard, *Wellington: The Iron Duke*, Harper-Collins, London, 2003.

Kent, Peter, *Fortifications of East Anglia*, Terence Dalton Ltd, Suffolk, 1988.

Peverley, John, *Dover's Hidden Fortress*, AR Adams & Sons, Dover, 1996.

Pocock, Tom, *Horatio Nelson*, The Bodley Head, London, 1987.

White, Colin (ed.), *The Nelson Companion*, Alan Sutton Publishing Ltd, 1995.

Yeoman, Peter, *Edinburgh Castle*, Historic Scotland, 2014.

Internet Sources

www.nelson-society.com – Produced by a highly informed group of enthusiasts, this is an excellent source of information about Nelson.

https://historicengland.org.uk/listing/the-list/list-entry/1017322 – This specific link refers to Berry Head Fort and other works but Historic England contains links to other Napoleonic fortifications.

www.martellotowers.co.uk – A useful site for detailed information about Martello towers.

www.waterlooassociation.org.uk – This excellent site has a well-informed members' forum exploring many aspects of the Napoleonic period.

Index